Anglican Theology

Anglican Theology

Mark D. Chapman

t&t clark

Published by T&T Clark International
A Continuum Imprint
The Tower Building, 11 York Road, London SE1 7NX
80 Maiden Lane, Suite 704, New York, NY 10038

www.continuumbooks.com

British Library Cataloguing-in-Publication Data
A catalogue record for this book is available from the British Library

ISBN13: 978-0-567-25031-5 (Hardback)
         978-0-567-00802-2 (Paperback)

Typeset by Deanta Global Publishing Services, Chennai, India
Printed in Great Britain

Contents

Preface

This book offers an interpretation of Anglican Theology which has been cultivated in a very distinctive environment: for the past nineteen years I have taught at Ripon College, Cuddesdon, just outside Oxford. Cuddesdon, which used to house the palace of the bishops of Oxford, has had a theological college since 1854. For a small Oxfordshire village it is surprisingly well known across the Anglican Communion. Cuddesdon College used to keep an album of photographs of all its bishops, many of whom served as early bishops of the new Anglican churches, which had begun to emerge throughout the world in the nineteenth century. On visiting the diocesan office at Johannesburg, for instance, I encountered the very familiar face of James Buchanan Seaton, sometime Rector of St Mary's Parish and Archdeacon, and afterwards Principal of Cuddesdon, whose portrait I greet several times a day. Or again, a few years later I was invited to Colombo by the inspirational and courageous Bishop Duleep de Chickera to give the clergy lectures. Bishop Duleep's earnest Anglo-Catholic predecessor, Mark Carpenter-Garnier, lies buried in the village churchyard. His solar topee, complete with purple episcopal band, is currently in my office as a physical reminder of the complex set of relationships between British Imperialism, Anglicanism, and my own college.

Over the years, as I have taught church history and doctrine to future clergy in this peculiar place, I have become increasingly aware of how the traditions of the Church of England were reshaped and reformed in the nineteenth century partly through encounter with other cultures and partly through efforts to understand and interpret the English past. This book is an attempt to bring those nineteenth century historical visions into a dialogue with the history and theology of the Reformation and the seventeenth century and also with the issues facing the Anglican Communion today. It is not a systematic theology but it is a very particular reading of historical theology. My reading of history will probably not appeal to all Anglicans, but I hope it will at least help readers think through some of the complexities of history and its impact on theology. My ideas have been stimulated by students who have often clamoured for a theological identity or who have wanted to know precisely what the Church of England and the Anglican Communion stand for. While this book might not give them too many answers, it should assist them in understanding why Anglicanism has a very distinctive set of problems.

The thinking behind this book emerged from lectures in Cuddesdon as well as many presentations, seminars and talks I have given in many different places in England and elsewhere: I am grateful to all those who have invited me. I hope I said something worthwhile. By name I would like to thank Professor Angela Berlis of the University of Bern, who provided a visiting lectureship and a great deal of hospitality in that beautiful Reformed city where the bulk of the text was written in glorious spring weather. Presenting a few lectures on Anglican theology in Switzerland was both highly enjoyable and stimulating. I would also like to thank those who read through the entire text: my colleagues Bishop Stephen Pickard and Martyn Percy, as well as my former doctoral student Andrew Atherstone. Finally, I am not sure that when we married my wife Linda Collins ever expected the extraordinarily varied and full life we have had at Ripon College Cuddesdon and for that matter neither did I. But I thank her for putting up with that microcosm of Anglican history that is Cuddesdon, as well as with me and my obsessions, and for keeping us both in touch with the world outside.

Mark Chapman
The Feast of Richard Hooker, 3 November 2011

Chapter 1

Anglican Theology and Some Myths of Anglicanism

The Fog in the Channel

Once upon a time, there was no 'Anglican theology'; and neither was there such a phenomenon as Anglicanism. There was, however, a Church of England, which maintained as vigorous a theology as the other churches that grew out of the Reformation (even if such theology failed to become embedded in a university culture in quite the same way as Germany). But whether this theology could be described as 'Anglican' is altogether another question. Even using the minimal and rather banal definition of Anglican as a synonym for 'English', it is not clear that the theology developed by the leading figures following Henry VIII's break with Rome was any more distinctively English than Zwingli's was Swiss or Luther's was German. While there were obviously local differences, it is also fair to say that in the sixteenth century, the fog in the channel had not yet cut off mainland Europe from theological discourse, much of which was conducted in the international lingua franca of Latin. While theology might have addressed some specifically English problems, it was still defined by its contact with the international guild of theologians and churchmen on the continent, a number of whom were even brought to England, including some of the leading figures of the continental Reformation, such as the Italian Peter Martyr Vermigli and the Strasbourg reformer Martin Bucer.[1] Even during the Elizabethan years, when some claim might be made for the beginnings of a distinctively English theology, the leading theologians including John Jewel, the first great defender of the 1559 Settlement, kept up a regular correspondence with their continental counterparts. As evidence of the international dimension of English theology,

1

parish churches were supposed to purchase their own copy of the *Paraphrases on the Gospels*, the biblical commentary by the great humanist Erasmus of Rotterdam.[2] At a time when Latin was still an important medium, English theologians were frequently published in continental Europe, and many of the debates that dominated theological discussion in England were much the same as those taking place on the continent. And the formularies, liturgies and documents that were produced from the 1530s were certainly not purely domestic developments but were deeply influenced by protestant[3] ideas that emerged from beyond England's shores. The Reformation may have occurred in national context,[4] but those contexts frequently merged into each other.

Myths about a pure English Reformation unsullied by influences from the continent[5] are matched by equally dubious claims about continuity, which regarded the religious changes of the sixteenth century as little more than clearing away some medieval popish clutter in order to return to the true church of the apostles that had survived more or less intact in England. This approach is what Diarmaid MacCulloch has called 'The Myth of the English Reformation'.[6] For many nineteenth-century writers, he claimed, the Reformation simply 'did not happen', or if did happen, 'it happened by accident rather than design or . . . was half-hearted and sought a middle way between Catholicism and Protestantism'.[7] Such a myth lies behind the grandiose claim of some nineteenth-century figures who viewed Anglicanism as the English branch of the Church Catholic alongside – and perhaps even superior to – Roman Catholicism and Orthodoxy and quite distinct from the heresies of Continental Protestantism.[8] While this is about as gross a distortion of history as it is possible to make, it was deeply influential on the perception and identity of Anglicanism, not least in its approach to theology, as well as in the closely related fields of liturgy and architecture.

And yet, there are still some contemporary Anglicans who continue to make such claims about the past: history matters to Anglicans, but that history is often the product of a creative mind rather than a scientific discipline. As I will demonstrate through the course of this book, trawling though the past in the hope of finding an elusive Anglican identity became a common-place activity among the different parties that emerged from the eighteenth and nineteenth centuries. This was particularly true for many of those labelled as Evangelical and Anglo-Catholic. And some of the ideas that got stuck in the nets have proved rather bigger catches than others. The biggest fish of all is something called 'the historic episcopate, locally adapted to needs' of the Lambeth Quadrilateral of 1888, which has come to be one of the badges of Anglican identity and theology. However, as I will show in the final chapter, even that is not quite as simple as it may seem.

Much has been written on the invention of tradition in the nineteenth century, particularly as this relates to the development of ideas of nationhood associated with the decline of the great empires.[9] What was true of the invention of national tradition during the massive changes affecting Europe after the defeat of Napoleon was equally true for the different European churches, many of which, including the Church of England, set about clarifying their identity often by returning to a vision of the past. History became a place of security amid the flux of rapid social change.[10] Many consequently sought to establish the identity of the Church of England on the basis of history. The assimilation of history led to the production of historical texts as well as the adoption of 'historical' symbolic practices and architectural forms. All of these contributed to the leading contours of the formative traditions behind the contested notion of Anglican identity. Yet, this was not a simple process, because it was far from clear where precisely the identity of the Church of England was to be found. It is not difficult to read the literary and symbolic productions of the nineteenth and twentieth centuries in the Church of England and other 'Anglican' churches – as part of the formation of a variety of 'ideal types' of what might be called 'Anglican theology' or Anglicanism (even if the title itself was used only by a few in the nineteenth century).

Yet any such historically rooted identity was highly contested: the history of the Church of England and the communion it spawned could be read in many different ways, and there were (and are still) clearly competing versions as to what counts as authentic historical Anglicanism. Different canons of 'Anglican theology' were constructed, which were of particular importance in a Church that had not developed a universally recognized canon of resources for doing theology, even if there were a number of key texts that had come to be regarded as classics. While most churches that emerged from the Reformation could rely on a long history of carefully argued dogmatic theology that expounded the meaning of Scripture and a key set of confessional writings, the Church of England lacked such a clear-cut theological tradition. There was no Luther, no Zwingli, no Calvin and no period of dogmatic orthodoxy as had developed among Lutherans and Calvinists in the seventeenth and eighteenth centuries. John Pearson's *Exposition of the Creed* (1659),[11] for instance, which remained very popular through the nineteenth century, can hardly be compared with the lengthy works of professorial scholarship emanating from the continent.

In contrast to other European countries, there were remarkably few people who could be classified as 'professional theologians' in the post-Reformation Church of England. Until the mid-nineteenth century, there were only two English universities (Oxford and Cambridge), but even there the study of theology as a distinct undergraduate subject was not on the curriculum (although all students were required to take compulsory courses in theology). Given this historical background, it is no surprise that there were virtually no universally recognized classics or 'normal texts' of theology on which to base Anglican theology, apart from Scripture, the writers of the early church and the liturgical and doctrinal resources including the Articles of Religion contained in the Book of Common Prayer that reached its final form in 1662. All that was required to complete the theological parts of the BA at Oxford University in the early nineteenth century (which was a solely Anglican institution until the 1870s) was a knowledge of the Gospels in Greek, the Thirty-Nine Articles and Bishop Butler's *Analogy of Religion* of 1736,[12] a book that proved deeply influential on a number of leading nineteenth-century figures including John Henry Newman and the Prime Minister, William Ewart Gladstone,[13] who edited a critical edition towards the end of his life.[14]

Apart from this extremely limited canon, there was little agreement about the norms and methods of Anglican theology in its formative period following the break with Rome. The possible exception is Bishop John Jewel's *Apology*, which gained semi-official status in late Elizabethan and Jacobean England and was bought by many parish churches as a 'very notable and learned confutation of all the principal points of popery',[15] and many would have added parts of Richard Hooker's *Laws of Ecclesiastical Polity*. It will become clear as I discuss the traditions of Anglican theology through the sixteenth and seventeenth centuries that those who sponsored and edited the production of classic texts in the nineteenth century, which reached a high point of activity in the 1840s and 50s, did so out of a desire to shape what some have misleadingly called the 'essence' of Anglicanism,[16] something which most at the time would have seen as identical to the Church of England. For many Victorians, the goal of theology was to provide the Church of England with clear markers of identity.

The Shape of the Book

This book does not present a conventional account of Anglican theology: it is too contested a phenomenon to allow for any straightforward presentation. Instead, it offers discussions of the different identities and theologies that have been regarded as characterizing Anglican theology. This means that it takes the form of a three-way dialogue between those who sought to make sense of their past as they created narratives of identity in the nineteenth century with that past as it might be understood from the vantage point of today. The formative past then is mediated through the nineteenth century. For this reason, the world of Victorian Romanticism and its odd combination of scholarship, fantasy and myth – and in which overseas mission played a secondary yet vital role – are as important to 'Anglican theology' as anything written during the sixteenth and seventeenth centuries, although what was written in the past contributed to the making of that myth. Throughout the chapters that follow, I ground my discussion of the past on the approaches to church and theological history that developed in the nineteenth century, but also in dialogue with contemporary scholarship.

Nineteenth-century approaches to history had many practical outworkings in liturgy and architecture, which in the long run are perhaps more important markers of identity than any literary texts. The nineteenth-century canon included art and architecture as well as theological and spiritual writings. Although they are not the main focus of the present study, some attention is given through the course of the book to some highly influential interpretations of medieval and Reformation history, such as Percy Dearmer's exhaustive, if somewhat eccentric, reading of precisely what was permitted in worship during the second year of the reign of Edward VI, which is discussed in Chapter 3. As will become clear, theology is not simply about the words of doctrine and controversy, but it is also about practice and participation in worship, which is why *culture* and *style* matter. Over the years, Anglicans have spent a great deal of time arguing over the deeply theological problem about what to wear in church: dressing up, as we shall see especially in Chapters 2 and 3, carries with it huge theological implications. Nevertheless, despite these frequent forays into the lived theology of liturgical action and ecclesiastical art, most of what I discuss through the course of this book is the writings of various theologians and church leaders – mainly but not exclusively English – as they engaged with the ecclesiastical conflicts and political disputes of their time. There were many events and campaigns that roused theologians from their scholarly meditations into fits of activity, some of which prove remarkably interesting as case studies of the application of theology.

As much of this book will demonstrate, Anglican theology was forged in the heat of controversy. Given the role of the Church of England as the monopoly state church at least until the seventeenth century, which came under the authority of the sovereign in parliament, its theology was always political and frequently addressed the issues of church and state. As will become clear, the practical theology of authority in matters of interpretation and church order (polity) was usually as important as controversy over doctrine (although there are frequent exceptions to this rule, especially over predestination in the late sixteenth and early seventeenth centuries, which is discussed in Chapter 6). While Scripture, as the Thirty-Nine Articles of Religion affirmed, was universally regarded as sufficient and containing all things necessary to salvation (Article VI), its interpretation and application were always open to debate. Furthermore, precisely what was contained in Scripture was hotly contested, as the debates over vestments and church order make clear. Who decides on these matters, and how one legislates for those things on which Scripture is silent, has been a perennial – perhaps even *the* perennial – issue in Anglican theology. It is for this reason that the key issue for Anglicanism is so often the doctrine of authority and order in the church. At least in its early years, as it forged its identity as a reformed church separate from Rome, it was often its approach to ecclesiology that gave Anglicanism – or at least the Church of England – its distinctiveness. Indeed, some forms of Anglicanism as they developed outside England described themselves as 'Episcopalian', emphasizing a particular aspect of their church order.

It is also important to remember that in their debates with one another, theologians of different periods in Anglicanism were frequently abusive and usually had little time for people with whom they disagreed. The benign, eirenic and inclusive comprehensiveness that developed after the Church of England lost its religious monopoly that shaped some of the debate about the nature of Anglicanism from the seventeenth century on is far from the norm. Instead, conflict is the normal state of 'Anglican' theology through history. While this way of doing things often makes later Anglicans wince, especially when it was frequently undertaken by rather unappealing zealots, it is important not to be too dismissive of the apologetic and polemic style of the past. As will become clear in Chapter 5, even apparently moderate figures, such as Richard Hooker, perhaps the most respected of the writers of the sixteenth century, whom many would regard as the Anglican theologian *par excellence* (but who never used the phrase *via media*), turn out to make use of rather unpleasant rhetoric.[17]

While attentive to this political and historical background, this book is for the most part about the clusters of often competing ideas that people have labelled as Anglican theology. Much aims at a historical account of the leading thinkers and their methods and motivations, particularly before the 1662 Act of Uniformity. But inseparable from this historical account is a discussion of later developments, especially in the nineteenth century, in what might more properly be called Anglicanism as a denomination, but one which was, as Samuel Wilberforce said in a different context, like 'grasping at a nebulosity or seizing upon a sepia'.[18] The art of doing Anglican theology is about holding two periods of history together, but always in relation to the present. Anglicanism, however, is clearly not identical any longer with the Church of England. Other churches labelled as Anglican have developed throughout the world, which share something of the inheritance of the Church of England's theology, but which have also grown quite independently and partly because of the vagaries of missionary and national histories have stressed different historical models of what constitutes authentic Anglicanism. At the same time, the different independent Anglican Churches have also developed ways of working with one another underpinned by a highly decentralized ecclesiology based upon a later nineteenth-century ideal of a national church. In the final chapter, I discuss this development as something quite distinct from the sort of Anglican theology discussed in the earlier chapters. I will conclude with a few reflections on whether it is possible to create a coherent theology for such a vague and contested phenomenon. Some ways of behaving that have been developed by the Anglican Communion could reasonably be described as 'doing Anglican theology', but they may have little to do with the sort of theology developed in the cut and thrust of Reformation polemics.

Finally, it is important to point out that those who might be reading this book to find out what Anglicans believe will come away with a good idea of what sorts of things have counted as doing Anglican theology in the past, particularly in the Church of England, and they should come away with a good idea about what some contemporary Anglicans think other Anglicans should believe. But they will be disappointed if they are looking for an Anglican systematic theology. While a few Anglicans have written systematic theologies[19] (and it is far fewer than in many other denominations), they have tended to write as theologians who happen to be members of Anglican churches, rather than as *Anglican* theologians. Anglican theology is thus unlikely to resemble a Lutheran or a Reformed dogmatics. The past functions very differently for most Anglicans: there is no key year or key text. Instead, everything is contested. Rather than being historicized in canonical or quasi-canonical texts, Anglican theology instead emerges from a combination of text, institution, context and practice, both ecclesiastical and secular and drawn

from a number of key periods. Consequently, although the
Church of England adopted much from the Augsburg Confession,
coupled with a number of more Reformed statements, as part
of its theological self-definition in the Thirty-Nine Articles of
Religion (see Chapter 3), the authority accorded to the text –
even one eventually ratified by an Elizabethan Parliament – was
quite unlike that given to the Augsburg Confession by Lutherans.
Anglican theology is not usually done primarily through
exposition of its historic formularies. Although some might prefer
it if it did, being Anglican does not usually mean subscription
to a text and its subsequent interpretation (as might be the case,
for instance, in the Presbyterian Church of Scotland where the
Westminster Confession still functions as the doctrinal norm).
What should become clear through the course of the book is
that 'Anglicanism' and 'Anglican theology' are highly contested:
sometimes the boundaries between historical myth, ecclesiastical
ideology and theology are remarkably thin. This is why doing
Anglican theology is such a complicated, sometimes infuriating,
but usually exciting task.

Chapter 2

The Reformation and Anglican Theology

Contested Canons

In Chapter 1, I suggested that the early Victorian period was one of the most important periods in the formation of Anglican identity. It was a time of intense discussion and significant conflict over the nature of the Church of England provoked by massive social and political changes. The synthesis of church and state, which was embodied in the great institutions of the land from parliament to the two ancient universities of Oxford and Cambridge, was fundamentally altered through a series of parliamentary acts following the union of the British and Irish parliaments in 1801 and the defeat of Napoleon in 1815. This meant that at the end of the 1820s with the repeal of the Test and Corporation Acts in 1828, which allowed non-conformists to enter parliament and other public offices, and Catholic Emancipation the following year, there was a rapid and definitive change in the British Constitution. This was followed in 1832 by the Representation of the People Act that enfranchised significant numbers of the middle classes as well as tidying up some of the grossest abuses in the electoral system, including the abolition of the so-called 'pocket boroughs'. This was seen by some as the death knell of the 'confessional system' of the *ancien régime*.[1] The continuity of the identity of the Church of England, which was still ultimately dependent on parliament for its authority, could no longer be taken for granted. Writing on the changes to the electoral system in 1832, John Henry

Newman's friend, Hurrell Froude, and like him a tutor at Oriel College, commented that

> the extinction of the Irish Protestant Boroughs, and the great power accidentally given to Dissenters by the Reform Act, gave a concluding blow to the ancient system. And in 1833, we have witnessed the assembling of a parliament in which few perhaps can detect the traces of a Lay Synod of the Church of England.[2]

The Church of England could not rely on its protection from a parliament that was no longer composed solely of members of that Church. It was as if the 'umbilical cord' connecting church and state had been severed.[3] Some other foundation than the settlement that had held good since the time of Elizabeth and particularly after 1662 seemed necessary. Thus, as English political events in the 1830s had demonstrated, neither parliament nor the monarchy seemed willing or able to protect the particular privileges of the established church. For many, especially those of a more conservative disposition, it was thus crucial to re-narrate the history and theology of the Church of England.

The old Church of England hegemony was particularly well entrenched in the University of Oxford, which was still composed solely of members of the Church of England and which functioned as the main seminary for the Church of England. It was in that University that the Oxford Movement emerged as a theological and ecclesiastical response to the political changes of the 1820s and 30s. Its major protagonists, including John Keble, John Henry Newman and Edward Bouverie Pusey, set about re-establishing the Church of England on what they believed to be the far more stable foundation of Christian antiquity and apostolicity. They understood their Church as the true Catholic Church of England and as standing in continuity with the tradition upheld by the fathers of the church and their successors in the bishops. Although the Oxford Movement retained a strong sense of the union of throne and altar such as had been modelled in the sixteenth and seventeenth centuries, they nevertheless felt that the Crown had begun to betray its heritage. While they believed that it was proper for the State to uphold the teaching of the Church of England as the legitimate successor of the primitive church,[4] they were also aware that where it was failing in its duty it was necessary for them to find a different justification for the Church.[5]

Given this background, it is hardly surprising that the Tractarians should have been particularly attracted to the Christian past and to efforts at proving the continuity of the Church of England with the Church of the Fathers. To this end, there was a huge flurry of publishing activity that began in earnest from the middle of the 1830s. By the 1840s, this had developed into a period of unprecedented editing and republishing of texts from the earlier history of the Church. Many of the Tracts published by the Oxford Movement were themselves translations of the Fathers, and by the 1840s, the Oxford Movement had organized two major subscription publishing ventures, *The Library of the Fathers* and the *Library of Anglo-Catholic Theology*. Both these series, which will be discussed in more detail in Chapter 7, were aimed at defining the nature of Anglicanism in relation to the past. At the same time, a number of churchmen, who held to a very different view of the identity of the Church of England, formed the Parker Society to republish the works of the sixteenth-century reformers, which is discussed in more detail in Chapter 3.

The publishing activity of the 1840s and 50s was one aspect of a far deeper conflict about how the Church of England of the nineteenth century related to the past, and more importantly, precisely which past was formative. This meant that the historical identity of the Church of England was highly contested. By producing a canon of important and seminal texts, churchmen from different parties sought to locate an essence of Anglicanism through selective use of authors and by emphasizing different theological methods and styles. While some authors were as keen on producing texts from long before the separation of the English church from Rome in order to emphasize the continuity and catholicity of the church, others were equally keen to point to the links between the Reformed Church of England and the other protestant churches of continental Europe.

An added complication is that the texts that were republished by the different subscription societies made available a series of works that were themselves often controversial works concerned with very similar sets of issues. There was a complex cycle of struggles for identity where different periods of history interacted with one another. The majority of the texts that were republished, from Bishop Jewel (Chapter 3) to Archbishop Laud (Chapter 6), were themselves efforts to provide an identity in the face of opposition: the earlier theology of the Church of England from virtually all quarters was forged in the heat of controversy, rather than through systematic exposition of creeds and confessions. Following the Reformation, theology was something that had to be done precisely because there were many who disagreed with the identity and shape of the church. Its republication in Victorian England was an effort to relate those earlier attempts at forging an identity to the clamour for identity in a very different set of conditions. The interactions of nineteenth-century church history and theology with the history and theology of earlier periods are almost completely inseparable. To some extent at least, the republication of texts in modern editions was a political act: while it involved scholarship and dedication, it also required the belief that a text was important in defining a tradition, and that in turn meant that the organizers of the series had to develop techniques for persuading others to subsidize or to buy the new editions. Many who cared about the soul of Anglicanism in the mid-nineteenth century were prepared to support publishing ventures (and to be sent sometimes virtually unreadable annotated editions by half-forgotten authors).

The Role of the Reformation

There were different versions of the Church of England on offer in the nineteenth century. One version saw the Church as rooted in the Fathers of the early Church: the norms and sources of theology were not principally those that had been foisted on the church at the Reformation but were to be understood chiefly in terms of what the church had taught universally before its schisms and divisions. What Diarmaid MacCulloch writes about the study of Church history in the nineteenth century illustrates this approach by the leading figures of the Oxford Movement (although as I will demonstrate in Chapter 3, there were alternatives to an Anglo-Catholic understanding of history):

to the extent that the universities took any interest in the history of the Church of England, it was to the Anglo-Catholic tradition that they looked for an academically respectable view of the past: the tradition that made more of continuity than discontinuity, of conscious ties across the Reformation rather than of accidental survival.[6]

Characteristic of this sort of thinking that looked to the past was the emphasis on the so-called Vincentian canon of 434 AD, which saw the content of the Christian faith as simply that which has been believed everywhere, always and by all. The Reformation could easily be regarded as something of an embarrassment.

This attitude is not easy to explain, because despite its many complexities and particularities, the English Reformation achieved what might reasonably be understood as a doctrinal and liturgical settlement that resembled some of the Reformed settlements of continental Europe. As Hensley Henson put it unequivocally but accurately, 'the type of Christianity which the Prayer Book was compiled to express, and which the Thirty-nine articles explicitly affirmed, was the Reformed type'.[7] While admittedly there were many who wanted the Reformation to go much further in the reign of Elizabeth I, it is nevertheless reasonable to suggest that Elizabeth consolidated most of the religious policy of her half-brother, Edward VI, and his archbishop, Thomas Cranmer (1489–1556). As will become clear, perhaps the best way of conceiving the English Reformation is of a Reformation halted in progress, with many loose ends, not least in terms of Church order. While it may have been halted, perhaps in part because of Elizabeth's own conservatism, it nevertheless took place – and in many ways it was far more thoroughgoing than many of its continental counterparts, particularly in the Lutheran territories. And yet, although it is difficult to read the history of the sixteenth century as anything other than a relatively successful implementation of a reformed settlement on the Church of England, the role of the Reformation in Anglican identity was called into question in the nineteenth century in a way that was quite novel.

By the 1830s, there were some who had even begun to question the value of the Reformation altogether. Just as the publishing policy of the Oxford Movement sought to emphasize the continuity of the Church of England with the past, so it tended to underplay the Reformation, seeing it as at best a necessary evil to purge the Church of some of the worst excesses of Rome and at worst a wholesale distortion of the truth. By the end of the 1830s, approaches to the Reformation could be polemically charged. A good example is offered by Hurrell Froude, a close friend of John Keble and Newman, and one of the youthful leaders of the Oxford Movement in the 1830s, who had the misfortune to die prematurely of consumption in 1836 aged only 32. After his death, his often aphoristic writings were gathered together into two volumes and published by Newman, Keble and Mozley as *Remains of the Late Richard Hurrell Froude*.[8] In death Froude proved even more outspoken than in life, and the power of his rhetoric was to have a lasting impact on the reputation of his editors. In one of his most controversial statements, he remarked, 'The Reformation was a limb badly set – it must be broken again in order to be righted'.[9] The very reformed identity of the Church of England was being brought under question. In a passage from a long letter written from Barbados as he was recuperating from illness at the beginning of January 1834, he commented the following:

> You will be shocked at my avowal, that I am every day becoming a less and less loyal son of the Reformation. It appears to me plain that in all matters that seem to us indifferent or even doubtful, we should conform our practices to those of the Church which has preserved its traditionary practices unbroken.[10]

At the end of the following year, shortly before his death, he went even further in a letter to a friend:

> Really I hate the Reformation and the Reformers more and more, and have almost made up my mind that the rationalist spirit they set afloat is the *pseudoprophetas* of the Revelations.[11]

To label the reformers as the false prophets of the Book of Revelation was hardly likely to win over friends to the cause of Froude's editors, who themselves were increasingly under suspicion for their catholizing tendencies.

At much the same time as the publication of Froude's *Remains*, a number of more protestant-minded people under the leadership of Charles Portalès Golightly had sought to build a substantial memorial to the Oxford martyrs of the Reformation, Latimer, Ridley and Cranmer, which was to play a key part of the assertion of a reformed identity for the Church of England.[12] In response, Keble had written privately to Edward Bouverie Pusey, Regius Professor of Hebrew, in 1839:

> I cannot understand how poor Cranmer could be reckoned a *bona fide* martyr according to the rules of the Primitive Church. . . . Anything which separates the present Church from the Reformers I should hail as a great good, and certainly such would in a measure be the effect of a monument of acknowledgment that we are not Papists, without any reference to them. As to its uniting people, I do not in the least expect it. There is a deep doctrinal difference which cannot be got over.[13]

The physical memorializing of the Reformation symbolized the struggles between the parties of the early Victorian Church, many of which, as will be shown through the course of this book, were to be played out physically in architecture and liturgy. The theological inheritance of the Reformation for the Church of England remained crucial in these differences.

In the 1830s, Bishop John Bird Sumner of Chester, who became the first Evangelical Archbishop of Canterbury, pointed to what he regarded as the threat to the Church of England of those who denied the importance of the Reformation: 'Under the spurious pretence of deference to antiquity and respect for primitive models, the foundations of our Protestant Church are undermined by men who dwell within her walls, and those who sit in the Reformer's seat are traducing the Reformation'.[14] On such a picture, which was not wholly removed from the truth, as Newman's notorious Tract XC of 1841 revealed, the Tractarians were little less than fifth columnists seeking to remove the inheritance of the sixteenth century. This was noted by many at the time. For instance, after reading a review of this final Tract, which sought to explain the Thirty-Nine Articles of Religion quite differently

17

from how their framers had intended, the broad churchman Charles Kingsley wrote to his mother in 1841: 'Whether wilful or deceived, these men are Jesuits, taking the oath to the Articles with moral reservations, which allow them to explain them away in senses utterly different from those of their authors – All the worst doctrinal features of Popery Mr Newman professes to believe in'.[15]

Even today, the question of the interpretation of the Reformation still provokes controversy. While many might have thought (and hoped) that the heated passions of the nineteenth century had disappeared from discussions of the Reformation, recent debates about the role of the Bible and the exercise of authority in the Anglican Communion have highlighted its continued importance in struggles over Anglican identity. Accusations of 'neo-Puritanism', for instance, have been levelled on attempts to establish a doctrinal minimum across the Anglican Communion in an Anglican Covenant.[16] Doctrinal boundaries and confessions of faith still provoke powerful responses from across the different strands of opinion. In such a situation, it is of course hard to be objective about the Reformation and its status in Anglican theology and identity.

The History of the Reformation

Even without these complicating factors of nineteenth- and twentieth-century clamours for identity, it is not easy to be clear about the precise contours of the English Reformation. The religious changes of the sixteenth century continue to be one of the most hotly contested issues in the study of English history. What holds sway for one generation of historians is revised in the subsequent generation, only to be revised again in the next. Even today, historians sometimes approach the Reformation with a modicum of romanticism, especially about the nature of 'popular' religion.[17] For the remainder of this chapter, I will seek to explain what happened to the Church of England from around 1529 to the death of Edward VI. In doing so, while I shall try to clear away some of the ideological deposits of the nineteenth century, the question still remains as to precisely how the strange combination of events shaped the identity and theology of Anglicanism, and how it continues to shape contemporary controversies and debates. Like so much else in Anglican theology, the legacy and influence of the Reformation turn out to be complicated, contested and inherently uncertain.

It would be impossible in a book of this scope to offer a complete explanation of the English Reformation. My focus remains on theology, both doctrinal and practical, although there are political and economic aspects that play such an important factor in the development of theological method in the sixteenth century that they cannot be ignored. The character of the monarchs (two kings in this chapter and two queens in the next) also plays a crucial factor in shaping English theology. Had Mary I or Edward VI lived longer, the English religious settlement might well have been significantly different. In a non-democratic polity, particular personalities could have an even more powerful effect on the course of events than they might do today. For this reason, it is reasonable to claim that the Reformation was personality driven. The protestant sympathies – or otherwise – of the people mattered far less in the Reformation period than the views and opinions of those in positions of power in the state and in the church.[18] And of course, had Henry VIII acquired a male heir by his first wife, Katherine of Aragon, then perhaps Anglican theology would have been little more than a distinctive and possibly rather insular form of Roman Catholicism. Such speculations point both to the centrality of Acts of State and also to the whims of monarchs in the progress of the English Reformation. While this does not mean that theology was unimportant, it is necessary to put it in the context of a much wider set of issues. Thus, according to one recent writer (even though he might be slightly exaggerating the differences), there were at least three Reformations – popular, political and ecclesiastical – which perhaps had little to do with one another.[19]

What I offer in this chapter is a brief overview of the main contours of the early part of the Reformation with some more detailed discussions of how theology was done in response to particular issues. While these are more illustrative than comprehensive, they nevertheless reveal some of the tensions and conflicts over the question of the identity of the Church of England. Despite the different ways in which later authors might have read and even idealized the period, it is crucial to remember that even in 1559, the year of the Elizabethan Settlement and the re-imposition of the Book of Common Prayer after the reign of the Roman Catholic Mary I, it would be quite misleading to speak of 'Anglican theology' – the struggle for Anglican identity was far from settled. The course of the Reformation into the reign of Elizabeth and the Stuarts is characterized by repeated controversy as people with a variety of viewpoints tried to impose their will on the shape of the Church of England. There was significant conflict over doctrine, church order and the relationships between church and state among those who would have professed themselves to be loyal churchmen. As will become clear, some succeeded and others did not, even where they might have expected to have done so.

Although inevitably any periodization involves a simplification of a complex web of events, it would not be too far off the mark to suggest that the English Reformation happened in three distinct stages: first, the separation from Rome under Henry VIII, which was accompanied by the suppression of the monasteries and the first tentative efforts at doctrinal reform. Secondly, the period under Edward VI, which marked a rapid and wholesale adoption of reformed liturgy and doctrine: the brevity of his reign and the accession of his half-sister Mary under the terms of Henry's will meant that whatever achievements for the protestant cause had been made could be rapidly undone. The third period, which will be discussed in the next chapter, was that of the consolidation of the Reformation in the Elizabethan Settlement when to all intents and purposes the Reformation came to an end, despite the strong wishes of many both in church and in parliament. As Christopher Haigh writes, it was only in this final period that 'the Protestant breakthrough came . . . through the evangelistic efforts of a new generation of university-trained ministers'.[20] Elizabeth's reign saw the consolidation of the Edwardian position, coupled with many efforts to continue the Reformation still further. It was here that the adolescent and even mature theology of the Church of England began to take shape.

Henry VIII

To use an anachronistic analogy, Henry VIII succeeded in national-
izing the Church of England and removing from it any vestige
of papal authority – he also stripped it of many of its assets and
distributed them to many of his supporters. While the precise
circumstances of the break with Rome do not need to be rehearsed
in detail,[21] Henry sought an annulment of the 1503 dispensation
he had received from Pope Julius II in order to marry his brother
Arthur's widow, Katherine of Aragon. The legal problems were
great, and the matter was complicated by the fact that Katherine
was the aunt of the Holy Roman Emperor, Charles V, whose troops
had sacked Rome in 1527 and who held Clement VII captive.
Under these circumstances, Henry soon began denouncing the
pomp of the Roman curia and asserting an 'authority imperial',
claiming to be 'not only prince and king, but set on such a pinnacle
of dignity that we know no superior on earth'. A collection of
texts, the *Collectanea satis copiosa*, was assembled from the Fathers
and the later traditions of the church, which purported to show
that the King was sovereign over the church: the King particularly
appreciated the letter supposedly written by Pope Eleutherius to
the legendary King Lucius of Britain where the King was to rule
by a law above that of Rome.[22]

Not long afterwards, at the beginning of 1531, Henry
presented to the Convocation of Canterbury the demand that
they recognize him as 'sole protector and supreme head of the
English Church and Clergy', which passed after the ambiguous
'as far as the law of God allows' had been inserted. At the
same time, he secured the passage of the Act for the Pardon
of the Clergy where the clergy were forced to pay £100,000
for alleged transgression of the law of *praemunire*, which stated
that no cases could be heard outside English courts. During
this period, Thomas Cromwell, a friend and accomplice of the
Boleyn family, had emerged as a key figure, who assured the King
that England had a jurisdictional independence from Rome. At
the same time, the prominent lawyer Christopher St Germain
published a tract called *Doctor and Student: Or Dialogues Between
A Doctor of Divinity and a Student in the Laws of England* where he
drew on the work of the fourteenth-century Paduan jurist and

defender of the Emperor, Marsilius, who had famously asserted that the only legitimate functions of the clergy were limited to the realms of piety, consecration and sacrament (the *potestas ordinis*); all other areas were included under the *potestas jurisdictionis* and were to be exercised purely by the secular authority. St Germain denied that the goods of the spiritual realm belong to the domain of the 'Spiritualty' (church) but instead were 'things merely temporal, and keeping the body' and were consequently part of the civil domain. Society is thus not to be divided into two realms, the sacred and the secular, but rather was composed of 'Spiritual Men . . . deputed and dedicated to the service of God . . . and secular men or lay men' who, 'though they walk in the way of God', are yet 'occupied about such things as pertain to the Commonwealth and to the good order of the people'. The crucial aspects here are the understanding of authority and the division between things temporal and spiritual. While it can hardly be dignified with the name of theology, the logic of his thinking led St Germain to assert that the king in parliament was 'high sovereign over the people, which hath not only charge on the bodies but also on the souls of the subject'.[23]

As Henry sought to put the theory of supreme headship over the church into practice, so it gradually mutated into a form of total royal control of the church.[24] This was enacted through a series of what can only be described as bullying measures to ensure the submission of the clergy who eventually gave way to the royal supremacy in May 1532.[25] What emerged through the crisis was a very clear statement of the King's authority over the church. He would settle for no halfway house, telling the Speaker and twelve members of the House of Commons:

> Well-beloved subjects, we thought that the clergy of our realm had been our subjects wholly, but now we have well perceived that they be but half our subjects, yea, and scarce our subjects; for all the prelates at their consecration make an oath to the Pope, clean contrary to the oath that they make to us, so that they seem to be his subjects. And not ours. The copy of both the oaths I deliver here to you, requiring you to invent some orders, that we be not thus deluded of our spiritual subjects.

Through the assertion of his own unfettered authority the King thus gained control over the church courts, which meant that the way was cleared to proceed to the royal annulment, which became increasingly urgent since Anne Boleyn was pregnant. Whether the assertion of royal supremacy was a pragmatic act by a King needing to get his own way or a premeditated series of manoeuvres planned over many years remains uncertain: what is clear, however, is that it offered unprecedented opportunities. 'Perhaps there was little to be said for a tainted papal primacy, and a lot to be said for an untried but promising royal supremacy'.[26]

The legislation introduced at the beginning of 1533 paved the way for a local decision to be made. The clearest formulation of the Crown as the sole authority over church and state was made by Thomas Cromwell in his famous preamble to the Act in Restraint of Appeals, which boldly asserted that 'this realm of England is an Empire ... governed by one supreme head and king, having the dignity and royal estate of the imperial crown of the same, unto whom a body politic, compact of all sorts and degrees of people, divided in terms and by names of spirituality and temporality, be bounden and owe to bear, next to God, a natural and humble obedience'. What this meant was straightforward: the final court of appeal in all matters was to be found 'within the king's jurisdiction and not elsewhere'. Shortly afterwards, Thomas Cranmer, who had replaced William Warham as Archbishop of Canterbury in 1532, went on to declare the annulment of Henry's marriage to Katherine on 23 May 1533, and five days later, the marriage to Boleyn was declared lawful.

Cranmer is a complex character whose opinions changed through his career as Archbishop, which was undoubtedly expedient if he was to survive alongside a king of strong, and sometimes erratic, views. One thing is certain about him: he retained a strong belief in Royal Supremacy that made him the King's ideal agent, especially through the rapid changes of the 1530s. As Jasper Ridley wrote many years ago, 'if the known facts of Cranmer's life are impartially examined, nearly all the apparent contradictions disappear and a consistent personality emerges. Like most of his contemporaries . . . Cranmer believed in Royal absolutism'.[27] The extent of the transfer of sovereignty to the monarch can be gleaned from Cranmer's own collection of quotations from Canon Law probably made around 1533. All were overturned through the 1530s:

> He that knowledgeth not himself to be under the Bishop
> of Rome, and that the Bishop of Rome is ordained by God
> to have primacy over all the world, is an heretic; . . . Prince's
> laws, if they be against the canons and decrees of the bishop
> of Rome, be of no force nor strength; The see of Rome hath
> neither spot not wrinkle in it, nor cannot err; . . . The bishop
> of Rome is not bound to any decrees, but he may compel, as
> well the clergy as laymen, to receive his decrees and canon-
> law; . . . The bishop of Rome hath authority to judge all men
> . . . but no man hath authority to judge him; . . . The bishop
> of Rome hath the authority to excommunicate emperors
> and princes, depose them from their states; . . . the emperor
> is the Bishop of Rome's subject; . . . There can be no council
> of bishops without the authority of the see of Rome; and the
> emperor ought not to be present at the council; . . . Nothing
> may be done against him that appealeth to Rome; The bishop
> of Rome is judge in temporal things, and hath two swords,
> spiritual and temporal; laymen may not be judges to any of
> the clergy; . . . The clergy ought to give no oath of fidelity to
> their temporal governors, except they have temporalities of
> them.[28]

Given that this whole list was fundamentally transformed in a matter of only a few years, it was clear that something profound was happening to the relationships between church and state.

A number of further acts cemented the Royal Supremacy over matters ecclesiastical. These were brought to a conclusion in the Act of Supremacy of 1534, which described the King as Head of 'the Church called *Anglicana Ecclesia*'. Within this church, the Crown was given authority to visit (or inspect) the clergy, 'to correct, restrain, and amend' their 'errors, heresies, abuses, . . . and contempts', both for the 'increase of virtue of Christ's religion' and for 'the conservation of the peace, unity and tranquillity of this realm'. While the King did not gain the power to ordain clergy or to administer the sacraments, in virtually everything else his authority was unlimited. As Geoffrey Dickens observed, the Crown gained 'power to correct the opinions of preachers, to supervise the formulation of doctrine, to reform the canon law, to visit and discipline both regular and secular clergy, and even . . . to try heretics in person'.[29] Here in embryo was an emphasis on order and peace, which proved such a strong theological theme in the controversies that emerged later in Tudor England.

The King quickly put these near-absolute powers into practice through Cromwell as his vice-gerent. Yet, he was undoubtedly also his own man when it came to religion: he had strong if not always completely coherent views of his own.[30] Cromwell ordered preaching in defence of supremacy, and the civil authorities, the sheriffs and JPs were instructed to keep an eye on bishops, who were soon replaced to reflect the changed religious policy. Where in 1530 the King had burnt Tyndale's works, by 1535 there were translations of the Bible in existence, which were soon encouraged to be placed in churches. This was accompanied by the dissolution of the monasteries, where the King asserted his right to confiscate and redistribute the lands of the church. What for Cranmer and Cromwell was a pious fraud was for Henry a lucrative source of revenue.

The mid-1530s also saw some tentative reforms in church doctrine, during a time when Henry was seeking continental alliances that made him move closer to the Lutheran territories. This led to the production of the *Ten Articles* in 1536, which were closely related to the so-called Wittenberg Articles[31] that had emerged out of exchanges with the Schmalkaldic league led by Bishop Edward Foxe of Hereford and Richard Heath.[32] The Articles are a somewhat hastily drawn up compromise between some of the cardinal principles of Protestantism (including the reduction of the sacraments to baptism, Eucharist and penance 'without which no man could be saved'), but they were also traditional in retaining a strong sense of real presence.[33] At this stage, the episcopal bench was divided between conservatives (such as Stephen Gardiner and Cuthbert Tunstall) and the reform-minded, including Cranmer and Hugh Latimer. The Articles were divided into two parts, the first five expressing those 'things necessary to our salvation' and the second five describing 'such things as have been of a long continuance for a decent order and an honest policy . . . though they be not expressly commanded of God, nor necessary to our salvation'. This distinction, which was maintained by the Reformers, became central to debates later in the sixteenth century, especially over ministry.

Of the first five articles on matters necessary to salvation, the compromise is perhaps strongest in Article V on Justification, which asserted that, while it was 'through the merits of Christ's passion' that justification was obtained, this was to be accompanied by 'contrition and faith joined with charity', which moved beyond the Wittenberg blueprint. The bluntness of the Lutheran insistence on Justification by Faith is thereby toned down. In addition, while the real presence was strongly affirmed, no particular theory was mentioned. Similarly, Article IV remained conservative in its theology, stating that 'under the form and figure of bread and wine . . . is verily, substantially and really contained and comprehended the very selfsame body and blood of our Lord and Saviour', yet it did not prescribe a particular theory of such a substantial presence. Among the indifferent matters in the second five articles – which were nevertheless expedient – were images in churches, honouring the saints, prayers to saints and prayers for the dead, with the caveat that 'such abuses be clearly put away, which under the name of purgatory hath been advanced, as to make men believe that through the Bishop of Rome's pardons souls might clearly be delivered out of purgatory'. Article IX offers a good summary of the general shape of the articles: the rites and ceremonies of Christ's Church are to be used as things 'good and laudable', but 'none of these ceremonies have the power to remit sin, but only to stir up our minds unto God, by whom only our sins are forgiven'. Haigh's assessment of the Ten Articles, as the first official statement of a theological settlement for the English Church, seems accurate: 'Though Henry had sanctioned admission of a good deal of Luther into his church (probably to quieten Cranmer, Latimer (Worcester), and their friends), he did not intend it to make much difference in practice. Sacraments and ceremonies – and, doubtless, superstitions – were to continue as before. The Ten Articles had brought more Reformation but only a little more'.[34]

In 1537, a follow-up called *The Godly and Pious Institution of a Christian Man* or the *Bishops' Book* was published by the bishops to help clarify the doctrinal settlement of the Ten Articles. While affirming seven sacraments, it went marginally further in its Lutheran teaching on justification. It was perhaps influenced by Melanchthon whose *Loci Communes* had been dedicated to Henry VIII in 1535. Its status, however, was unclear. It was adopted for a three-year period 'without the . . . power and licence of your majesty', with the bishops admitting that 'we knowledge and confess that we have none authority'. Henry disapproved of much in the book, reaffirming the importance of good works and also – perhaps surprisingly given his track record – the importance of the sacrament of marriage. He was also critical of the discussion of 'holy orders'. The *Bishops' Book* had appeared to limit the rights of the King in matters of ecclesiastical appointment and in excommunication: 'We may not think that it doth appertain unto the office of kings and princes to preach and teach, to administer the sacraments, to absolve, to excommunicate, and other things belonging to the office and administration of bishops and priests'.[35] While he may not have claimed sacramental authority, he remained anxious about any curtailment of his powers in the government of the church. As a sign of the ambiguity of the period, however, the *Bishop's Book* was also significant in rearranging the Ten Commandments so that the injunction against images became a commandment in its own right, a way of formulating the commandments that betrays the influence of Reformed thought.[36]

Again it was perhaps because of the perceived threats to his own authority that the King outlawed the cult of St Thomas à Becket in 1538 (who had challenged the authority of Henry II). In the same Act, he showed more caution about the Bible and other books, lest they should challenge the royal supremacy, regulating their import from the Continent. The King also defended the practice of creeping to the cross on Good Friday, which was highly suspect to the reform-minded. It looked as if the brief and circumspect foray into Reformation doctrine in the mid-1530s was over, even if many held out that it would later return. What the period also clearly illustrates is the influence of both strong reform-minded voices among the bishops and the importance of international diplomacy, something which continued unabated throughout the remainder of Henry's reign. The ill-fated marriage to Anne of Cleves illustrates one aspect of this policy, as does the anti-papal pageant on the River Thames in June 1539. Yet soon afterwards, following the quarrels between France and the Emperor, the need for an alliance with Lutherans became less important, which resulted in a rapid change in Henry's religious policy. Where the reform-minded Anne Boleyn, Cromwell and Cranmer had been his chief religious influences in the mid-1530s, the conservatives Stephen Gardiner and the Duke of Norfolk became central to his policy after 1538, even if the 'Teflon prelate'[37] Cranmer remained in office.

What emerged was a rather eccentric version of a *via media*. The King was remarkably even-handed in his punishments of protestant heretics and Catholics. Although he perhaps misleadingly sees Henry's policy as the precursor of the Elizabethan Settlement in that Elizabeth's mean was between rather different extremes, G. W. Bernard summarizes Henry's later religious policy clearly: 'He was anti-papal, against the monasteries, against superstitious and idolatrous abuses, but he was also opposed to novelties, to justification by faith alone, and upheld something like traditional teaching on the mass'.[38] In July 1540, for instance, three preachers, Robert Barnes, who had helped produce the Wittenberg Articles, William Jerome and Thomas Garrett, were burnt for heresy, and three Catholic priests – Richard Fetherstone, Edward Powell and Thomas Abel – were hanged on the same day. Other opponents wisely left the country, escaping to cities that had experienced the Reformation, including Strasbourg, Basel and Zürich. The French Ambassador observed afterwards:

> It is no easy thing to keep a people in revolt against the
> Holy See and the authority of the Church, and yet free from
> the infection of the new doctrines, or, on the other hand, if
> they remain orthodox, to prevent them from looking with
> attachment to the Papacy.[39]

While anti-papalism may not have been an easy policy, it was nevertheless put into effect by the unbridled assertion of the Royal Supremacy. As Cromwell said to the parliament in 1540 shortly before his own demise, the King leant 'neither to the right nor the left hand . . . but set the pure and sincere doctrine of the Christian faith only before his eyes'. He even saw himself both as Josiah purging the temple and as David leading his people in worship. As late as 1545, he denounced the two types of extreme clergy before parliament: those who were 'too stiff in their old mumpsimus' and those who were 'too busy and curious in their new sumpsimus'.[40]

There was also a conservative reaction in doctrine. On 16 May 1539, the Duke of Norfolk asked the House of Lords to consider the six controversial issues of transubstantiation, communion in one kind, vows of chastity, votive masses, clerical celibacy and auricular confession. Unity was to be achieved by the careful regulation of official confessions, by setting out 'plain and sincere' doctrine and, as the Act of Six Articles (1539) has it, by legislating for 'abolishing of diversity in opinions', a diversity which Henry feared.[41] What emerged was a conservative restatement of traditional doctrine and practices, which was accepted by both parliament and convocation. Article I, for instance, affirmed the real presence and claimed that 'after the consecration there remaineth no substance of bread and wine, nor any other substance but the substance of Christ, God and man'. Article II affirmed communion in one kind, Article III maintained clerical celibacy and Article IV permitted vows of chastity. Article V upheld private masses and Article VI auricular confession. The sting in the tail was that the Act was used to promote uniformity of practice and was called by some 'the whip with six strings'. Under its provisions, charges of heresy could be brought before both common law courts and ecclesiastical courts.

Cromwell was denounced on the grounds of treason and heresy and was executed on 28 June 1540. Henry then married Katherine Howard, a member of the conservative faction. A new committee on doctrine drew up *The Necessary Doctrine and Erudition for Any Christian Man*, the so-called *King's Book* in 1543. This summarized the teaching of the Church and was highly traditional. It began by noting that the King and his clergy 'by the help of God and his word have travailed to purge and cleanse our realm' of idolatry and superstition.[42] But this purging did not result in any move towards Reformation doctrine. On justification, for instance, it noted the alliance of faith and good works:

as it is taken in scripture, signifieth the making of us righteous afore God . . . And albeit God is the principal cause and chief worker of this justification in us, without whose grace no man can do no good thing . . . yet it so pleaseth the high wisdom of God, that man . . . shall be also a worker by his free consent and obedience . . . in the attaining of his own justification.

However, although the doctrine may have been conservative, the *King's Book* continued the Royal Supremacy in ecclesiastical appointments and the administration of the church:

there is no certain rule prescribed or limited by the word of God for the nomination, election, presentation or appointing of any such ecclesiastical ministers, but the same is wholly left unto positive laws and ordinances of every Christian region, provided and made or to be made in that behalf, with the assent of the prince and ruler.[43]

In 1543, there were also restrictions placed on reading the Bible in English with the Act for the Advancement of True Religion. Those of the rank of yeomen or below, as well as all women who were not members of the nobility or gentry, were forbidden from having access to the Bible or to 'dispute or argue, to debate discuss or expound' it.[44] At least in the rhetoric of later years, the old practices seem to have continued in the popular piety of the common people. As John Foxe put it, describing the martyrdom of William Mouldon, these were 'those days of King Henry':

when the mass most flourished, the altars with the sacrament thereof being in their most high veneration, that to man's reason it might seem impossible that the glory and opinion of that sacrament and sacramentals, so highly worshipped and so deeply rooted in the hearts of many, could by any means possible so soon decay and vanish to nought.[45]

Liturgically, there were few innovations, although in 1544, Cranmer produced his English Litany to be used in processions, which might indicate a certain weakening of the conservative influence at court. The King had observed that people 'understode no parte of suche prayers or suffrages as were used to be songe and sayde'. He therefore commissioned Cranmer to 'set forthe certayne godly prayers and suffrages in our natyve Englyshe tongue'. The litany was based on medieval precedents, even if it reduced the number of saints in the suffrages. It also presented a version of the King's *via media*, maintaining a balanced rejection of papacy and heresy. One suffrage, which was dropped from later editions, read: 'From all sedycion and privey conspiracie, from the tyranny of the bisshop of Rome and all his detestable enormyties, from all false doctrine and heresye, from hardnes of hearte, and conmtempte of thy worde and commaundemente: Good lorde deliver us'. Similarly, a *Primer* was written for the instruction of young people in some basic and traditional prayers, which also purified some aspects of traditional piety.[46]

Towards the end of Henry's reign, the Conservative party remained in the ascendency, which prompted Christopher Haigh to assert that the theological changes under Edward VI were accidental: 'if Henry had died in September 1546, when conservatives were in the ascendant and reformers had their backs to the stake, English history would have been very different'.[47] When he died on 28 January 1547, the King died 'a catholic, though a rather bad catholic',[48] leaving £666 to the poor to pray for his soul and a further endowment of £600 for a chantry of two priests at Windsor to celebrate four solemn requiem masses a year. However, even though there was an attempt at a Howard regency, the Earl of Hertford managed to neutralize Stephen Gardiner, and Norfolk was sent to the Tower on 12 December 1546. This regime change proved crucial for the development of Anglican theology. Under his son, Henry's modestly reformed Catholicism without the Pope quickly mutated into something very different.

Edward VI and the Protestant Reformation

Edward VI was only nine years old when he succeeded his father. This meant that a regency had to be set up. The Earl of Hertford, who was shortly afterwards made Duke of Somerset, was named as the protector of the realm on 31 January 1547, and on 12 March, he became virtual regent with near sovereign powers: while the precocious king was not uninterested in affairs of church and state, the Royal Supremacy was exercised on his behalf by a faction interested in further protestant reform. In July 1547, Thomas Cranmer issued a series of injunctions requiring the removal of images from churches as well as the acquisition of an English Bible and a copy of Erasmus' *Paraphrases* in each parish. In addition to the Primer and the Litany, a *Book of Homilies* had been produced towards the end of Henry's reign, which functioned as official sermons that could be read out in churches on Sundays. As might be expected, obedience to the King was a strong theme, but Cranmer also reintroduced doctrine that was strongly opposed to the *King's Book*, not least on justification. His understanding of justification in the *Book of Homilies* was clear and unequivocal:

> For all the good works that we can do be unperfect,
> and therefore not able to deserve our justification: but
> our justification doth come freely by the mere mercy of
> God ... But justification is the office of God only, and is not
> a thing which we render unto him ... yet we must renounce
> the merits of all our said virtues, of faith, hope, charities and
> all other good deeds, which we either have done, shall do,
> or can do, as things that be far too weak and insufficient
> and unperfect, to deserve remission of our sins and our
> justification.[49]

While some bishops, especially Bishop Stephen Gardiner, opposed these religious changes, Somerset ensured conformity and Gardner was eventually deprived of his bishopric. The ground was being prepared for further reform: parliament introduced a statute requiring communion in both kinds and introduced an order for communion in 1548 that offered English translations of some parts of the Mass to allow for congregational participation. At the same time, there was no weakening of the Royal Supremacy over the church. The Act implementing religious change asserted that 'All authority of Jurisdiction, spiritual and Temporal, is derived and deducted from the King's Majesty, as supreme head'. Royal control also extended over the ecclesiastical courts, which were to 'be kept by no other power, or authority, either foreign or within the Realm'.

In the summer of 1548, a significant amount of discussion took place over the doctrine of the Eucharist, which helped pave the way for the first of the two Books of Common Prayer that were to appear during the reign of Edward. There was a desire by Cranmer to remove the complexity of the past so that everything was 'plain and easily' understood. The production of a new Prayer Book also gave him the opportunity for experimenting in the liturgical expression of reformed doctrine, which, hardly surprisingly, was focused on the Eucharist. Cranmer, it seems, had moved increasingly away from a belief in the real and corporal presence of Christ in the mass at the very end of Henry's reign.[50] Nicholas Ridley seems to have been principally responsible for this change of heart, and Cranmer began to affirm a spiritual presence. The first Prayer Book did not proceed as far as it might have done, partly because of the desire not to upset the balance of the delicate international situation in which Calvin and Bullinger were seeking an agreement on the Eucharist. This resulted in the *Consensus Tigurinus* of May 1549 that brought a significant degree of harmony to the Eucharistic doctrine of the Swiss churches, which made it far easier for discussions between English and Swiss churchmen later in the Reformation.[51] In December 1548, a four-day set piece debate on the Eucharist was held in the House of Lords in which Protector Somerset participated, briefed by Peter Martyr, who had been installed as Regius Professor in Oxford. Cranmer also appointed Martin Bucer (1491–1551), the Strasbourg reformer to the equivalent chair in Cambridge.

Thomas Cranmer had spent much of his archiepiscopate wrestling with doctrine, not least in the discussions with Lutherans in which he was actively engaged in 1538 and which influenced the Forty-Two Articles of 1553: the protectorate gave him the opportunity to produce a statement of faith along with new liturgical resources for a reformed church, which would move away from the conservatism of the later years of Henry VIII. Cranmer was far from insular and sought an international alliance among reformed churches. Writing to Calvin in March 1552, he urged him to convene a meeting to 'handle all the heads of ecclesiastical doctrine'.[52] Now resident in England, both Peter

Martyr and Martin Bucer corresponded with Cranmer in the production of the Prayer Book: Bucer seems to have understood the Eucharist in terms of a drawing up to heaven by the believer where the spiritual food is received, and Peter Martyr asserted that the substance of the bread and wine were unchanged.[53]

Nevertheless, there was a certain reticence about the first Book of Common Prayer that was published early in 1549 and that had been purchased by nearly all parishes by June. For instance, the order for the Eucharist was called 'The supper of the Lord and the holy Communion, commonly called the Mass'. Nevertheless, it represents significant developments in theology from the old order of the mass. Most importantly, the offering of Christ on the cross was separated completely from any sense of Eucharistic sacrifice. The prayer of consecration affirms the singularity of Christ's atonement (and is mainly repeated in the second Prayer Book of 1552):

> God heavenly Father, which of thy tender mercy didst give thine only Son Jesus Christ, to suffer death upon the cross for our redemption, who made there (by his one oblation, once offered) a full, perfect, and sufficient sacrifice, oblation, and satisfaction, for the sins of the whole world, and did institute, and in his holy Gospel command us to celebrate, a perpetual memory of that his precious death, until his coming again.[54]

In relation to the presence of Christ, Cranmer outlines his understanding of the spiritual presence of Christ in the Eucharist in one of the lengthy exhortations before receiving communion. Here he states the following:

> if with a truly penitent heart, and lively faith, we receive that holy Sacrament; (for then we spiritually eat the flesh of Christ, and drink his blood, then we dwell in Christ and Christ in us, we be made one with Christ, and Christ with us).[55]

At the same time, however, the words at the distribution of communion implied a degree of ambiguity about the presence of

Christ in the sacrament: 'The body of our Lord Jesus Christ which was given for thee, preserve thy body and soul unto everlasting life'. This simple formula could obviously be read in different ways. Because of these ambiguities, it is best to see the 1549 Prayer Book as an interim rite, which, as Bucer wrote, 'was only to be retained for a time' while 'the people . . . may be won over'.[56] For some, the book's attachment to the past rendered it unusable. Thus John Hooper, who was one of the more radical figures on the English bench of bishops and who was a pure memorialist in his Eucharistic doctrine,[57] threatened to excommunicate himself unless the book, which he regarded as 'manifestly impious', was further reformed. After expressing hope that the new Bishop of London, Nicholas Ridley, would 'destroy the altars of Baal', he wrote to Heinrich Bullinger in Zürich: 'I am so much offended with that book . . . If it be not corrected, I neither can nor will communicate with the church in the administration of the supper'.[58]

Shortly after the publication of the Prayer Book in 1549, there was further discussion over doctrine in both Oxford and Cambridge in the early summer. In Oxford in an influential debate, Peter Martyr made the case for further reform. The proceedings of the debate sold well in England and Switzerland. The young King was sufficiently interested in what was going on to annotate his own copy.[59] Key to the theology that had been developed by the continental figures was a doctrine of a spiritual presence of Christ in the sacrament that is discerned only by faith. In his criticism of the Prayer Book text, Bucer was keen that ordinary bread should be used, rather than wafers, and also that any left over should be taken home for personal use by the celebrant.[60]

Despite the change of leadership with Somerset's replacement by the Earl of Warwick (who became the Duke of Northumberland) in October 1549, the reformation continued. Cranmer himself published his *Defence of the True and Catholic Doctrine of the Sacrament of The Body and Blood of Our Saviour Christ with a Confutation of Sundry Errors Concerning the Same, Grounded and Stablished Upon God's Holy Word, and Approved by The Consent of the Most Ancient Doctors of the Church* in 1550.[61] After Stephen Gardiner had attacked the book, Cranmer replied in 1551 with the less than subtly titled *Answer to a Crafty and Sophistical Cavillation Devised by Stephen Gardiner against the True and Godly Doctrine of the Most Holy Sacrament of the Body and Blood of Our Saviour Jesus Christ*.[62] Cranmer's basic understanding of the sacrament was that spiritual presence was available by grace to those whom God had elected for salvation: 'For as Christ is a spiritual meat, so is he spiritually eaten and digested with the spiritual part of us, and giveth us spiritual and eternal life, and is not eaten, swallowed, and digested with our teeth, tongues, throats, and bellies'.[63] The sacraments, however, were not bare signs but were means of grace where believers received spiritual food: 'For the sacramental bread and wine be not bare and naked figures, but so pithy and effectuous, that whosoever worthily eateth them, eateth spiritually Christ's flesh and blood and hath by them everlasting life'.[64] This resembles closely the theology of Bullinger, Zwingli's Zürich successor, who modified Zwingli's pure memorialism by emphasizing instead the spiritual reception of Christ in the heart of the believer.[65]

Along with this spiritual receiving, however, Cranmer was also keen to stress the materialism of the sacraments that played on the senses of taste, smell, touch and sight in much the same way as the Word did to the hearing. Thus, he wrote that Christ

> hath also ordained one visible sacrament of spiritual
> regeneration in water, and another visible sacrament of
> spiritual nourishment in bread and wine, to the intent that, as
> much as is possible for man, we may see Christ with our eyes,
> smell him at our nose, taste him with our mouths, grope him
> with our hands, and perceive him with all our senses.[66]

For Cranmer, then, 'Christ is present in the sacrament, as . . . he is present in his word, when he worketh mightily in the hearts of the hearers'.[67] Displaying the influence of Bucer, who had introduced him to the theology of Chrysostom, he wrote that we ascend into heaven to be with Christ: Chrysostom 'saith also in many places, "That we ascend into heaven, and do eat Christ sitting there above"'.[68] It comes as no surprise that Cranmer remained deeply critical of any sense of a propitiatory sacrifice offered up by the priest in the mass. He was equally vehement in his criticism of transubstantiation and sacrifice:

> The very body of the tree, or rather the roots of the weeds, is
> the popish doctrine of transubstantiation, of the real presence
> of Christ's body and blood in the sacrament of the altar (as they
> call it), and of the sacrifice and oblation of Christ made by the
> priest for the salvation of the quick and the dead.[69]

The only sense of sacrifice beyond what had been offered once
and for all by Christ was the 'sacrifice of praise and thanksgiving'
by which 'we offer ourselves and all that we have, unto him and
his Father'.[70]

These liturgical and doctrinal discussions fed into the
production of the second Book of Common Prayer, which was
published in 1552. It contained a drastically altered communion
service: the title 'mass' was completely removed and it became
simply 'The Order for the Administration of the Lord's Supper, or
Holy Communion'. The shape of the service was also transformed
(although many of the words remained much the same and
continue to be used regularly even in the twenty-first century).
The Lord's Prayer, for instance, was said after communion in case
the reference to 'Give us this day our daily bread' should be seen
as referring to the Eucharist. Similarly, the prayers for the 'church
militant' in earth (intercessions) were separated from the prayer of
consecration, emphasizing the living rather than the dead which
meant that there could be no misinterpretation of any intercessory
role for the service as a means of offering up prayer. To emphasize
the penitential character and worthy reception of communion,
the Ten Commandments were introduced at the beginning of the
service.

At the distribution of Communion, the bread was handed
out with very different words from the earlier service, which
were far less ambiguous about real presence and verged on mere
memorialism: 'Take and eat this in remembrance that Christ died
for thee, and feed on him in thy heart by faith, with thanksgiving'.
And lest there should be any misunderstanding about Eucharistic
doctrine, the so-called 'Black Rubric' was added. It was inserted at
the last moment, which it why it had to be printed in black rather
than red, after complaints about the implications of the rubric
to kneel when receiving Communion. What it stressed in no
uncertain terms was that such a posture did not imply any sense of

adoration of the presence of Christ in the bread and wine. Indeed any sense of 'real and essential presence' was explicitly ruled out:

> we do declare that it is not meant thereby, that any adoration is done, or ought to be done, either unto the Sacramental bread or wine there bodily received, or unto any real and essential presence there being of Christ's natural flesh and blood. For as concerning the Sacramental bread and wine, remain still in their very natural substances, and therefore may not be adored, for that were Idolatry to be abhorred of all faithful Christians. And as concerning the natural body and blood of our saviour Christ, they are in heaven and not here. For it is against the truth of Christ's natural body, to be at one time in more places than one, at one time.

By clearly rejecting the Lutheran doctrine of ubiquity, this rubric stresses the solely spiritual dimension of the sacrament. Thus, even though the 1552 Book of Common Prayer fell far short of the more purified liturgical forms of the Swiss, significant changes were made to emphasize the reformed character of the liturgy. Elsewhere in the book, the exorcism and anointing were omitted from Baptism, and communion and prayers for the dead were removed from the Burial service.

The doctrine of the Eucharist expressed in the Books of Common Prayer was accompanied by rapid changes to the architecture and practices of the church. By 1550, stone altars, which implied the sacrifice of the mass offered by the priest, were denounced by Hooper in Gloucester, and there was a campaign for their removal in London under Ridley and in Bath and Wells under William Barlow. Across the country, Churchwardens' accounts reveal the dismantling of altars was swift. Instead of an altar, a table was to be placed in the church that would serve as a place where for the believer 'spiritually to eat [Christ's] body and spiritually to drink his blood'.[71] While it is hard to know precisely what the people made of such actions as well as the imposition of two new prayer books in three years, many reformers were reluctant to listen to any opposition, which they regarded as little more than evidence of lingering popular suspicion. On 5 February

1550, for instance, Hooper wrote to Bullinger that the people, that 'many-headed monster, is still wincing, partly through ignorance and partly fascinated by the inveiglements of the bishops, and the malice and impiety of the mass-priests. Such then is the present state of things in England'.[72]

Cranmer also revised the ordination services along lines suggested by Martin Bucer: even though the word 'priest' was retained ministry was increasingly rooted in the body of the faithful, and by 1552, the old symbols of the sacraments – the giving of the chalice and paten to the priest – had been replaced with the presentation of a Bible as the source of authority. For some, however, reform had not gone far enough. In his set of sermons on Jonah preached soon after the publication of the Ordinal in 1550, Hooper objected to the prescribed attire of black chimere and rochet (the 'habit and vesture of Aaron and the gentiles rather than the ministers of Christ') as well as to swearing the oath. He urged the King and his councillors to remove these abuses.[73] Shortly afterwards, Hooper was offered the bishopric of Gloucester but declined. He sought counsel from some of his friends, including Martin Bucer and Peter Martyr.[74] In his lengthy reply, Bucer expressed his concern about various abuses from indolent clergy who are either 'Papists or epicures' and whose services might as well have been in the 'Afric or Indian tongue'. He went on:

> the abuse of apparel and of all other things will be utterly
> abandoned, and all the badges and shadows of Antichrist
> would vanish away ... if any of the churches would give
> ear to me, surely they should retain none of these garments
> which the Papists have used in their superstitious service.

Nevertheless, Bucer remained convinced that such clothing was not in and of itself inevitably tainted:

> But to say that these garments are so defiled by the abuse
> of Antichrist, that no church may use them, albeit how
> much soever some one of them worship their Saviour
> Christ, and know the liberty of all things, I dare not be

so bold; . . . That any ceremony is wickedly Aaronical or Antichristian, standeth not in any creature of God, in any garment, in any figure, in any colour, or any work of God, but in the mind and profession of those which abuse Gods good creatures to wicked significations. . . . As for these things, touching the *place,* the *time,* the *apparel,* to minister or receive the holy communion, of admitting women to the Lord's table, of the manner of prayers and hymns unto God; so also of apparel, and other things pertaining to outward comeliness, I doubt not but the Lord gave free liberty to his churches to appoint and ordain in these things that which every church shall judge most available for the people, to maintain and encrease the reverence towards al the divine service of God. . . . Whatsoever you see of the abuse of these garments, that is not in the garments, but sticketh in unclean minds. . . . I pray God, that he so moderate, or else remove this controversy, lest any way it hinder the necessary cleansing of the Church; and lest they be divided either in opinion or in ministration, whom God in such sort hath coupled and joyned to set forward the salvation of the people.[75]

Bucer's points were later taken up by John Whitgift in his conflict with Cartwright, which grew out of another conflict over vestments in the mid-1560s.[76]

Explaining to Bullinger, Hooper claimed that he had done so, 'both by reason of the shameful and impious form of the oath, which all who choose to undertake the function of a bishop are compelled to put up with, and also on account of those Aaronic habits which they still retain in that calling, and are used to wear, not only at the administration of the sacraments, but also at public prayers'. Since he had declined the King's offer, he was summoned before the Privy Council 'to state my reasons, that it might be seen whether I could justly and lawfully decline the royal favour'.[77] Bullinger wrote to Cranmer pleading with him to bring an end to the controversy, although Cranmer did not respond until long after the consecration (and after Hooper had also become Bishop of Worcester).[78] The Council briefly imprisoned Hooper in the Fleet Prison on 27 January 1551 for his act of disobedience, but, after a lengthy debate with Ridley, he was eventually persuaded to conform, writing to Cranmer on 15 February. He was consecrated at Lambeth on 8 March.[79] Hooper wrote again to Bullinger, whom he called his 'much honoured gossip' in August 1551, reporting that he had been much occupied with the question of 'habits' over the past year: 'I very properly, if I am not mistaken, found fault with the use of them in the church, and contended for their entire removal. He [Ridley], on the other hand, most urgently and pertinaciously defended their use'.[80] The debates between Hooper and Ridley function as a precursor to one of the most formative controversies at the beginning of the reign of Elizabeth a few years later, as Whitgift noted.[81] Indeed, disputes about matters indifferent and obedience to the canons and regulations of the church came to characterize the conflicts of the church in the next generation.[82]

Cranmer also drew up a collection of Forty-Two Articles of Religion to which royal assent was given in 1553 (although parliament never saw them), which aimed to outline the doctrine of the new reformed Church of England.[83] Cranmer's reform of Canon Law, which began in 1552 under a commission that included Peter Martyr (which was later called the *Reformatio Legum Ecclesiasticarum*),[84] however, was never passed. This would have introduced a completely new code of canon law and abolished the medieval system. A new system of synods would have been introduced on the Swiss model, which would have been made up of clergy as well as laity. It would have amounted to a form of Presbyterianism adapted to an episcopal church. Even in parishes, a group of 'seniores' or elders would have worked with the clergy to ensure discipline. These proposed reforms, which were rejected by Northumberland, provided a possible blueprint for reform in the church for many in the generations to come.

Though it cannot be said that the Reformation was complete under Edward, the substance was nevertheless there. While there was an abrupt halt under Mary who succeeded her half-brother under the terms of Henry's will after the unexpected failure of the attempt to put the Protestant Lady Jane Grey on the throne, the seeds were sown for the Elizabethan consolidation of Reformation, which is discussed in the next chapter. Had Mary lived longer, things might have turned out very differently, and the Tractarians might have been able to write the Reformation out of the history of the Church of England. But Elizabeth's reign would prove far more difficult to ignore in the formation of Anglican identity. It was this point that was stressed by the opponents of the Oxford Movement as they set about republishing many of the key texts of the Reformation.

Chapter 3

Settling Anglican Theology: Elizabeth I, John Jewel and the Thirty-Nine Articles

The Parker Society

As I suggested at the beginning of the last chapter, the role of the Reformation presents a key issue in the formation of the identity and theology of the Church of England. The example of the Oxford Martyrs' Memorial offers a good example of a physical representation of the importance of the Reformation among Victorian churchmen. At the same time, many sought to ensure that the key texts of the Reformation were available in popular and cheap editions. Some Evangelicals had become increasingly aware of their protestant heritage, which they regarded as under threat from what they often regarded as the Romanizing tendencies of the Oxford Movement. As a counterblast to the publishing projects emanating from Anglo-Catholics with their very distinctive understanding of the identity of the Church of England in the Church of the Fathers and later of the High Churchmen predominantly of the seventeenth century, a number of more protestant-minded churchmen of the mid-nineteenth century under the leadership of the leading Evangelicals, Anthony Ashley Cooper, seventh Earl of Shaftesbury (1801–85) and Edward Bickersteth (1786–1850), established the Parker Society in 1840.

The society was named after Matthew Parker, Elizabeth I's first Archbishop of Canterbury, and aimed to republish the writings of the English Reformers as well as some of their continental influences, such as Heinrich Bullinger's *Decades*. Like many of their Evangelical contemporaries, both Lord Ashley and Bickersteth were convinced of the imminence of the coming judgement, which gave this publishing venture a degree of urgency (which was also expressed in some of their other enterprises including the conversion of the Jews).[1] Both were also strongly opposed to what they regarded as 'popery' in all its guises.[2] Bickersteth had produced a polemic in 1836, published as *The Progress of Popery*, which left little to the imagination:

> To maintain the purity of the gospel, to be full of zeal and godly jealousy on this point, is a great part of our fidelity as *stewards of the mysteries of Christ.* Especially does it become us to be so when there is reason to think that the grossest corruption of the gospel that the world has ever yet seen, is again reviving among us. [3]

While he had in mind the Roman Catholic Church, he also had doubts about the Oxford Movement, which to many Evangelicals was a veritable cuckoo in the nest. The conflicts over the establishment of a joint English and Prussian bishopric in Jerusalem helped polarize opinion between Lord Ashley and Bickersteth and the Oxford Movement, especially Pusey and Newman. At the same time, Ashley became chairman of the committee that prevented the election of the Tractarian Isaac Williams to the Oxford Professorship of Poetry in 1841–2.[4] The Parker Society represented another aspect of this polarization between the church parties over the nature of Anglicanism.

Under the oversight of the General Secretary and Librarian, the Revd John Ayre ((1801–69), Domestic Chaplain to the Evangelical benefactor, the Earl of Roden (1832–69) and Minister of St John's, Hampstead (1834–55)), and James Scholefield (1789–1853), general editor, the Parker Society attracted approximately seven thousand subscribers who paid a mere £1 per year for the fifty-three volumes published between 1841 and 1854. The General Index and the Latin originals of the 'Original Letters Relative to the English Reformation' (1847) were extra. With twenty-four editors responsible for the different volumes, there was naturally an unevenness in quality, and some of the volumes originally planned did not materialize. Despite the omissions from what had originally been planned, the end product succeeded in making available to a general readership a huge range of hitherto obscure material in cheap editions. As was emphasized by the full title of the society, to subscribe to the Parker Society was to identify with a particular idea of Anglicanism based on 'the works of the Fathers and the early writers of the Reformed English Church'.

The purpose of the Society was made explicit in the report of the final meeting of the Council of the Society that prefaced the General Index, where it was noted that the volumes

> comprise the complete works of the most eminent prelates, and others, who suffered imprisonment, exile, or death, in the sixteenth century, for the gospel's sake; and those of their immediate successors when religion was re-established under Queen Elizabeth.[5]

Quite clearly, the essence of the Church of England was established on the faith of those who were willing to suffer persecution and even death during the Reformation. It was this example that continued to provide the weaponry to combat Roman Catholicism and Anglo-Catholicism in the nineteenth century. The series included the writings of the Marian martyrs such as Cranmer, Ridley, Latimer and Hooper as well as Elizabethan conformists such as Jewel and Whitgift. In addition, there were a number of volumes of letters and writings of some of the continental Reformers who exerted a particular influence on the Church of England. The Parker Society were not Little Englanders when it came to the understanding of the English Reformation: it was very much part of a wider European phenomenon. For instance, in 1843, Steuart Adolphus Pears (1815–1875), who became the headmaster of Repton School, was sent to search the libraries of Zürich for correspondence relating to the English Reformation and succeeded in making a number of new and important discoveries.[6] Other works by continental Reformers included four volumes of the Decades of 'Henry' Bullinger, the Zürich Reformer. Other volumes included liturgical texts as well as earlier writings, including those of William Tyndale, who was put to death in 1536.[7] While admitting that there had been a degree of controversy over precisely why certain texts had been published when others remained unpublished, the final report of the Committee was clear about the purpose of the volumes in illuminating the identity of the English Church:

> In closing the proceedings of the Parker Society, the Council desire to express their thankfulness to God that a very important object has been attained, that the works of the leading English Reformers have been made for all future time easily accessible to the theological student, and a fuller light thereby thrown upon the principles of the Church of England.[8]

The volumes, which had been 'distributed through the United Kingdom, the colonies, and many foreign countries', amounted to a 'library in themselves'. Most importantly, they contained theological resources in the battle with Rome, or what were called

> proved weapons for the whole encounter with popery, and maintain the doctrine and order of the Church of England against those who afterwards rose up from her own bosom to assault her. They have shed light upon contemporary history. They are documents, which have already been frequently appealed to in the Ecclesiastical Courts, and which will ever remain as evidences of Reformation truth.[9]

This presented a version of Anglicanism capable of fighting those with those of different views both inside and outside the Church of England. A great deal was therefore at stake in the reading of the past and the construction of an Anglican canon. Both the Parker Society and the Libraries produced by the heirs of the Oxford Movement could lay claim to be the authentic voice of Anglicanism, but it was an authenticity that was imposed on a past through the creation of a canon with particular concerns for the present. In the reading of the Elizabethan Settlement offered in the next two chapters, most of the texts used are those published by the Parker Society. And yet there are strands that emerge in the Settlement which came to be of crucial importance in the liturgical revival of the late nineteenth century.

Mary I and Elizabeth I

While Mary I hardly had time in her brief reign to turn the clock back completely to the 1520s, the country returned to Roman Catholicism even if this was made more complex because of the European situation. Mary was married to Charles V's son, Philip II of Spain, which drew England into international politics, especially as after 1555, Pope Paul IV pursued a strongly anti-Spanish policy. Reginald Pole, Papal Legate, and Archbishop of Canterbury after Cranmer's execution, who might have proved one of the leading reformers in the Catholic church, was hampered by international rivalries. A return to Roman obedience did not prove universally popular, especially when accompanied by burnings of about 280 protestants including Bishops Hooper, Latimer and Ridley, who were so vividly portrayed in John Foxe's great piece of protestant hagiography, *Acts and Monuments* (1563), usually referred to as Foxe's 'Book of Martyrs'. Just under 800 others wisely sought refuge abroad where they were able to gain first-hand knowledge of the Reformation. Ironically, it was perhaps the brief return to Roman Catholicism and the widespread persecution that did most to shape the theology of the Elizabethan period: suffering and martyrdom did much to help forge an English protestant identity[10] which was often defined against Roman Catholicism. Yet had Mary not succumbed to cancer after only five years on the throne it is impossible to say what might have happened: the thirteen bishops appointed during her reign showed far more concern for pastoral care and simple living than many of their predecessors. 'Death', as Diarmaid MacCulloch writes, 'was the greatest enemy of the struggle for Catholic restoration'.[11]

Following the death of her half-sister, Mary I, Elizabeth succeeded to the throne on 17 November 1558. It was during her reign that the theology of the Church of England consolidated into what came to be called the Elizabethan Settlement. The period has been the source of many of the myths of Anglican theology, not least the *via media* and the three-legged methodological stool of scripture, tradition and reason.[12] However, as I will show in Chapter 7, such ideas need to be treated with a great deal of caution. Much about the Elizabethan era is the product of a Victorian re-reading of the past in the light of their own concerns.

Whatever the Queen's predilections – and these were important in halting further reform – the church that emerged in her reign was undoubtedly reformed in its theology. But once again, as in the reign of her father and half-brother, theological method was determined as much by the political and ecclesiastical situation as by doctrine. As Patrick Collinson writes, 'Religion in Elizabethan England was a political matter because the Elizabethan state was unable for lack of resources, or unwilling for lack of conviction and commitment, to enforce the strict religious uniformity which was supposed to obtain'.[13]

Ruling a society which retained a degree of diversity did not prove easy, which is one reason why so often order and uniformity were of central importance in Elizabethan theology. While there were many things debated which were 'matters indifferent' and which were certainly not matters of one's eternal salvation – such as wearing a 'comely surplice with sleeves' – they were nevertheless treated as anything but indifferent matters. For most of Elizabeth's theologians theological method focused on the question of authority. In relation to those issues that were not explicitly prescribed or proscribed in scripture and which therefore could not be said to be matters of salvation, the solution was simple: if the due authorities had decided that something should be done, then it should be done. Some even sought to clarify the sources of authority in these sorts of questions – somewhat subversively, some asked: where did the due authorities receive their authority from?

For many, the answers were clear: the traditions and the Fathers of the Church seemed to be directly relevant to many issues and helped to clarify the meaning of scripture. Others – most importantly Richard Hooker, whose theology is discussed in Chapter 5 – sought to locate the authority for decision-making in the church in a God-given faculty of reason, which meant that the laws of creation filled in when scripture was silent. Others theologians, however, begged to differ: if something was not explicitly prescribed in scripture, then it should not be done. Hardly surprisingly, there was significant conflict about what precisely was contained in scripture. Yet, it would be wrong to regard the Elizabethan period as a time when matters were completely polarized between extremes, with a few enlightened souls attempting to steer a *via media*. It was instead a period when theology was *in via*, as it responded to new situations and new problems. Indeed, as in the nineteenth century, English theology was struggling for its identity.

With Elizabeth's accession, many of those who had been exiled during Mary's reign began flocking back home.[14] Among them were three future archbishops, Edmund Grindal, Edwin Sandys and Thomas Young, as well as 119 theological students. Their experiences had introduced them to many new ideas, some of which appeared to be worth trying in the English context.[15] Zürich under Bullinger, Geneva under Calvin, and Strasbourg, where Peter Martyr had fled, all proved attractive. At Frankfurt, where the future bishops John Jewel and Richard Cox had fled, the English congregation had used the 1552 Prayer Book. Such practices had led to disagreements with John Knox over discipline and vesture. As will be discussed in the next chapter, it was not long into Elizabeth's reign that such controversies would be repeated in England. Indeed, as Solt writes, 'It is an ironic twist that the English sovereign who achieved the reputation of being the greatest enemy to Protestantism should have inadvertently caused Englishmen to carry out religious experiments in continental laboratories that would inspire succeeding Puritan generations'.[16]

There were high hopes among some exiles for Elizabeth. John Jewel described her 'as a wise and religious queen, and one too who is favourably and propitiously disposed towards us'.[17] She was, after all, Anne Boleyn's daughter, and she had appointed William Cecil (afterwards Lord Burghley), a known protestant, who had been active in her brother's reign, as her principal secretary. Her sympathy for the protestant cause had been noted earlier. During her brother's reign, the Marian martyr, John Hooper had written to Bullinger, that the King's

> sister, the daughter of the late king by queen Ann, is inflamed with the same zeal for the religion of Christ. She not only knows what the true religion is, but has acquired such proficiency in Greek and Latin, that she is able to defend it by

the most just arguments and the most happy talent; so that she encounters few adversaries whom she does not overcome.[18]

Given the centrality of the role of the sovereign, Elizabeth's religious opinions were of crucial importance. However, as many historians have discovered to their cost, her own views are particularly difficult to gauge: where one generation saw her as a protestant who was forced into compromises with her conservative bishops,[18] later in the twentieth century she had mutated into a conservative forced to compromise by a number of radical MPs.[19] This in turn has been challenged, and the source of opposition has been relocated to the House of Lords and among the bishops.[20] However, even if Elizabeth was not prepared to push forward with reform as far as many of the exiles might have wanted, it is difficult to see her as anything other than a (relatively moderate) protestant in doctrine.[21] At the same time, there is good evidence to suggest that she remained something of a liturgical conservative. Indeed, as Collinson writes: 'There seems little doubt that the reinstatement of a cross and candlesticks in the royal chapel in the autumn of 1559 was a calculated retort to the unauthorised holocaust of roods and rood imagery in the Visitation of the previous summer'.[22] Along with a liking for images, the Queen also had a distaste of clerical marriage.

Such conservatism was found wanting by some of her own bishops. Writing in 1560 to Peter Martyr, for instance, Bishop Edwin Sandys of Worcester commented that while the Eucharist had been restored in its purity, the Queen's attitude to the figures of the medieval rood screen, the crucifix with Mary and John the Beloved Disciple, gave cause for concern:

The doctrine of the Eucharist, as yet by God's blessing unimpugned, remains to us, and we hope will continue to remain, pure and inviolate. For both myself and my episcopal brethren will maintain it, by God's help, to the utmost of our power, as long as we live. We had not long since a controversy respecting images. The queen's majesty considered it not contrary to the word of God, nay, rather for the advantage of the church, that the image of Christ crucified, together with Mary and John, should be placed, as heretofore, in

some conspicuous part of the church, where they might
more readily be seen by all the people. Some of us [bishops]
thought far otherwise, and more especially as all images of
every kind were at our last visitation not only taken down,
but also burnt, and that too by public authority; and because
the ignorant and superstitious multitude are in the habit of
paying adoration to this idol above all others. As to myself,
because I was rather vehement in this matter, and could
by no means consent that an occasion of stumbling should
be afforded to the church of Christ, I was very near being
deposed from my office, and incurring the displeasure of
the queen. But God, in whose hand are the hearts of kings,
gave us tranquillity instead of a tempest, and delivered the
church of England from stumbling blocks of this kind: only
the popish vestments remain in our church, I mean the copes;
which, however, we hope will not last very long.[23]

Sandys' optimism proved wrong: such stumbling blocks remained
and were to be the source of major controversy only a few years
later. The Queen's conservatism continued to prove a thorn in the
flesh for many years to come. By 1576, Archbishop Grindal was
so disturbed by the Queen's views that he was forced to speak
out, which cost him his job: 'But God forbid, Madam, that you
should . . . go about to diminish the preaching of Christ's gospel:
for that would ruinate all together at the length'.[24]

Despite her apparent conservatism over religious practice and
images, however, one thing is certain about Elizabeth: she proceeded
with caution, primarily out of political considerations and the
need to conciliate her divided and still wincing population.[25]
She seems to have been both an astute and cautious politician:
'Unlike her father, there is not much evidence that Elizabeth
modelled herself on the biblical figure of Melchizedek, who was
both priest and king. She was not an ayatollah'.[26] Her caution was
noted at the time: Jewel wrote to Peter Martyr, with whom he had
worked in Oxford when he was Regius professor, explaining that
'though she openly favours our cause', she 'is wonderfully afraid of
allowing any innovations . . . She is however prudently, and firmly,
and piously following up her purpose, though somewhat more
slowly than we could wish'.[27]

The Elizabethan Settlement

The religious settlement which emerged over the first few months of Elizabeth's reign displays her caution. Before anything else she sought to achieve a regulation of religion, including both its preaching and liturgy. Thus on 27 December 1558 the Queen issued a Proclamation which pointed to the underlying issue of what was called 'unfruitful dispute in matters of religion, but also contention and occasion to break common quiet'. Elizabeth was thus keen to re-establish a uniformity of doctrine and order. While the proclamation permitted the use of the English Litany, it also at the same time forbade unlicensed preaching lest it should pose a challenge to her authority. For the queen, it was a matter of some urgency that there should be consultation with parliament

> for the better conciliation and accord of such causes, as
> at this present are moved in matters and ceremonies of
> religion . . . The true advancement whereof to the due
> honour of Almighty God, the increase of virtue and godliness,
> with universal charity and concord amongst her people, her
> majesty most desireth, and meaneth effectually, by all manner
> of means possible, to procure and to restore to this her realm.
> Whereunto as her majesty instantly requireth all her good,
> faithful, and loving subjects to be assenting and aiding with
> due obedience, so if any shall disobediently use themselves
> to the breach hereof, her majesty both must and will see
> the same duly punished, both for the quality of the offence,
> and for example to all others neglecting her majesty's so
> reasonable commandment.[28]

Shortly afterwards there was 'An acte restoring to the crown the ancient jurisdiction over the state ecclesiastical and spiritual and abolishing all foreign power repugnant to the same'. This returned all ecclesiastical authority to the crown.

On taking office clergy were required to take an oath 'that the queen's highness is the only supreme governor of this realm and of all other her highness's dominions and countries, as well in all spiritual or ecclesiastical things or causes as temporal, and that no foreign prince, person, prelate, state, or potentate hath or ought to have any jurisdiction, power, superiority, pre-eminence, or authority, ecclesiastical or spiritual, within this realm'. While obviously aimed principally against the claims of the Roman Catholic Church, the location of all authority in 'the imperial crown of this your realm' meant that all alternative voices in the church were equally silenced. Despite the change in title from supreme head to supreme governor, which was probably to appease those – including herself[29] – who not unreasonably supposed Christ to be the head of the Church, the royal supremacy continued unabated through the Elizabethan period. She saw it as her duty to help the ministers of the church to 'retain our people in obedience to their Almighty God and to live as Christians to the salvation of their souls which Christ hath redeemed'.[30] As an astute politician Elizabeth was aware that she could not share her father's claim to be a 'crowned theologian, confounding parliaments and bishops with God's learning' but was far more 'an adroit and devious politician, operating through the interstices of statute law'.[31]

The Act of Settlement also allowed the Queen to appoint 'such persons' by letters patent – that is, by her own authority – 'to visit, reform, order, or correct any errors, heresies, schisms, abuses or enormities'. They were to make use of criteria for what counted as heretical based on

> the authority of the canonical scriptures, or by the first four
> General Councils, or any other general council wherein the
> same was declared heresy by the express and plain words of
> the said canonical Scriptures, or such as hereafter shall be
> ordered, judged, or determined to be heresy by the high
> court of parliament of this realm, with the assent of the clergy
> in their convocation.

The Crown was thus charged with deciding on matters of heresy, which meant that the independent voice of the church was severely curtailed. The initial attempt to pass the Act of Settlement failed to gain the support of a single bishop, and convocation and the House of Lords continued to protest.[32] Although Elizabeth had initially been hopeful that a number of Mary's bishops would change their allegiance, this proved false. It was only after the bishops had been removed that the Act passed into law after

Easter. In the end, there was a change of all but one bishop, the 'timeserver'[33] Anthony Kitchin of Llandaff. Elizabeth appointed Matthew Parker (1504–75) as the Archbishop of Canterbury, who had been chaplain to her mother, Anne Boleyn. Through the course of her reign, Elizabeth was to appoint seventeen bishops who had been in exile during her sister's reign. These included Richard Cox at Ely, Edmund Grindal at London and John Jewel at Salisbury.

Matthew Parker is an interesting figure in the formation of the identity of Anglican theology. His chief literary work, which was published in 1572, was a collection of the early narratives of the British Church which sought to show that the Church of England was the most ancient of all territorial churches and did not depend for its primary evangelization on the Church of Rome, despite what admirers of Augustine of Canterbury might claim.[34] While fanciful, this demonstrates the effort to create a history for a national church detached from papal interference: the myth of continuity was not simply a Victorian creation.[35] In the following century, Archbishop Ussher of Armagh tried to do something similar for Ireland, publishing *A Discourse on the Religion Anciently Professed by the Irish and British* in 1631.[36] He surveyed Irish history in detail to show how much closer the ancient Celtic Church was to Protestantism than it was to Rome. These examples again show how the theology of the Church of England (and Ireland) depends upon sometimes competing approaches to national history. Such history inevitably interacts with other histories, not least of which are those of the other countries and churches in Europe, and, as the recent history of the Anglican Communion demonstrates, across the world.

Together with the Act of Settlement, the Act of Uniformity of 1559 revived the religion of the last year of the reign of Edward VI. It imposed harsh penalties on clergy who refused to adopt it as well as a fine of 'twelve pence . . . to the use of the poor of the same parish' for those who did not attend divine service on Sundays and Holy Days. Fifty-seven injunctions, which were based on those issued during the reign of Edward VI, were issued in July 1559 to ensure that the country fell into line. The aim was the 'suppression of superstition throughout all her highness's realms and dominions, and to plant true religion to the extirpation of all hypocrisy, enormities, and abuses'. Particular strongly worded was Number XXIII: the clergy 'shall take away, utterly extinct, and destroy all shrines, coverings of shrines, all tables, candlesticks, trindals, and rolls of wax, pictures, paintings, and all other monuments of feigned miracles, pilgrimages, idolatry, and superstition, so that there remain no memory of the same in walls, glass windows, or elsewhere within their churches and houses'. Article VI stated that Churches were also to buy a Bible in English as well as the paraphrases of Erasmus. One modest concession was contained under Article LIII, which noted where 'altars be not yet removed . . . there seems no matter of great moment, so that the Sacrament be duly and reverently ministered'. Nevertheless, the Holy Table was to be moved for the service of Holy Communion and 'placed in good sort within the chancel, as whereby the minister may be more conveniently heard of the communicants in his prayer and ministration'. After the service, it was 'to be placed where it stood before'. This was hardly evidence of total iconoclasm or high sacramentalism.[37]

The modestly revised Prayer Book of 1559 made a number of concessions to more conservative opinion. The litany was revised to remove the petition again the Bishop of Rome's 'destestable enormities', and where the 1552 Prayer Book forbade all vestments except the rochet and surplice, the new Ornaments Rubric ordered the minister somewhat ambiguously to 'use such ornaments in the church as were in use by authority of parliament in the second year of the reign of king Edward the VI'. The Act of Uniformity explicitly repeated this instruction 'by authority of Parliament'. In the Communion Service, the 1549 words of administration were added to those of the 1552 book, resulting in a lengthy hybrid that allowed for a diversity of interpretation. In addition, the Black Rubric was removed. These changes allowed for the possibility of a greater degree of sacramentality and, at several different points, became of crucial importance in liturgical controversy. However modest these seemed, to some these could be understood as an attempt to introduce a *via media*.

Much later on, what Patrick Collinson called the 'Trojan Horse'[38] of the ornaments rubric allowed some ritualist clergy to create a form of liturgical practice and decoration for the Church of England based upon an idealized vision of the form of worship of the second year of the reign of Edward VI. Given that the Prayer Book commanded that 'Chancels shall remain as they have done in times past' and ministers were to use the vestments of the second year of Edward, there was ample scope for liturgical archaeology and historicism. The best known and most influential example was Percy Dearmer's *Parson's Handbook*,[39] first published in 1899, which contained detailed instructions about what to do and where to stand based on what was happening in 1548.[40] This was followed by many other publications on liturgical reform, as well as hymn books based on similar principles including the *English Hymnal*. Dearmer's idealization of the 'English use' helped create a pattern that proved deeply influential on English church architecture – his study of art, particularly of the period around the break of Rome, led him to design model altars, surrounding them with riddles and large supporting posts, usually with two massive candlesticks. He and the Warham Guild designed ecclesiastical costume based on designs from the golden age. The shadow side of his project was an often scarcely submerged anti-Romanism. On genuflection, for instance, after a few pages of detailed exposition of different meaning of the term, he concludes that

> we have no precedent for ministers or people dropping on one
> knee when passing the Holy Sacrament; but that both natural
> reverence and our Anglican canons, rubrics, and tradition
> do suggest that they should bow when approaching for
> communion . . . . I have given rather fuller references to this
> matter, because it is one in which all modern directories have
> gone astray, by recommending a particular form of reverence
> that is without justification either from those primitive
> customs to which the Prayer Book makes so strong an appeal,
> or from formal directions of the late medieval books.[41]

This comment is typical of Dearmer's tendency to distance his understanding of the English use from that of Rome, and he frequently verged on the nationalistic. In the conflicts of his own time he provided a way forward which offered the clarity of a reconstructed (or constructed) historical myth which allowed for the reformed services of the Prayer Book to be practised with the utmost dignity in a medieval church. What is obvious to the historian of theology, however, is that he passes over the often bitter conflict that the retention of ornaments and vestments produced in the Elizabethan church.

One of the most prominent Marian exiles, John Jewel expressed a degree of anxiety about the matter of ecclesiastical dress in a letter to Peter Martyr written shortly after Elizabeth came to the throne. His view of the vestments used in the second year of the reign of Edward VI was a very long way from that of Dearmer:

> As to religion, it has been effected, I hope, under good auspices, that it shall be restored to the same state as it was during your latest residence among us, under Edward. But, as far as I can perceive at present, there is not the same alacrity among our friends, as there lately was among the papists. So miserably is it ordered, that falsehood is armed, while truth is not only unarmed, but also frequently offensive. The scenic apparatus of divine worship is now under agitation; and those very things which you and I have so often laughed at, are now seriously and solemnly entertained by certain persons, (for we are not consulted,) as if the Christian religion could not exist without something tawdry. Our minds indeed are not sufficiently disengaged to make these fooleries of much importance. Others are seeking after a *golden* or as it rather seems to me, a *leaden* mediocrity; and are crying out, that the half is better than the whole.[42]

Jewel's exasperation over the leaden mediocrity of a lack of reform was met with an invitation from William Cecil to compose an *Apology for the Church of England*,[43] which soon became one of the key texts in the formation of Anglican identity. In 1609, during the reign of James I, Archbishop Richard Bancroft organized a collection of Jewel's work in a single volume with a foreword by John Overall. All parishes were instructed to buy a copy. It is interesting to note that those, including Bancroft, who were associated by later writers with moving the Church of England away from the Edwardian Reformation could see the *Apology* as a standard work of doctrine. Similarly, Lancelot Andrewes in a Latin text republished in the *Library of Anglo-Catholic Theology* elevated it to a status equivalent to the Articles and the Prayer Book catechism.[44]

While Jewel may have had some assistance in its composition, it seems likely that he was the main author.[45] The *Apology* was first written in Latin early in 1561 and published on 1 January 1562. It was rapidly translated into English by Ann, Lady Bacon,[46] and was also read widely abroad. On receiving a copy from Bishop Grindal, for instance, Peter Martyr noted to Jewel that Bullinger and the church leaders of Zürich thought the book was 'so wise, admirable, and eloquent, that they can make no end of commending it, and think that nothing in these days hath been set forth more perfectly'.[47] As early as 1570, the book had been translated into French, Italian, Dutch and Spanish.[48]

The Theological Defence of the Elizabethan Settlement: Jewel's Apology

On 26 November 1559 as Bishop-elect of Salisbury, Jewel had preached a famous sermon at Paul's Cross.[49] Here, he put forward a challenge to his Roman Catholic opponents, with whom he continued to engage at length throughout his writings (particularly Thomas Harding, Bishop Stephen Gardiner's confessor and a former canon treasurer of Salisbury Cathedral).[50] The style of Jewel's sermon was extremely direct. He called on his catholic opponents 'to bring any one sufficient sentence out of any old Catholic Doctor, or Father; or out of any old General Council; Or out of the Holy Scriptures of God'[51] to prove the legitimacy of catholic practices such as private masses or communion in one kind. The sermon was repeated on 17 March the following year before the Court and again just before Easter, once again at Paul's Cross. This gave it a particular prominence in the early months of Elizabeth's reign. The sermon demonstrates already the methods he was to use in the *Apology*: he does not simply dismiss Catholics, whom he likens to the Jews of Jesus' time, but engages with them directly, asking them to prove their practices from antiquity and Scripture. Indeed, a few years later, in a reply to Harding, he went as far as claiming: 'If the church of Rome would now faithfully keep the traditions and doctrines of the apostles, we would frankly yield her all that honour that Irenaeus giveth her'.[52]

For Jewel, Roman Catholics were indeed a pious people, but quite misguided: echoing the standard interpretation of his age, he wrote, 'The Jews had a zeal for God, and yet they crucified the

Son of God'.[53] Similarly, Roman Catholics in the end 'proceed as far as the scribes and Pharisees, that for the maintenance of their own traditions, despised and brake the commandments of God'.[54] In order to engage with Roman Catholics, Jewel makes use of an apologetic method where the Fathers become sources to justify the purification of the Church. It is important to remember that Jewel's theological studies at Merton and Corpus Christi Colleges in Oxford in the last years of Henry VIII had focused on the new editions of the Fathers that Erasmus had made available. Jewel's mentor, Peter Martyr Vermigli, had also made an extensive study of patristics: the costs of bringing his books from Basel to London was £126 7/6. Jewel remained close to Martyr, going as far as calling him 'my father, my pride, even the half of my soul'.[55]

The Paul's Cross sermon provided the foundation for what was to follow in Jewel's later works. 'The mere sermon of November 1559', according to Southgate, 'became in the spring of 1560 the introductory chapter and thesis of what was to be a vast corpus of controversial writing extending over the next decade'.[56] The sermon's challenge was taken up by Henry Cole, Mary's Dean of St Paul's. The letters that were exchanged between Jewel and Cole[57] provide the background for the *Apologia*, and help to explain its particular anti-Catholic stance: it soon became the standard work in defining 'Anglican' theology – the word was used in the title of the original Latin *Apologia Ecclesiae Anglicanae* – against Roman Catholicism. As in the sermon Jewel's method in the *Apology* is to use a vigorous apologetic that aims to prove the truth of the Church of England on the basis of Scripture and the Fathers of the early church. In this he seeks to show how truly it 'agreeth with Christian Religion'.[58] In Jewel's method, the Church of the Fathers of the first six centuries or so played a crucial part,[59] but above all it was Scripture that was normative: The true test for doctrine is the scriptural test. Thus for Jewel, as for all protestants, the Scriptures were

> the very might and strength of God to attain to salvation;
> that they be the foundations of the prophets and apostles
> whereupon is built the church of God; they be the very sure
> and infallible rule, whereby may be tried whether the church
> doth stagger or err, and whereunto all ecclesiastical doctrine

ought to be called to account; and that against these scriptures neither law nor ordinance nor any custom ought to be heard.[60]

For this reason, he asks, 'If we be heretics then why do the catholics not convince us and master us by the divine scriptures?'[61]

Despite his reverence and respect for the Fathers, Jewel never regarded them as of the same status as the Scriptures. Following the standard line of the Reformers, Jewel claimed that the authority of tradition could never be compared with the authority of scripture.[62] There was never a time at which there was a *consensus patrum*. The Fathers were interpreters of the Word of God but could not be regarded as the Word itself. He put this poetically in a sermon preached at Salisbury towards the end of his life:

> But what say we of the fathers, Augustine, Ambrose, Hierome, Cyprian etc.? What shall we think of them, or what account may we make of them? They be interpreters of the word of God. They were learned men and learned fathers; the instruments of the mercy of God and vessels full of grace. We despise them not, we read them, we reverence them and give thanks unto God for them. They were witnesses unto the truth, they were worthy pillars and ornaments in the church of God. Yet may they not be compared with the word of God. We may not build upon them; we may not make them the foundation and warrant of our conscience; we may not put our trust in them. Our trust is in the name of the Lord . . . They are our fathers, but not our fathers unto God; they are the stars, fair and beautiful and bright; yet they are not the sun: they bear witness of the light, they are not the light.[63]

For Jewel, then, the Church of England – like all authentic churches – was grounded in antiquity, but above all in Scripture. This meant that it was neither one of the 'sundry sects',[64] nor had it fallen into the immorality of the Roman church. Jewel thus sought to 'shew it plain, that God's holy Gospel, the ancient bishops, and the primitive Church do make on our side, and that we have not without just cause left these men, and rather have returned to the apostles and old catholic fathers'.[65] He thus uses the writings of the Fathers to defend both the antiquity and the authenticity of his own church:

> As for our doctrine which we might rightlier call Christ's catholic doctrine, it is so far off from new that God, who is above all most ancient, and the Father of our Lord Jesus Christ, hath left the same unto us in the Gospel, in the Prophets' and Apostles' works, being monuments of greatest age. So that no man can now think our doctrine to be new, unless the same think either the Prophets' faith, or the Gospel, or else Christ Himself to be new.[66]

For Jewel, the Church of England was not a new church that began at the Reformation, but 'we are come, as near as we possibly could, to the Church of the Apostles and of the old catholic bishops and fathers'.[67] Furthermore, he contended, where Scripture was silent, the authority of the Fathers was central:

> We have searched out of the Holy Bible, which we are sure cannot deceive, one sure form of religion, and have returned again unto the primitive church of the ancient fathers and apostles, that is to say, to the first ground and beginning of things, as unto the very foundations and headsprings of Christ's Church.[68]

Using similar arguments, Jewel goes on to counter the notion of papal primacy. Indeed through the course of his apologetic, he directly challenged the Pope:

> Tell us, I pray you, good holy Father, seeing ye do crake so much of all antiquity, and boast yourself that all men are bound to you alone, which of all the fathers have at any time called you by the name of the highest prelate, the universal bishop, or the head of the Church? Which of them ever said that both the swords were committed to you?[69]

Again he asks Catholics to prove the antiquity of their religion by using the Fathers, rebutting them with his own patristic knowledge. Thus, drawing on the writings of Jerome and Cyprian in particular, he claims – in terms familiar from the time of Henry VIII – that the Pope took upon himself the name of the head of the church, by 'usurping he took upon himself the right and authority of other folk's churches'.[70] Earlier in the book, he was less guarded in his language, calling the Pope the 'Lucifer which prefereth himself before his brethren'.[71] Antiquity and Scripture, he held, would come down firmly on the side of the protestants.

> For our parts, if we could have judged ignorance, error, superstition, idolatry, men's inventions, and the same commonly disagreeing with the Holy Scriptures, either to please God or to be sufficient for the obtaining everlasting salvation; or if we could ascertain ourselves, that the word of God was written but for a time only, and afterward again ought to be abrogated and put away: or else that the sayings and commandments of God ought to be subject to man's will, that whatsoever God saith and commandeth, except the Bishop of Rome willeth and commandeth the same, it must be taken as void and unspoken: if we could have brought ourselves to believe these things, we grant there had been no cause at all why we should have left these men's company. As touching that we have now done to depart from that Church, whose errors were proved and made manifest to the world, which Church also had already evidently departed from God's word: and yet not to depart so much from itself, as from the errors thereof; and not to do this disorderly or wickedly, but quietly and soberly; we have done nothing herein against the doctrine either of Christ or of His Apostles.[72]

However, while he claims that the Church of Rome had 'forsaken the fellowship of the Holy Fathers',[73] at least for apologetic purposes he is more sympathetic to the Eastern Churches. He goes as far as to suggest that

> those Greeks, who ay this day profess religion and Christ's name, have many things corrupted amongst them, yet hold they still a great number of those things which they received from the apostles. They have neither private masses, nor mangled sacraments, nor purgatories, nor pardons.[74]

Even if it was its main purpose, the *Apology* was not simply concerned with denunciation of Roman Catholics. Jewel was also keen to prove that the changes that had been made in the previous twenty years or so had been properly authorized. The book was written against the background of Elizabethan government considering the possibility of admitting a papal nuncio and sending representatives to the Council of Trent. In such a context, the authority of councils was of particular importance. Consequently, Jewel emphasizes the fact that nothing had happened in the English Church without parliamentary sanction. Parliament served as a kind of lay synod operating in conjunction with bishops:

> Yet truly we do not despise councils, assemblies, and conferences of bishops and learned men; neither have we done that we have done altogether without bishops or without a council. The matter hath been treated in open parliament, with long consultation, and before a notable synod and convocation.[75]

Jewel claimed that it was only the civil power that had the authority to convene a Council, a teaching which had already been incorporated into Cranmer's articles (Art. XXI). Besides, he noted, 'Whatsoever it be, the truth of the gospel of Jesus Christ dependeth not upon the councils'.[76] The Council of Trent thus fell far short of a truly ecumenical council since it was principally concerned to bolster papal authority. Similarly, it refused to listen to the voices of the Reformers. It became a Council 'where our prince's ambassadors were contemned; where not one of our divines could be heard . . . And in very troth we have not tarried for, in this matter, the authority or consent of the Tridentine council, wherein we saw nothing done uprightly, nor by good order; where also everybody was sworn to the maintenance of one man'.[77] The claims of the Council of Trent are thus tested by the standard of the primitive church. Again they are found wanting.

The Church of England, however, like the other protestant churches, had not ignored the importance of councils. Indeed it had introduced changes through a 'provincial convocation', since there was no alternative to shake off the 'yoke and tyranny of the

bishop of Rome, to whom we were not bound'.[78] It is important
to note that Jewel writes in the plural. A pan-protestant identity
would be important to counter the charges that the different
strands of the Reformation could not agree. While Catholics
might point to differences between the diverse strands of the
Reformation, Jewel was keen to point to its overriding unity, even
if his optimism seems somewhat unfounded in hindsight:

> And as for those persons, whom they upon spite call
> Zuinglians and Lutherians, in very deed they of both sides
> be Christians, good friends and brethren. They vary not
> betwixt themselves upon the principles and foundations of
> our religion, nor as touching God, nor Christ, nor the Holy
> Ghost, nor of the means of justification, nor yet everlasting
> life, but upon one only question, which is neither weighty
> nor great: neither mistrust we, or make doubt at all, but they
> will shortly be agreed. And if there be any of them which
> have other opinion than is meet, we doubt not but ere it be
> long they will put apart all affections and names of parties,
> and that God will reveal it unto them: so that by better
> considering and searching out of the matter, as once it came
> to pass in the Council of Chalcedon, all causes and seeds of
> dissension shall be thoroughly plucked up by the root, and be
> buried, and quite forgotten for ever.[79]

Finally, Jewel paved the way for the characteristic debates of the next
generation. Like many of his protestant contemporaries, he discussed
the question of how authority was to be exercised in matters of
discipline and doctrine on which Scripture was silent. Such
'indifferent' areas, which included forms of worship and ecclesiastical
dress, were aspects of a wider order and uniformity expressed in both
church and state.[80] Echoing the solution to the Hooper controversy
during the reign of Edward VI, Jewel was clear that obedience
and conformity were of the utmost importance in the church. In
defending the retention of those practices of the church, which had
neither the warrant of scripture nor tradition, he asserts:

> Nevertheless we keep still and esteem, not only those
> ceremonies which we are sure were delivered us from the

apostles, but some others too besides, which we thought might be suffered without hurt to the church of God; because we had a desire that all things in the Holy Congregation might (as Paul Commandeth) 'be done with comeliness, and in good order;' but as for all those things which we saw were either very superstitious or unprofitable, or noisome, or mockeries, or contrary to the Holy Scriptures, or else unseemly for honest or discreet folks, as there be an infinite number nowadays where papistry is used, these I say, we have utterly refused without all manner exception.[81]

'Comeliness' and 'good order' become criteria for assessing the legitimacy of certain practices. And, in turn, as might be expected, Jewel locates the authority for making such definitions in the doctrine of Royal Supremacy. Christian princes were to serve as governors of the Church in their territories: 'A Christian prince hath the charge of both tables committed to him by God, to the end he may understand that not temporal matters only but also religious and ecclesiastical causes pertain to his office'.[82] Quoting the prophet Isaiah, he notes that the King should be 'patron and nurse of the church', suggesting explicitly that 'we ought to obey princes as men sent by God'.[83]

Three key themes emerge from Jewel. While none is any sense a surprise, each presents an important aspect for the future development of theology in the Church of England. First is the authority and supremacy of Scripture in matters of salvation. This doctrine, which was shared with the other churches of the Reformation, was accepted by virtually all what proved more controversial was what was to be done – and by whom – about those matters on which Scripture was silent. Related to this was the question of who should decide on whether Scripture was silent or not. Secondly, Jewel offers an apologetic example of what became a prominent feature of Anglican theology: its use of the Fathers and understanding of the traditions of the undivided church. Again this was far from uniquely Anglican, but for various reasons, not least of which was the relative conservatism of the English queen and the ambiguities of the Prayer Book liturgy, the Fathers gained a particular status even if they were never to be equated with Scripture. Finally, Jewel is clear about the legitimacy of the civil rulers exercising authority over the church in non-sacramental matters. There was a single, divinely granted order in both Church and State. It was this final factor, which is obviously closely related to the other two, that was to prove to be the most important in the development of Anglican identity and theology through the remainder of Elizabeth's reign and into the next century.

The Thirty-Nine Articles[84]

While Jewel might have provided the first extended defence of the Church of England against Rome, it was not until 1563 that the formal doctrinal statement for the church, the Thirty-Nine Articles of Religion, was ratified, although it did not finally receive Royal Assent until 1571. The Articles were closely based on the Forty-Two Articles from ten years earlier. Their genesis was complex and extended over many years. Many of the opening articles are closely modelled on the first seventeen articles of Philipp Melanchthon's 1536 formulation of the Augsburg Confession – the Wittenberg Articles – which had been delivered to Edward Foxe (Bishop of Hereford) and Nicholas Heath during the negotiations over membership of the Schmalkaldic league in Henry VIII's reign. In turn, these articles were remodelled in the abortive thirteen articles of 1538, which had been drawn up by Cranmer after the King's excommunication in that year.[85]

When they were originally discussed in 1552, there had been forty-five, but these were revised to forty-two. The 'Articles agreed on by the Bishops and other learned men in the Synod at London in the year of our Lord God 1552, for the avoiding of controversy in opinions, and the establishment of a godly concord, in certain matters of Religion', were published in May 1553, receiving Royal Assent on 19 June, although they were not ratified in parliament. While much is dependent on Lutheran formularies, there was some similarity in some of the more controversial areas of grace to more Reformed Confessions. This is hardly surprising since it is likely that Cranmer was assisted in their production by Peter Martyr Vermigli as well as Richard Cox (Dean of Westminster and the King's Almoner), and Thomas Goodricke (Bishop of Ely and Lord Chancellor). On Elizabeth's succession, a version of the Articles was introduced to Convocation for debate by Matthew Parker. After much discussion and some substantial reform, they were adopted in January 1563. Some changes fleshed out a few gaps in the original collection, and a few articles were omitted. For instance, an article on the Holy Spirit was added (Art. 5) as was an explicit statement on the consubstantiality of the Son (Art. 2). In these revisions, a strong influence was the adaptation of the language of the Augsburg Confession made by Johannes Brenz in the Württemberg Confession of 1552, which was offered as a statement of the unity and antiquity of the teaching of the protestant churches to the Council of Trent.[86] The articles on justification and free will were amended, although neither significantly changed the thrust of Cranmer's original. After the bishops had agreed the final text, it was sent for royal approval. In her careful reading the Queen omitted Article XXIX on wicked communicants 'in no wise' being 'partakers of Christ' from the draft text,[87] which would have been unacceptable to Lutherans, since it seemed to make the presence of Christ in the sacrament solely a matter of faith.[88] This article was restored in 1571, when the Articles received the Royal Assent, since the possibility of an alliance with Lutherans looked highly unlikely.

Much of the content of the Thirty-Nine Articles cannot be regarded as controversial. The first five articles, for instance, simply state the orthodox western doctrines of the Trinity and Christ in terms of the first four ecumenical councils. The next three articles cover the authority and content of Scripture and its sufficiency to salvation. These display more explicit anti-Catholicism than in the Forty-Two Articles, including a differentiation of the apocryphal books from the Scriptural books which alone are regarded as canonical (Art. VI). Articles IX to XIX discuss matters of salvation and consequently engage with the key sixteenth-century controversies of original sin, freedom, grace, justification, works and predestination. There are strong hints of more Reformed doctrine, especially Article XVII on 'predestination'. However, in a manner resembling Bullinger and Martyr, the article avoids the more tendentious aspects of the doctrine, including the thorny issues of irresistible grace and limited atonement, which came under the spotlight later in the century. Similarly, there is nothing in the articles on the invisible church of the elect.

Articles XX to XXX discuss the doctrine of the church and the sacraments. As might be expected, they attack transubstantiation (XXVIII) and the 'Romish' doctrine of purgatory (XXII). In contrast, the criteria for assessing all rites and ceremonies of the church are laid down by Scripture in a standard protestant manner: this meant that although the Church 'hath power to decree Rites or Ceremonies, and authority in Controversies of Faith' nothing could be done which was 'contrary to God's word written'. Even though the church had an important role as 'witness and keeper of Holy Writ . . . it ought not to decree any thing against the same, so besides the same ought it not to enforce any thing to be believed for necessity of salvation' (XX). At the same time, many of the most contentious issues between protestants are avoided in Article XXVIII on the Lord's Supper, (although there was an implicit condemnation of Zwingli's views with the phrase that the sacraments are 'not only signs' and with the emphasis on the 'partaking' of the body of Christ). Any sense of real presence was qualified by the following clause which stated that 'The body of Christ is given, taken, and eaten in the Supper, only after an heavenly and spiritual manner'. This understanding betrays the influence of many of the continental reformers with whom the English had mixed, including Bullinger, Bucer and Peter Martyr, as well as Calvin. This article was a significant alteration from its predecessor in 1553, since it omitted the explicit denial of the real presence. In words reminiscent of the Black Rubric, the earlier version had stated:

> that the body of one and the selfsame man cannot be at one
> time in diverse places, but must needs be in some one certain
> place: Therefore the body of Christ can not be present at
> one time in many and diverse places. Forasmuch as the truth
> of man's nature requireth, And because (as holy Scripture
> doth teach) Christ was taken up into Heaven, and there shall
> continue unto the end of the world, a faithful man ought
> not, either to believe or openly to confess the real and bodily
> presence (as they term it) of Christ's flesh and blood in the
> Sacrament of the Lord's supper.[89]

While Lutherans might still not be satisfied with the later version, it certainly endeavoured to be rather more comprehensive than Cranmer's original.

Articles XXXI to XXXVI centre on the discipline, worship and ceremonies of the church. Here is much that is explicitly anti-Roman, as with the sacrifice of the mass (XXXI), and the legalization of clerical marriage (XXXII). A second set of homilies published in 1563 was also added to the first (Art. XXXV), which tackled a wide range of subjects ranging from 'An Homily of the Worthy Receiving and reverent Esteeming of the Sacrament of the Body and Blood of Christ'[90] through 'A Sermon against Whoredom and Uncleanness'[91] to 'An Homily on Repairing and Keeping Clean and Comely Adorning of Churches': the church was 'a house of prayer, not a house of talking, of walking, of brawling, of minstrelsy, of hawks, of dogs'.[92] The teaching on the Eucharist resembled that of the Articles: 'It is well known that the meat we seek for in this Supper is spiritual food, the nourishment of our soul, a heavenly refection and not earthly, an unvisible meat and not bodily, a ghostly sustenance and not carnal'.[93]

Perhaps the most interesting of all the articles, however, is Article XXXIV on traditions and ceremonies, which echoes the preface to the 1549 Prayer Book, which had stated that 'although the keeping or omitting of a ceremony (in itself considered) is but a small thing: Yet the wilful and contemptuous transgression, and breaking of a common order, and discipline, is no small offence before God. Let all things be done among you (sayeth Saint Paul) in a seemly and due order'. While the Article states that it 'is not necessary that traditions and ceremonies be in all places one or utterly alike . . . and may be changed according to the diversity of countries, times, and men's manners', nevertheless those who refused to obey the 'common authority' in these matters indifferent offend 'against common order of the Church', hurt 'the authority of the magistrate', and 'wound the conscience of the weak brethren'. Order, obedience and authority were thus of central importance in the doctrinal settlement. As the full title of the Articles emphasizes, they were written for 'avoiding diversities of opinions, and for the stablishing of consent touching true Religion'. Order and uniformity were further stressed in the final three Articles which discuss the role of the civil ruler and the political duty of Christians. Article XXXVII asserts that the Queen 'hath the chief power in this Realm of England, and other her Dominions, unto whom the chief Government of all Estates of this Realm, whether they be Ecclesiastical or Civil, in all causes doth appertain, and is not, nor ought to be, subject to any foreign Jurisdiction'. Nevertheless the clause that 'The Civil Magistrate is ordained and allowed of God; wherefore we must obey him, not only for fear of punishment but also for conscience sake' was dropped from the 1563 text. Article XXXVII also allows the death penalty and permits the bearing of arms and serving in wars. Article XXXVIII forbids the common ownership of property and explicitly condemns anabaptists, and the final article permits the swearing of oaths.

The Articles as a statement of doctrine clearly demonstrate the wider European context: there is little that is distinctly English. While much derives from Lutheran confessions, for the most part they would be acceptable to both sides of the Reformation divide. Indeed, Cranmer had originally hoped in 1552 that there might be a pan-protestant statement about all the controversial issues. He wrote to Calvin on 20 March 1552:

As nothing tends more injuriously to the separation of the churches than heresies and disputes respecting the doctrines of religion, so nothing tends more effectually to unite the churches of God, and more powerfully to defend the fold of Christ, than the pure teaching of the gospel, and harmony of doctrine. Wherefore I have often wished, and still continue to do so, that learned and godly men, who are eminent for erudition and judgment, might meet together in some place of safety, where by taking counsel together, and comparing their respective opinions, they might handle all the heads of ecclesiastical doctrine, and hand down to posterity, under the weight of their authority, some work not only upon the subjects themselves, but upon the forms of expressing them .... It cannot escape your prudence, how exceedingly the church of God has been injured by dissensions and varieties of opinion respecting this sacrament of unity; and though they are now in some measure removed, yet I could wish for an agreement in this doctrine, not only as regards the subject itself, but also with respect to the words and forms of expression.[94]

This desire for an ecumenical consensus might explain the delay in the production of the original articles. Nevertheless, despite the Lutheran background to many of the Articles, on the more controversial issues on predestination and the Eucharist a moderate Reformed influence is clear. The Articles also have the virtue of relative brevity, which allowed for a degree of diversity in interpretation (even if there has been a tendency among some commentators for theological labelling). As a key defining moment in Anglican theology, they have been discussed ever since.[95]

What remained unclear in the Articles was their precise status, and this remains a contentious issue even today. Initially, Archbishop Parker had hoped that they might function as rules whereby preachers could be held to account. He had also intended that they should be read out twice a year in churches, which probably proved too much for the Queen's sensibilities.[96] When they were granted Royal Assent on 29 May 1571, subscription to the Articles was required by all clergy who had been ordained in the reign of Queen Mary, since their ordination had not been according to the Edwardian ordinal. Similarly, when clergy were presented to livings they were required to subscribe. In 1571 the Bishops issued a series of canons, which never received royal assent, to enforce subscription. These regarded the Articles as a statement of the church's public teaching, and as a test for what was acceptable for preachers. Clergy who refused to subscribe were to be deprived of their living. However, it was not clear that the laity were so tied to the articles. And of course while most clergy were able to subscribe, many were no doubt hopeful that they would not be the last word on Anglican theology. This became obvious in the years that followed, as will be discussed in the next chapter.

Chapter 4

Challenges to the Settlement

Churches Restored

The previous chapter showed that the Elizabethan Settlement gave a statutory closure to the English Reformation: religious change was complete, and the Act of Uniformity imposed the disciplines of the Book of Common Prayer across the country. Shortly afterwards, the theology of the Church of England was defined in the Thirty-Nine Articles, which were imposed on all those holding ecclesiastical offices. In theory, England could be regarded as a 'confessional state'. The limits of 'Anglican theology' were thus drawn, which means that this book could come to a hasty conclusion. And yet, of course, theological debates continued, and very quickly they became very heated. Given that they were inextricably linked with politics, it is once again impossible to give an account of theology that fails to devote attention to the problems of power and authority in church and state. The presenting issue for the theological controversy was over what to wear and do in church, which has been something of an Anglican fixation ever since. Some of the most bitter conflicts of the nineteenth century have a certain déjà vu to them.

From the 1840s, huge numbers of English churches were restored or rebuilt, and to cope with the rising population, many new churches were also built. The prevailing style was the 'Christian' style so beloved of the Gothic revivalists, particularly the Early English style. A vision of the medieval, pioneered by A. W. N. Pugin among others, began to replace the alternatives. Although most parish churches had been adapted to meet the demands of a word-based worship following the Edwardian and Elizabethan reforms, very few churches were able to withstand the historicizing influence of church restoration conducted according to so-called Ecclesiological principles.[1] Various societies were set up to promote church rebuilding along historical lines, the most prominent of which was the Cambridge Camden Society, which was set up in May 1839 by two Cambridge undergraduates, Benjamin Webb and John Mason Neale. By 1843, it had two archbishops, 16 bishops, 31 peers and MPs as patrons and a membership of 700. Its publication *The Ecclesiologist* proved influential on church rebuilding, and quickly architects and artists turned to medieval ideas for inspiration. In an often polemical way, the writers sought to restore churches on what they believed to be historical lines and to introduce as much ceremonial as possible.[2] Before long, designs for church ornaments and furniture had been published.[3]

For the Ecclesiologists, the church was to become a place of symbolism. In an edition of *The Ecclesiologist*, they thus wrote: 'A Church is not as it should be, till *every* window is filled with stained glass, till every inch is covered with encaustic tiles, till there is a rood screen glowing with the brightest tints and with gold, nay, if we would arrive at perfection, the roof and walls must be painted and frescoed'.[4] To assist this process, in 1843 Neale and Webb translated a thirteenth-century manual of symbolism by William Durandus, the *Rationale Divinorum Officiorum*. The 'material fabric symbolizes, embodies, figures, represents, expresses, answers to, some abstract meaning'.[5] This meant, for instance, that the nave and two side aisles represented the Holy Trinity,[6] and the tiles on the roof were 'the soldiers, who preserve the church . . . from enemies'.[7] In their lengthy introduction, the translators were clear about the purpose of restoring church buildings and liturgy:

> We assert, then, that *Sacramentality* is that characteristic which so strikingly distinguishes ancient ecclesiastical architecture from our own. By this word we mean to convey the idea that, by the outward and visible form, is signified something inward and spiritual . . . This Christian reality, we would call SACRAMENTALITY; investing that symbolical truthfulness, which it has in *every* true expression, with a greater force and holiness, both from the greater purity of truth which it embodies.[8]

This meant that it was important to see architecture not simply as a profession but as 'the study of the devout ecclesiastic':

We are not saying that none but monks should design churches . . . But we do protest against the merely business-like spirit of the modern profession, and demand for them a more elevated and directly religious habit of mind.[9]

Such a high view of sacramentality and symbolism had a rapid impact on buildings throughout the country, which deeply offended many. The implications of the Ecclesiological Movement were even noted by Pugin in 1843:

It is most delightful to see the feeling reviving in the Anglican Church for the sanctity and depths of chancels; and as a preliminary step to better things, it should receive all possible encouragement, but those who think merely to build chancels, without reviving the ancient faith, will be miserably deceived in their expectations . . . if the present revival of Catholic antiquity is suffered to proceed much further, it will be seen that the Common Prayer or the ancient models must be abandoned.[10]

Francis Close, vicar of the Evangelical stronghold of Cheltenham, preached a sermon on Guy Fawkes Day in 1844 under the title 'The Restoration of Churches is the Restoration of Popery: proved and illustrated from the authentic publications of the Cambridge Camden Society'. Court cases were rapidly brought, which led to the formation of the English Church Union in 1859 'To afford counsel and protection to all persons, lay or clerical, suffering under unjust aggression or hindrance in spiritual matters'. Six years later, the Church Association was formed to finance legal actions. After the 1874 Public Worship Regulation Act, several prosecutions led to a number of imprisonments, including Fr Tooth of Hatcham (1877). Some Evangelicals found ritualist worship little different from paganism. In 1866, Lord Shaftesbury, for instance, visited Fr A. H. Mackonochie's church of St Alban's, Holborn. He had had been reprimanded for using lit candles and for mixing water and wine in the chalice. Shaftesbury commented:

In outward form and ritual, it is the worship of Jupiter and Juno . . . [it was] such a scene of theatrical gymnastics, and singing, screaming, genuflections, such a strange movements of the priests, their backs almost always to the people, as I never saw before even in a Romish temple. . . . The communicants went up to the tune of soft music, as though it had been a melodrama, and one was astonished, at the close, that there was no fall of the curtain.[11]

By 1857, various practices had been declared legal including use of the credence table, the cross on the chancel screen, the unrestricted use of the cross as a symbol, frontals of various colours and the altar cross. It was ruled that stone altars were still illegal, as was the omission of the Ten Commandments from the chancel. *The Ecclesiologist* commented on the verdicts of 1857:

With an altar or holy table, be it of wood or stone, vested according to the Christian season, surmounted with a cross and reredos on the east wall, furnished with super-altar and altar lights, flanked by a credence table, with a chancel separated by a high screen and gates, and the chancel itself furnished with stalls, and above all, this altar served by priest and deacon in their distinctive vestments, it will be very difficult to persuade, be it friends or foes of the church of England, that with all this pomp and dignity of ritual permitted and enjoined, our Church does not hold the very highest doctrine, even though the Christian sacrifice be celebrated on a wooden altar, and even though the east wall be decorated with the decalogue in unintelligible black letter, or though there be a judgment prohibiting – without defining – the additional splendour of two yards of 'bone lace'. If puritanism considers this decision a victory, we can only wish its advocates a few more such triumphs.[12]

The debates that emerged at the Reformation continued to shape the conflicts of three hundred years later: the authors of the article in *The Ecclesiologist* derided their opponents as puritans, and opponents of the ritualists were happy to label them as Romanists. While the ultimate failure of the courts in regulating religion reveals the changed circumstances of late Victorian England, the fact that visible forms of worship and architecture continued to provoke conflict well into the twentieth century reveals the profound weakness of both the Elizabethan Act of Uniformity and its 1662 successor in imposing uniformity on a church that was so often bent on reinterpreting the nature of its identity. While the number of medievalists like Neale and Webb was small, their impact on the church was nonetheless profound. At the same time, they represent simply one aspect of the wider nineteenth-century struggle for the location of Anglican identity in an idealized history.

On Surplices and Caps: A Theology of Dressing Up[13]

Ecclesiastical practices and ornaments were divisive from the very beginnings of the reign of Elizabeth. What brought matters to a head was a refusal among some clergy to wear the vestments which had been laid down in the Elizabethan legislation, which had emerged once before during the consecration of John Hooper in the reign of Edward VI. In Oxford two prominent Marian exiles had refused to wear the surplice, seeing it as a sign of the popish priesthood.[14] These were Laurence Humphrey, President of Magdalen College and Regius Professor of Divinity, and Thomas Sampson, Dean of Christ Church, who had track record, having also refused to wear vestments at his ordination in 1550. Similarly, at Cambridge the Vice-Chancellor had informed Archbishop Parker that one fellow of Christ's College, and 'sundry' at St John's, 'will be very hardly brought to wear surplices'.[15] Such disobedient practices provoked Elizabeth's counsellors. Thus, after hearing about the 'sundry varieties and novelties, not only in opinions but in external ceremonies and rites' that had crept into the Church, Cecil wrote to Parker on 25 January 1565 on behalf of the Queen. Complaining about the lack of discipline in the church, he urged him to use his metropolitical powers as archbishop to compel uniformity throughout his province.[16] What was important, Cecil noted, was that there should be 'one rule, form, and manner of order in all their actions . . . without diversities of opinions or novelties of rites and manners'. Lack of uniformity presented 'an open and manifest disorder and offence to the godly wise and obedient persons, by diversity of opinions and specially in the external, decent, and lawful rites and ceremonies to be used in the churches'.[17] He thus told the archbishop to 'proceed by order, injunction, or censure, according to the order and appointment of such laws and ordinances as are provided by act of Parliament, and the true meaning thereof, so as uniformity of order may be kept in every church, and without variety and contention'.[18] Within a few weeks Parker had written to the bishops asking for reports on conformity in their dioceses, and had drafted a 'book of articles' to enforce the injunctions.

For many of the 'godly' or 'precisianist' clergy who came to be known as Puritans, however, the surplice could not be freed from its popish associations, which made them particularly reluctant to wear the offending garment. And since it was a matter indifferent – often referred to by the Greek term 'adiaphoron' (plural 'adiaphora') – on which the Bible was patently silent, the argument against wearing the surplice seemed sound. The problem, however, was that it had been legislated upon by the duly appointed supreme authority of the land. The dilemma was between the dictates of Scripture and obedience to authority. A number of clergy had written to their friends on the Continent asking for advice on how to proceed. Humphrey, for instance, wrote to Heinrich Bullinger in Zürich asking whether wearing the 'round cap and popish surplice' which 'are now enjoined us, not by the unlawful tyranny of the pope, but by the just and legitimate authority of the queen' be 'matters of indifference'. Could 'habits of this kind ... be worn in church by pious men, lawfully and with a safe conscience?'[19] Similarly, Sampson asked Bullinger whether 'the nature of things indifferent admits of coercion; and whether any violence should be offered to the consciences of the many who are not yet persuaded'; and 'Whether any new ceremonies may be instituted, or superadded to what is expressly commanded in the word'.[20] The problems of practice required a continental theological opinion.

Bullinger responded at length to these letters on 1 May 1566 where he was less than sympathetic to the puritan cause. He suggested that 'for the sake of decency, and comeliness of appearance, or dignity and order, some such regulation may be made' about the dress of the clergy.[21] Against the charge that such vestments were papist he responded: 'it is not yet proved that the pope introduced a distinction of habits into the church; so far from it, that it is clear that such distinction is long anterior to popery. Nor do I see why it should be unlawful to use, in common with papists, a vestment not superstitious, but pertaining to civil regulation and good order'.[22] For Bullinger, clothes were not quite so inherently grubby as for his Oxford correspondents. Besides, he suggested, things needed to be put into proportion. He concluded by emphasizing the importance of staying obedient to the church, since leaving would simply play into the hands of their conservative opponents:

> in my opinion great caution is to be observed lest this dispute, and clamour, and contention respecting the habits should be conducted with too much bitterness . . . It appears indeed most extraordinary to me, . . . that you can persuade yourselves that you cannot, with a safe conscience, subject yourselves and churches to vestiarian bondage; . . . because, by the relinquishment of your office, you will expose the churches to wolves.[23]

This letter was copied to Robert Horn, Bishop of Winchester, with a cover note from Bullinger asking him to forward the letter to Grindal and a number of other bishops. He also encouraged them to show respect to Humphrey and Sampson and to do their best to try to bring about reconciliation.[24]

Grindal was so encouraged by Bullinger's support that he had the letter printed in English and Latin to help put his case. He wrote to Bullinger (whom he did not know) informing him of what he had done on 27 August 1566: 'It is scarcely credible how much this controversy about things of no importance has disturbed our churches, and still, in great measure, continues to do'. While many clergy had been on the verge of leaving the ministry, he claimed, the publication of Bullinger's letter had helped them return 'to a better mind . . . . Some of the clergy, influenced by your judgment and authority, have relinquished their former intention of deserting their ministry'. In a telling passage, Grindal went on to indicate the compromises that he had been forced to make on returning to England from exile:

We, who are now bishops, on our first return, and before
we entered on our ministry, contended long and earnestly
for the removal of those things that have occasioned the
present dispute; but as we were unable to prevail, either
with the queen or the parliament, we judged it best, after
a consultation on the subject, not to desert our churches
for the sake of a few ceremonies . . . But these unseasonable
contentions about things which, as far as I am able to judge,
are matters of indifference, are so far from edifying, that they
disunite the churches, and sow discord among the brethren.[25]

For Grindal decency and good order required compromise.
Although he made it clear that he would prefer not to minister
in a cope or surplice at St Paul's, he nevertheless was prepared to
do so 'for order's sake and obedience to the prince'.[26] It would
appear that Grindal's circulation of the letter had the effect of
keeping some people in the church.[27] He continued to make
use of the letter in later disputes with those who had refused to
conform.[28]

In a joint letter written in July 1566 Humphrey and Sampson
replied to Bullinger repeating their complaints about the
actions of the English bishops: 'how can that habit be thought
consistent with the simple ministry of Christ, which used to set
off the theatrical pomp of the popish priesthood?'[29] In short,
they claimed, 'in the rites nothing is discretionary'. Citing Martin
Bucer as an authority, they noted that compulsion on matters
indifferent was inconsistent with Christian liberty.[30] At the end of
the letter, they enumerated the 'blemishes which still attach to the
Church of England', which included 'exquisite singing' and the
playing of the organ, the use of the sign of the cross at baptism,
the possibility that women might baptize in private, the wearing
of the cope and surplice, as well as 'popish' habits out of doors,
kneeling to receive communion, and the use of unleavened bread.
Assent to such ceremonies brought with them the loss of 'free
liberty of preaching'. Finally, they complained that 'the article
[XXVIII] . . . which expressly oppugned and took away the real
presence in the Eucharist, and contained a most clear explanation
of the truth, is now set forth among us mutilated and imperfect'.[31]
All these complaints were to resurface only a few years later.

This joint letter and Grindal's publication of his earlier reply prompted Bullinger to write back to Grindal on 6 September 1566 to seek to distance himself from seeming to approve of the offending vestments. He summarizes his main point: 'The sum of our judgment', he notes, 'was this, that churches redeemed by the blood of Christ ought on no account to be deserted for the sake of caps and gowns, which are to be regarded as mere matters of indifference'.[32] He goes on to express his grief that the advertisements were being enforced with such vigour, and that episcopal power was silencing the right of the individual pastor 'to deliver his opinion in ecclesiastical affairs'.[33] Shortly afterwards, Bullinger wrote again to Humphrey and Sampson expressing his hope that his private concerns about the vestiarian controversy would not be taken out of context in order to bring about 'the restoration of things that every pious person, who is acquainted with our writings, has long known us to disapprove of'.[34] Bullinger seems to have regretted interfering in a controversy, whose political implications he perhaps failed to grasp in their entirety. However, the seeds of future theological debate were clearly sown during this controversy. Theologians of different viewpoints had begun to do theology as they interpreted the formularies and liturgies of their church – and as a consequence from the very beginning of Elizabeth's reign a few were forced to leave that church.

Despite Cecil's encouragement to Archbishop Parker to enforce conformity, the Royal Assent was not given to the so-called Advertisements when they were sent to him on 3 March 1565. It is not clear precisely why this was not granted, although it is possible that the Queen did not wish to be directly associated with what might prove an unpopular policy, or – perhaps more likely – she felt sufficient authority had already been given in the 1559 Injunctions (and the Advertisements had modestly weakened them). Furthermore, the Queen seems not to have wished to interfere with what she probably regarded as the proper authority that she had delegated to her archbishop.[35] Parker showed a degree of exasperation with the refusal of the Queen to intervene, especially as some bishops, including Bishop Grindal, had turned a blind eye to lack of conformity.[36] In 1565 Parker tried unsuccessfully to persuade the Queen to write to Grindal to ensure conformity in London, which, he felt, would have been an important gesture to enforce conformity 'throughout the realm'.[37] For Parker this lack of discipline had simply made matters worse: indeed, had Grindal taken action in 1559, he wrote to Cecil, then he would have survived with 'both his reputation better saved and my poor honesty not so foully traduced'.[38] Ironically, perhaps, it was only after Grindal had openly disobeyed her in 1575 as Archbishop of Canterbury that the Queen began to intervene directly in church affairs.

Parker had begun to enforce conformity even before the Advertisements were issued. Thus in 1565, he challenged Sampson and Humphrey to wear the appointed vestments: he wrote to Cecil that it was a question of 'either conformity or depart'.[39] They were 'to wear the cap appointed by Injunction, to wear no hats in their long gowns, to wear a surplice with a non-regent hood in their quires at their Colleges, according to the ancient manner there, to communicate kneeling in wafer-bread'.[40] In the end, Humphrey retained his offices, but Sampson, who held a Crown appointment, was deprived as Dean of Christ Church on 26 May 1565.

After another attempt to gain Royal Assent for the Advertisements met with the same result a year later, Parker issued them on his own authority. He wrote to Cecil on 28 March 1566: 'I am now fully bent to prosecute this order, and to delay no longer . . . where the Queen's Highness will needs have me assay with mine own authority what I can do for order, I trust I shall not be stayed hereafter, saving that I would pray your honour to have your advice to do that more prudently in this common cause which must needs be done'.[41] Although the Advertisements made some concessions to the sensitivities of the precisianists in that the old mass vestments were not insisted upon (although copes were prescribed for cathedrals), it was nevertheless clear that 'every minister saying any public prayers, or ministering the sacraments or other rites of the Church, shall wear a comely surplice with sleeves'; the people were to receive communion kneeling; and in addition 'all ecclesiastical persons or other, having any ecclesiastical living, do wear the cap appointed by the Injunctions'.[42] In the spring of 1566 a campaign was conducted throughout the country and most bishops toed the line.[43] Grindal issued a summons to 98 of his clergy on 26 March, demanding that they give written guarantees that they would conform. Thirty-seven refused and were suspended for three months in the hope that they might come to their senses.[44] Across the country, others lost their livings, including William Turner, Dean of Wells.[45] The vestiarian crisis emphasized the conflict between matters indifferent and those things necessary to salvation: as so often with efforts at legal enforcement, the situation hardened. It seemed, as John Jewel commented to Bullinger, that

> the affair of the habits has at this time occasioned much disturbance . . . some of our brethren are contending about this matter, as if the whole of our religion were contained in this single point; so that they choose rather to lay down their functions, and leave their churches empty, than to depart one tittle from their own views of the subject. They will neither be persuaded by the very learned writings either of yourself and Gualter, or by the counsels of other pious men.[46]

For some of the former exiles who were hoping that the Reformation would continue, the Church of England seemed to be betraying the Gospel: the vestiarian controversy was simply the thin end of the wedge. During the investigations of the deprived London clergy, a number of them appeared before the Ecclesiastical Commissioners in June 1567. In their answers, some of them looked back to the reign of Queen Mary, which began to seem like a golden age for 'God's saints'. A certain John Smith commented on how those who had refused to conform had come to their decision:

> we remembered that there was a congregation of us in this city in Queen Mary's days; and a congregation at Geneva, which used a book and an order of preaching, ministering of sacraments and discipline, most agreeable to the word of God; which book is allowed by that godly and well-learned man, Master Calvin, and the preachers there; which book and order we now hold. And if you can reprove this book, or anything that we hold, by the word of God, we will yield to you, and do open penance at Paul's Cross; if not, we will stand to it by the grace of God.[47]

For such men, there were other ways to do things in church that did not smack of the popish past – and it was possible that the Church of England could change its ways and continue a Reformation that had been so abruptly halted, or even reversed, by Elizabeth. However, with a Queen and set of bishops so intent on enforcing in matters indifferent, alternative theological visions brought with them significant threats. Furthermore, the importance of ensuring a properly protestant identity for the Church of England became more pressing after Elizabeth's excommunication by the Pope in 1570 and the threat of sedition from the many Roman Catholics in the country who had been enjoined in the accompanying Bull 'not to obey her, or her orders, mandates and laws'.[48]

At the same time, it is important to remember that during the campaigns for enforcement in 1566 and again in 1571 over subscription to the articles, most clergy remained within the Church of England however reluctantly: outward uniformity was accompanied by internal dissent. The struggle for the theological identity of the Church of England was for the most part carried on from within (although often given added momentum from those outside). And to complicate matters further, there was often fundamental agreement on some of the major controversial issues that occupied theologians on the continent. 'The contrast between the godly and conformists in England', Felicity Heal writes, 'was more one of temperament, of the intensity of commitment to spiritual regeneration, than of doctrinal substance'.[49] However, such spiritual regeneration returned over and again to two simple and closely related theological questions: who had the authority to decide in matters indifferent? And who made the final judgement on whether or not something was contained in Scripture? In practice, as J. W. Allen pointed out long ago, the questions could often amount to much the same thing:

> It was fully admitted that the Supreme Government of
> the Church was bound by Scripture. Yet, if you accepted
> the Elizabethan system, you could not deny that it was
> for the Queen, or for the Queen in Parliament, to declare
> authoritatively what sacraments and what doctrines are
> indeed in scripture . . . The authority of the Scriptures
> became a kind of legal fiction.[50]

From the 1570s onwards, different interest groups in the church and state, some inevitably more powerful than others, spent much of their time doing theology as they engaged with the identity of the Church of England. Who precisely made decisions came to be seen as increasingly central to the independent identity of the church. This set in motion a struggle that continues till today. Indeed, despite the Act of Uniformity of 1662 that ended the project of comprehension, it is not clear that the identity of Anglicanism has ever been settled, as the telling example of the nineteenth-century ritualists with which I began this chapter revealed.

Admonitions, Whitgift and Cartwright: The Struggle for Church Identity

The question of clerical dress was the presenting symptom of a much larger problem. The fact that Cranmer's attempt to provide a more accountable model of episcopacy in the *Reformatio* had never been approved meant that bishops survived with many of their medieval powers intact. Indeed some saw the survival of bishops and their despotic rule as an obstruction to the authentic preaching of the Word of God. Parliament was chosen as a suitable route for reform. Furthermore, the Book of Common Prayer contained much that seemed to contradict the purest form of the Gospel. The Dean of York, Matthew Hutton, commented in 1573 to William Cecil, who had been elevated to the peerage as Lord Burghley: 'At the beginning it was but a cap, a surplice, and a tippet; now, it is grown to bishops, archbishops, and cathedral churches, to he overthrow of the established order, and to the Queen's authority in causes ecclesiastical'.[51] Already in April 1571 some Puritans led by William Strickland had introduced a Bill into the House of Commons for Reformation of the Book of Common Prayer.[52] In Elizabeth's fourth parliament in May 1572, a further Bill was introduced that aimed at reforming the rites and ceremonies of the Church in 'imitation of the ancient apostolical church and the best reformed churches in Europe'. It consequently promoted the introduction of a modified prayer book based on that being used in the French and Dutch churches in London, as well as the removal of what the Puritan sponsors regarded as various other abuses.[53] After the second reading on 19 May, the Queen objected to such matters being discussed in parliament,[54] and on 22 May the Speaker reported to the House of Commons that 'her Highness' Pleasure is, that from henceforth no Bills concerning Religion shall be preferred or received into this House, unless the same should be first considered and liked by the Clergy'.[55]

The rejection of the Bill in parliament provoked a not inconsiderable reaction. Two young London Puritan clergymen John Field, already suspended from the ministry, and Thomas Wilcox quickly produced *An Admonition to the Parliament*,[56] which provoked a significant theological discussion in what can be regarded as one of the key formative periods for the identity of the Church of England. Field and Wilcox had appeared in the Star Chamber in May 1573 with Edward Dering, who had initially been a protégé of Whitgift. Notorious for his sermon which accused the Queen of neglecting her church,[57] in his answers Dering was to claim that while 'princes have full authority over all ecclesiastical and civil persons', nevertheless there is 'in the church no lawgiver but Christ Jesus'.[58] He wrote to Burghley after his suspension that 'the worldly power of the prince hath no place' in the spiritual sphere. His strongest attacks, however, were reserved for bishops: 'The Lordship of the bishop hath been even a plague sore in the state of a kingdom and is at this day a swelling wound of corruption in the body of a commonwealth . . . [it] is utterly unlawful in the church of God'.[59] The *Admonition* proper, which was written by Wilcox, offered what they called 'a true platform of a church reformed',[60] which amounted to a complete abolition of the papal inheritance, including a significant reform of the ministry. It boldly suggested that the 'popish mass mongers', 'King Henry's priests . . . should . . . be utterly removed' from the church,[61] to be replaced with a more ancient form of ministry where the congregation would have the authority to pick ministers. They would not be 'tied to any form of prayer invented by man',[62] but 'preaching in season and out of season'.[63] There should be no hierarchy, which meant that parliament was called on to

remove advowsons, patronages, impropriations, and the
bishops' authority, claiming to themselves thereby right to
ordain ministers, and to bring in that old and true election,
which was accustomed to be made by the congregation. You
must displace those ignorant and unable ministers . . . and
in their rooms appoint such as both can, and will by God's
assistance feed the flock. . . . Remove homilies, articles,
injunctions, a prescript order of service made out of the
mass book. Take away the Lordship, the loitering, the pomp,
the idleness, and livings of bishops, but yet employ them to
such ends as they were in the old Church appointed for. Let
a lawful and a godly Seignorie look that they preach, not
quarterly or monthly, but continually: not for filthy lucre sake,
but of ready mind.[64]

In ecclesiastical discipline, Wilcox and Field followed a Presbyterian
model, seeking to introduce 'seniors, or elders, and deacons'
whose office was to govern the church.[65] Thus, they argued for an
abolition of hierarchy:

Instead of an Archbishop or Lord bishop, you must make
equality of ministers. . . . This regiment consisteth especially
in ecclesiastical discipline, which is an order left by God
unto his Church, whereby men learn to frame their wills
and their doings according to the law of God, by instructing
and admonishing one another, yea and by correcting and
punishing all wilful persons, and contemners of the same.[66]

The model of a godly church, they claimed, had been revealed by
fully reformed churches in France and Scotland.[67] The *Admonition*
was accompanied by a summary written by John Field of the
'Popish Abuses Yet Remaining in the English Church, for the
which Godly Ministers Have Refused to Subscribe'.[68] This part
had a 'bitterness of the stile' which Wilcox was later to disown.[69]
Field enunciated a by now familiar list of abuses: the Book of
Common Prayer was described as 'an unperfect book, culled &
picked out from that popish dunghill, the Mass book full of all
abominations'.[70] It attacked saints' days, kneeling for communion,

the use of the term 'priest', the sign of the cross at baptism, the use of the term 'worship' at the marriage service, confirmation and much else besides. Two letters from Gualter in Zürich and Beza in Geneva which had been written to Bishop Parkhurst of Norwich in 1566 during the Vestiarian crisis were also published with the Admonition. Beza, with whom Cartwright had lived in Geneva, wrote in no uncertain terms about the Book of Common Prayer:

> as touching the Lord's supper, who can refrain tears, to declare how miserably it is transformed into that old stagelike frisking and horrible Idol gadding? . . . For who would not think, that the using of an altar, or some table were an indifferent thing? . . . They were not content with common and plain songs, and therefore . . . that busy and curious prickesong and descanting was brought in, more meet for stage plays, for the most part, than for an holy action.[71]

Despite the fact that Beza's letter had had little effect on the course of the Vestiarian Controversy, it was now being used to support the reform of the English Church in new circumstances.

Although the authority of the 'godly seignorie' was not denied in the *Admonition*, the question that was raised was whether such an authority should extend over the ordering of the church, or whether the church should be left to decide for itself in crucial areas, such as whether a minister should be appointed to an ecclesiastical living and who should be responsible for accusations of heresy. While a great deal of theological energy was expended in trying to prove the antiquity of the Presbyterian system, a more fundamental issue was how far should a church be able to rule for itself independent of the Royal Supremacy. The heart of the *Admonition* rested in its understanding of ecclesiastical discipline as a matter for the church unmolested by bishops and the state. The church polity outlined in the *Admonition* thus called for a disciplined church, autonomous in judgement and able to fulfil its apostolic calling: 'This regiment consisteth especially in ecclesiastical discipline, which is an order left unto God by his church, whereby men learn to frame their wills and doings according to the law of God'.[72] Once the church had been reformed, the kingdom itself would be transformed by the Word of God, which would lead to a more obedient and compliant population:

> Not that we mean to take away the authority of the civil Magistrate and chief governor, to whom we wish all blessedness, and for the increase of whose godliness we daily pray: but that Christ being restored into his kingdom, to rule in the same by the sceptre of his worde, and severe discipline: the Prince may be better obeyed, the realm more flourish in godliness, and the Lord himself more sincerely and purely according to his revealed will served than heretofore he hath been, or yet at this present is. Amend therefore these horrible abuses, and reform God's church, and the Lorde is on your right hand, you shall not be removed for ever.[73]

For others, however, the plea for the church's autonomy in deciding matters for itself presented an obvious challenge to the order and stability of the state.

Whitgift and Cartwright: The Limits of Scripture

Shortly after the publication of the *Admonition*, a second *Admonition*, which repeated the demands of the first book, was issued.[74] Although the style was less inflammatory, the issues remained the same. On the Book of Common Prayer, for instance, it issued the challenge to those in authority in the church to

> shewe us (if they can) by what aucthoritie they may enjoine us (if God his worde beare them to be magistrates) to observe the boke of Common prayers, bothe in matter and manner, as in their laste Canons they forbid their ministers to depart from one or other? it is wicked to say no worse of it, so to attribute to a booke, in deede culled out of the vile popish service booke, with some certaine rubrikes and gloses of their owne devise, suche authoritie as only is due to God his booke and inditements, imprisonments, and suche extremities used against them which breake it, is cruell persecution of the members of Jesus Christe.[75]

This second *Admonition* has often been mistakenly attributed to Thomas Cartwright (1535–1603),[76] one of the most articulate of the Puritan theologians. Cartwright had been a prominent figure in Cambridge, appointed to the Lady Margaret Chair in 1569, but deprived after the imposition of the new statutes drawn up by the Master of Trinity College, John Whitgift (1530–1604), who had succeeded to the office of Vice-Chancellor. Cartwright fled to Geneva where he worked alongside Theodore Beza. It was in the aftermath of this tense atmosphere in Cambridge that Whitgift responded to the *Admonition* in his *Answere to a Certan Libel Intituled, 'An Admonition'* (1573) to which Cartwright published *A Replye* (April 1573). In turn this prompted Whitgift's *The Defense of the Aunswere to the 'Admonition'*, which was followed by a further series of blasts and counterblasts. The controversy between the erstwhile Cambridge sparring partners drew out the full implications of the question of authority in matters indifferent, helping to point to the direction in which the Church of England was to travel in the next century.

Historically, this was a period of tension: in October 1573, John Hawkins, who had been mistaken for the Queen's advisor, Christopher Hatton, had been stabbed to death by Peter Birchett, a radical Puritan. Shortly afterwards, the Queen issued a proclamation that threatened imprisonment for those refusing to use the Book of Common Prayer. In a famous speech given in the Star Chamber on 28 November 1573, Burghley, the Lord Treasurer, stated that the Queen:

> doth understand by divers means, that of late years, by
> negligence of the Bishops and Clergy, having ecclesiastical
> jurisdiction, there are in sundry parts of her realm entered
> into ordinary cures of souls, that is, into rectories, vicarages,
> and such like, and into places of preaching and reading,
> a number of persons young in years, but over-young in
> soundness of learning and discretion, which according to
> their own imaginations and conceits, and not according to
> the public order established by law, having not only in the
> common services of the church, and in the administration
> of sacraments, made sundry alterations, but also, by their

example and teaching, have enticed their parochians, and their auditories, being her Majesty's subjects, to conceive erroneous opinions, in condemning the whole government of the Church and order ecclesiastical, and in moving her Majesty's good subjects, to think it a burden of conscience to observe the orders and rites of the Church established by law; a matter pernicious to the state of government, that her Majesty cannot, for the charge committed to her by Almighty God, but by speedy good means procure the stay of the danger that must needs follow, and provide for the reformation.[77]

While Cartwright and Whitgift framed their debate in theological terms, discussions of church order and uniformity had direct political implications.

For Cartwright, the Bible was to be the rule of everything, which effectively meant that virtually nothing was indifferent. Everything was to be ordered by scriptural authority; it was the church which was to be the final court of appeal in matters of dispute. Similarly, the church was governed according to its own laws and not by the laws of the magistrate. The magistrate's role was merely to confirm and implement the action of the church, if necessary by the use of law:

> The church is governed with that kind of government which the philosophers that write of the best commonwealths affirm to be the best. For, in respect of Christ the head, it is a monarchy; and, in respect of the ancients and pastors that govern in common and with like authority amongst themselves, it is an aristocraty, or the rule of the best men; and, in respect that the people are not secluded, but have their interest in church-matters, it is a democraty, or a popular estate.[78]

To some extent what Cartwright sought was a system where the church determined the running of the state and in turn expected the state's protection. This need for a strong law code required taking the whole of the Bible seriously, including the Old Testament. Cartwright made the point forcefully:

Whereas you say 'there is a great difference between the severity of the law and lenity of the Gospel,' methinks I smell a spice of error of the Manichees . . . that there is a good and an evil, a gentle and a severe God, one under the law and another under the Gospel. For to say that God was a sever punisher of sin, and to say that now he is not at so great hatred with it, but that he will have it gentler and softlier dealt with, is even all one in effect with that which supposeth two Gods.[79]

In his first response to the *Admonition*, Whitgift asserted the right of the church to legislate in matters indifferent, proposing a quite different understanding of the limits of scriptural authority. He outlined the problem of matters indifferent and necessary to salvation clearly and succinctly:

Whether all things pertaining to the outward form of
the church be particularly expressed, or commanded in
the scripture, or no, is the question that we have now in
controversy . . . Affirmatively the argument is always good of
the authority of the scripture; as, God hath there commanded
it to be done; therefore it must be done: or, The scripture
affirmeth it to be so; *ergo* it is so. But negatively it holdeth not,
except in matters of salvation and damnation.[80]

Interestingly, he defends this statement not by recourse to the Fathers of the early church but by using the writings of the Reformers. He points in particular to Zwingli's *Refutation Against The Tricks of The Catabaptists*.

At the same time, however, Whitgift is keen to affirm the reformed doctrinal settlement enshrined in the Prayer Book, the Articles, and Jewel's *Apology*, which Whitgift had come to regard as an authoritative work. Together these provided a sufficient statement of matters necessary to salvation. He was utterly clear on this point:

It were but a needless labour to make any particular recital
of those points of doctrine which this Church of England
doth hold and maintain; for they be at large set out in sundry

English books, and especially in the Apology of the Church of England . . . summarily also collected together in the book of articles . . . This I dare boldly affirm, that all points of religion necessary to salvation, and touching either the mystery of redemption in Christ, or the right use of the sacraments and true manner of worshipping God, are as purely and perfectly taught . . . as ever they were in any church sithence the apostles' time, or now be in any reformed church in the world.[81]

For Whitgift, the theological issues raised by the *Admonition* involved matters indifferent rather than points of doctrine. His method was to go through the charges of the *Admonition* methodically, proving that matters of church order and ceremony were not laid down in Scripture and were therefore to be adapted to local conditions. Since there was much that the Bible does not mention, then the church had to legislate as it saw fit. As Article XXXIV expressed it, 'Every particular or national Church hath authority to ordain, change, and abolish, ceremonies or rites of the church ordained only by man's authority, so that all things be done to edifying'.

Thus, against the Puritans who understood vestments purely in terms of their similarity to the Popish priesthood, Whitgift was to repeat Bullinger's theme in his letter to Sampson and Humphrey:[82] 'When they were a sign and a token of the popish priesthood, then they were evil, even as the thing was which they signified: but now they be signs and tokens of the ministers of the word of God, which are good, and therefore also they be good'.[83] Similarly, where the Puritans insisted that Scripture laid down one distinct form of Church Government, Whitgift claimed that the government of the church was a matter for churches to seek out what was best suited to particular circumstances. This allowed for a diversity of church orders in different places: 'we do not take upon (as we are slandered) either to blame or to condemn other churches, for such orders as they have received most fit for their estates'. Thus against Cartwright he claimed that 'Those who would seek to reform the ministry,' and create a uniform ministry throughout the world were nothing more nor less than 'troublesome and schismatical defacers', rather 'than zealous and godly reformers'.[84] While *a* form of church government was undoubtedly necessary, its precise character was not.

This led Whitgift to distinguish between different types of necessity. Necessity meant either 'that without the which a thing cannot be', a category under which fell all those matters affecting salvation, or 'that without the which a thing cannot so well and conveniently be', which encompassed matters indifferent.[85] For Whitgift, because Scripture was silent on the subject, church order was classified under the second type of necessity:

> I confess that in a church collected together in one place, and at liberty, government is necessary in the second kind of necessity; but that any kind of Government is so necessary that without it the church cannot be saved, or that it may not be altered into some other kind thought to be more expedient, I utterly deny.[86]

For Whitgift, then, the important point was to show against Cartwright that church government was a matter indifferent and simply a question of finding the best mechanism for the particular circumstances. He proves his point on scriptural grounds:

> I find no one certain and perfect kind of government prescribed or commanded in the scriptures to the Church of Christ; which no doubt should have been done, if it had been a matter necessary unto the salvation of the church.[87]

This means that he was able to claim that the precise form of church government was not part of the essence of the visible church (which is simply 'a congregation of faithful men, in the which the pure word of God is preached and the sacraments be duly ministered according to Christ's ordinance in all those things that of necessity are requisite to the same'):[88]

> touching the outward form and perfection of it, yet is it not such a part of the essence and being, but that it may be the church of Christ without this or that kind of government; and therefore the 'kind of government' of the church is not 'necessary unto salvation'.[89]

For Whitgift, then, certain ecclesiastical practices, which while they are not necessary to salvation (as both the puritans and the papists claim on different occasions),[90] are nonetheless necessary for the proper order and decorum of the church. For this reason, they should be obeyed. He summarized his understanding of the importance of adiaphora under eight headings:

> [First,] God hath in scripture fully and plainly comprehended all those things necessary to salvation.
>
> Secondly, that in ceremonies and external discipline he hath not in scripture particularly determined any thing, but left the same to his church, to make or abrogate . . . as shall be thought from time to time most convenient for the present state of the Church; so that nothing be done against the general rule of St Paul, 1 Cor. xiv.: 'Let all things be done decently and in order'.
>
> Thirdly, that it is the duty of a Christian man without superstition willingly to obey such constitutions, not to contemn them, not to neglect them, much less stubbornly and arrogantly to break them.
>
> Fourthly, that the observing of them taketh not liberty from the conscience, because they be not made to be perpetual and inviolable, but to be altered as time, occasion and necessity requireth.
>
> Fifthly, they all ought to obey such ordinances, for charity' sake, though all stand not in need of them.
>
> Sixthly, that, if a man do violate them by ignorance or forgetfulness, he doth not offend; if by contempt or stubbornness, he doth greatly offend.
>
> Seventhly, that confusion (which is to suffer every man to do what he list) is the seed of contention and brawling.
>
> Last of all, that the true ministers of God be not contentious, neither yet the churches of God.[91]

Again proving his reformed pedigree, Whitgift claims that all the headings emerge from Calvin himself.[92] For Whitgift, then, the important point about matters indifferent was not that they do not matter, but rather that they were things which each and every national church had the authority to order and to alter in the due manner. But equally important was the Pauline injunction that what is laid down for matters indifferent should be obeyed for the decency and order of the church and state. (1 Corinthians 14: 40)

Cartwright answered Whitgift with remarkable speed, to which Whitgift responded with equal haste with his *Defence of the Answer to the Admonition*, where he tried to clarify some of the issues emerging from his earlier work, once again emphasizing the point that we

> know that all things necessary to salvation are much more plainly expressed in the Gospel than in the law: we are also well assured that Christ in his word hath fully and plainly comprehended all things requisite to faith and good life; but yet hath he committed certain orders or ceremonies, and kind of government, to the disposition of his church.[93]

Similarly, he stressed the point that not all things inherited from the Church of Rome were to be regarded as abominations. Thus, while claiming that 'Papists worship God otherwise than his will is, and otherwise than he hath prescribed, almost in all points of their worship' and 'give to the creature that which is due to the Creator', he nevertheless does not consider that they are 'in the third kind of idolatry', that is that they are worshipping 'false gods either in heart and mind, or in external creatures, living or dead, and altogether forget the worship of the true God'.[94] In its time, this could be considered something of an ecumenical gesture.

Whitgift moved on to discuss the thorny issue of how to reach a decision about how something was to be regarded a matter of salvation. Displaying a knowledge of the Fathers, he adopts the patristic criterion of the 'rule of faith', which was a short creedal-like statement that summarized what was central to the teaching of Scripture.[95] While it was used to distinguish matters necessary to salvation, it was silent about local customs:

> It is evident that Tertullian's rule is to be understood
> in matters of salvation, and of faith, and not in matters of
> ceremonies or kinds of government . . . (*de Virginibus Velandis* –
> 'This law of faith remaining, other things of discipline
> and conversation admit newness of correction' . . . So that

Tertullian thinketh that matters of ceremonies and discipline may be altered (the rule of faith remaining inviolable).[96]

Applying this patristic method to the contentious problem of church government, Whitgift reaffirmed his understanding of church order as a matter indifferent, which was subject to variation according to time and place. Unlike Cartwright, Whitgift believed Scripture did not prove the equality of ministers,[97] which allowed him to justify a hierarchical form of ministry on the grounds that it allowed for determinations to made 'according to the law and rule already by the church established'.[98] He moves on to defend the hierarchical system as it had been inherited by the Church of England on practical grounds in terms of the part it played in ensuring the order and discipline of both state and church. In contrast, he considered Cartwright's preferred Presbyterian system, with its equality of ministers, as 'the very highway to subversion and confusion'.[99] The burden of proof was left on those who would add the ministry to those things necessary to salvation. Thus, Whitgift challenged Cartwright:

> I contend not that the name of the archbishop was in the apostles' time; but you have not yet proved that the office was not then, or that there was no superiority among the clergy . . . your negative reason proveth nothing.[100]

To rub in his point, he differentiated his Scriptural and pragmatic method from that of the 'papists' who

> make their traditions necessary unto salvation; and therefore they are to be rejected, because the word of God containeth all things necessary to salvation. I make those offices part of decency, order, ecclesiastical government and policy, which admitteth alteration as the times and persons require, and are not particularly expressed in the scriptures, no more than divers other things be in the same kind.

He concluded by once again challenging Cartwright: 'You have not yet proved that either the name or office of archbishops is in any respect "oppugned" in the word of God'.[101] For Whitgift, a hierarchical system, and particularly the office of archbishop, although not a matter necessary to salvation, was nonetheless 'profitable to the government of the church'. God had 'appointed functions in his church both ecclesiastical and civil, as means to keep it in external peace, discipline and order'.[102] In an interesting parallelism, he emphasized the function of the archbishop as equivalent to that of the civil magistrate in upholding the peace of the realm:'The Archbishop doth exercise his jurisdiction under the prince and by the prince's authority. For, the prince having the supreme government of the realm, in all causes and over all persons, as she doth exercise the one by the lord chancellor, so doth she the other by the archbishops'.[103] Here again there is evidence of Whitgift's underlying belief of a fundamental unity in church and state.

This theme of the role of the civil authority in relation to the church is something to which Whitgift returns over and again throughout his writings. Within what amounts to a single social fabric of both church and state, he affirms that 'Among men the chief pillar that upholdeth the church is the Christian prince and magistrate'.[104] Cartwright, on the other hand, adopted a very different view, which made the civil magistrates subject to the authority and discipline of the church:

It is true that we ought to be obedient unto the civil magistrate which governeth the church of God in that office which is committed unto him, and according to that calling. But it must be remembered that civil magistrates must govern it according to the rules of God prescribed in his word, and that as they are nurses so they be servants unto the church, and as they rule in the church so they must remember to subject themselves unto the church, to submit their sceptres, to throw down their crowns, before the church, yea, as the prophet speaketh, to lick the dust of the feet of the church. Wherein I mean not that the church doth either wring the sceptres out of princes' hands, or taketh their crowns from their heads, or that it requireth princes to lick the dust of their feet (as the pope under this pretence hath done), but I mean, as the prophet meaneth, that, whatsoever magnificence, or excellency, or pomp, is either in them, or in their estates and commonwealths, which doth not agree with the simplicity and (in the judgment of the world) poor and contemptible estate of the church, that they will be content to lay down.[105]

Whitgift attacked this understanding with a defence of the godly King, whose role it was to legislate on behalf of the many. While admitting that in the apostles' time princes 'did not meddle in causes ecclesiastical' except to persecute, he explains this away with the observation that 'they were then infidels, not Christians'.[106] In distinction to Cartwright, Whitgift, who was a member of the Privy Council, claimed that the Christian king upheld the unity of the state far better than any multitude. In a somewhat shocking defence of royal absolutism, he displays no sympathy for democracy:

> Wherefore a wicked man directed by law governeth more indifferently than multitudes without law, be they never so godly. Moreover, one godly wise and learned man is much more hardly moved to any error than is the multitude, which naturally is prone and bent to the same; in whom not only philosophers, but singular divines also, have noted great inconstancy and disposition most unmeet to govern . . . So is one wise and prudent man, governed and directed by order and by law, further from corruption and error in government, than whole multitudes of people, of what sort soever they be.[107]

In the end, then, Whitgift's theology is grounded both in Scripture and in a high doctrine of law and order embodied in the person of the godly prince: 'I am fully persuaded . . . that there is no such distinction betwixt the church of Christ and a Christian commonwealth, as you and the papists dream of'.[108] A unified theory of church and state alone will maintain decency, decorum, good order and the rule of law in church and state. The power to make laws is certainly not something to be given to the multitude in either church or state. Indeed obedience to the law is far better than any alternative which inevitably results in anarchy. For the Puritans, however, the rule of law was grounded solely in Scripture, and the church had a duty to define it and to ensure it was protected.

The Royal Supremacy and Religion

To many – including the Queen – the Presbyterian form of church government threatened sedition and the breakdown of order. Through much of the 1570s, there were efforts to control 'prophesyings' and other unauthorized activity among the clergy. Prophesyings were highly regulated meetings where clergy took their turns to expound the scriptures, providing a kind of 'continuing education'.[109] They had developed in many parts of the country into a system of regular meetings and even a form of parallel jurisdictions, where local clergy appointed a leadership and system of oversight, sometimes with the approval of the bishop, as at Norwich.[110] Under Grindal, who became Archbishop of Canterbury in 1575 and who showed sympathy to some of the moderate puritans, tension increased between the Queen and her archbishop. Grindal defended the importance of prophesyings and felt that it should be the church rather than the Queen that should rule in matters of discipline. He challenged the Queen in no uncertain terms: 'Remember, Madam, that you are a mortal creature. . . . And although ye are a mighty prince, yet remember that He which dwelleth in heaven is mightier. . . . Wherefore I do beseech you, Madam, *in visceribus Christi* [Phil. 1.8], when you deal in these religious causes, set the majesty of God before your eyes, laying all earthly majesty aside: determine with yourself to obey his voice, and with all humility.'[111] Not surprisingly, Grindal was removed from his duties, although not from his post as archbishop.[112] This allowed for direct rule over the Church by the Crown. The development of theology was once again closely affected by the will of a Monarch who was increasingly involved in governing her church and whose zeal for order thwarted so many of the experiments in church reform.[113] At the same time, the Crown was also milking much of the revenue of the church, which meant that it was often difficult for bishops to exercise their ministry.[114]

In 1583, Whitgift replaced Grindal as archbishop. His sense of the importance of the Royal Supremacy and order meant that he soon set about enforcing conformity and subscription. The oath that the Book of Common Prayer contained nothing contrary to the Word of God in particular created significant opposition both in parliament and in the church, and many of the demands of the *Admonition* returned. A few years later, Anthony Cope introduced a Bill in February 1587 that would have abolished the Prayer Book and the Royal Supremacy in ecclesiastical matters and would also have returned revenue to the church which had been diverted to the Crown and lay impropriators. There was further controversy shortly afterwards after the publication of strong attacks on the church in the pseudonymous Martin Marprelate tracts of 1588–9. In the ensuing controversy, conformists attacked the demands for the reform of church government, which led Richard Bancroft, who later succeeded Whitgift as archbishop, to reaffirm the notion that the church had been governed by a hierarchy of bishops since apostolic times in a famous sermon preached at Paul's Cross on 9 February 1589. Where Whitgift had been keen to emphasize the point that the form of church government was not prescribed in Scripture, however, Bancroft was silent on this matter, which some thought amounted to a defence of Divine Right episcopacy.[115] The Tractarians were later to cite the sermon as one of the key moments in the formulation of the doctrine of apostolic succession: 'unto [bishops], as St. Jerome saith, ever since St. Mark's time, the care of Church government hath been committed; they had authority over the rest of the ministry'.[116] For Bancroft, it was hierarchy and order that were central to the ministry of the church. It was much easier to express the Royal Supremacy through bishops than other forms of ministry. This meant, as Heal says, that the 'monarch reigned and guided the Church by imperial right. Her commission for the regulation of that body was given directly to the prelates, who formed beneath her a spiritual hierarchy divinely ordained and legitimated'.[117] It was in this situation that Richard Hooker wrote his highly contested magnum opus as he sought to find a more adequate way of justifying obedience to law and order in the very constitution of the world.

Chapter 5

The Theology
of Richard Hooker

Richard Hooker and Anglicanism

Any book on Anglican theology needs to engage with the writings of Richard Hooker (1553–1600), not least because he is one of the most often cited but also one of the most hotly contested voices in the history of Anglicanism.[1] Perhaps for this reason, and the perceived need to return to the 'historical Hooker' to solve some of the issues in interpretation,[2] he has become the one Anglican theologian who has been subject to a full twentieth-century critical edition, a privilege that has not even been accorded to Newman. While the other writers of the Reformation and post-Reformation period exist only in nineteenth-century editions, Hooker can be read in the fully annotated version edited by William Speed Hill: the Folger Library edition of the works of Richard Hooker (1977–93).[3] This very fact elevates Hooker to a status above that of the run-of-the-mill Anglican theologian. And yet, despite his undoubted greatness, Hooker is neither a Luther nor a Calvin: he did not write catechisms or a systematic theology. Instead, his massive eight-book work is a discussion of the laws of ecclesiastical polity: its subject matter is the underlying theology of church order and practice as this relates to divine and human law and order. It owes its existence to the debates and discussions that had occupied theologians at least from the time of the Hooper's consecration.

The fact that he was not a systematic theologian means that it is possible to read his work in different ways and with various emphases, a process which began almost immediately after the publication of The Laws of Ecclesiastical Polity.[4] Indeed, it is the figure of Hooker who is credited with the creation of the distinctive emphasis of Anglican moderation, of formulating the carefully balanced three-legged stool of Scripture, Tradition and Reason as the sources of Anglican theology. Generations of Anglicans have honoured the 'incomparable'[5] or 'judicious Mr Hooker' as the architect of a theology and political theory that remains of relevance for their own day. Despite his relatively quiet career – which was not as quiet as all that[6] – he has been regarded as the 'first major exponent of the Anglican view'[7] and has even been put on the same level as Shakespeare.[8] A recent overview of Hooker's writing has dubbed him the 'Prophet of Anglicanism'.[9] Similarly, in an aside in his study of William Chillingworth, J. W. Packer hailed *The Laws of Ecclesiastical Polity* as 'one of the greatest apologies for Anglican doctrine that has ever been written'.[10] One of the twentieth century's archetypal Anglicans, Henry McAdoo claimed that in Hooker's work, 'something time-defying was created for Anglicans'.[11] Summarizing such an approach, William Haugaard observed that 'many Anglicans understand Hooker's role in the development of the theological temper of the Church of England and its daughters to be quite unique'.[12]

Given such hagiographic tendencies, Hooker has proved to be a useful ally to enlist in any presentation of Anglican identity. In the 1830s, for instance, in what was one of the key periods in the formation of the identity of modern Anglicanism, John Keble, at the height of the Oxford Movement, edited Hooker's writings in three volumes, partly in opposition to the edition of 1830, which had been produced by the Congregationalist, Benjamin Hanbury. Keble's Hooker stands in marked contrast to Hanbury's Reformed theologian: he was the pioneer of the *via media*, to whom 'we owe it, that the Anglican Church continues at such distance from that of Geneva, and so near truth and apostolical order'.[13] For Keble, as for many others, Hooker was treated as the Anglican theologian *par excellence*, the architect of the perfect mean between Romanism and Puritanism. Hooker gave 'to Anglican theology a tone and a direction which it has never lost'.[14] By being dubbed an *Anglican*, understood by the Tractarians as a position between Protestantism and Romanism and identified with a form of purged English Catholicism based on Antiquity, Hooker was enlisted as a proto-Anglo-Catholic in order to defend their understanding of the church.[15]

There are some obvious problems with Keble's reading of Hooker: there is a degree of circularity in this sort of thinking. Indeed, his interpretation may have less to do with Hooker himself and more to do with the need for a powerful supporter for Tractarian church reform. For Keble, if Hooker was an Anglican, and if he paved the way for those theologians so admired by the Tractarians and republished in the Library of Anglo-Catholic Theology,[16] then he could not have been fully committed to the Reformation. Yet, as many have pointed out, Hooker may be far less 'Anglican' than Keble might have wished. As Diarmaid MacCulloch suggests, 'nowhere in any of his writings does Hooker use either the word Anglicanism or the phrase *via media*. That may suggest that the legacy of Hooker is not as straightforward as it has sometimes been portrayed; indeed it may mean that Anglicanism and the *via media* are more interesting and fluid concepts than the complacent version of Anglican historiography has sometimes made them'.[17] Some sort of historical appraisal seems to be necessary to try to unearth the central themes of Hooker's work, and how these might be related to something that could be labelled as Anglican.

Hooker remains a figure of much academic and historical interest. His relationship to the Reformation and particularly one of its cardinal themes of *sola scriptura* continues to be a hotly contested topic. Underlying some of the interpretations are different understandings of Anglicanism. As Nigel Voak writes: 'Numerous writers have appealed to Hooker for support, thus further emphasizing the contentiousness of the subject, as reinterpreting Hooker has for some again become a way of reinterpreting Anglicanism'.[18] Thus, on the one hand, against the *via media* 'Anglican' version of Hooker, interpreters such as Nigel Atkinson[19] have seen Hooker as standing in continuity with the key tenets of the Reformation. Similarly, in a series of writings, W. J. Torrance Kirby maintains that in his Protestant Platonism Hooker adheres to the magisterial reformation.[20] From a different perspective, over many years, Egil Grislis has interpreted Hooker as a key figure in conservative ecclesial hermeneutics[21] and even analogous to Karl Barth,[22] and highly relevant for the present day.

On the other hand, from a historical perspective Peter Lake, in one of the most important and influential recent discussions, sees Hooker quite differently as the inventor of what emerged later as Anglicanism and as remodelling the arguments of the earlier conformist writers. He was indeed a pioneer of something quite distinct from his predecessors, 'Protestant but not Calvinist, episcopalian yet reformed, sacrament and ceremony centred although in no sense popish'.[23] Hooker is consequently understood as an innovator paving the way for the 'Anglicanism' of the post-Restoration church, by moving away from the Calvinist style of divinity which dominated the Elizabethan Church.[24] This move is exemplified by the fact that *The Laws* offer a detailed explanation of the ceremonies of the church, creating a 'sacrament- and prayer-centred piety'.[25] According to Lake, 'for all its judiciousness of tone' the *Laws of Ecclesiastical Polity* as a whole is 'the conformist equivalent of the Marprelate tracts'.[26]

Others have emphasized Hooker's medievalism.[27] Gunnar Hillerdal, for instance, sees Hooker as a systematic theologian on the model of Aquinas, who seeks to 'demonstrate that a harmonic cooperation is quite possible between the laws pertaining to revelation and those set forth in the natural law or by man's reason'.[28] A false doctrine of grace, however, meant he was ultimately irrational. Peter Munz sees Hooker as strongly influenced by Aquinas[29] with the idea of a hierarchically structured universe which 'mediates in a "gradual order" between man and God', which is obviously a problem for 'the Reformed doctrine of an immediate and inward union between the soul and God through the action of imputed righteousness'.[30] Others emphasize Hooker's humanism,[31] which also suggests a fundamental disagreement with the tenets of the Reformation.

These different styles of interpretation appear incompatible. As Nigel Voak writes: 'Hooker cannot on the one hand have philosophically articulated the establishment position of a Reformed English Church, and on the other have been a proto-Laudian Anglican'.[32] In his own interpretation, which begins from an understanding of grace, Voak seeks a synthesis between the opposing views, both of which, he claims, contain some truth.[33] Ultimately, however, he regards Hooker as a conservative radical: 'Hooker is . . . a most interesting and enigmatic figure, on the one hand conservative and nostalgic for the past, and on the other hand advancing rationalizing principles in the deceptively measured pages of the Lawes that would see much greater expression in the seventeenth century and beyond.[34] While there is not space to discuss these interpretative issues in detail, I will suggest in this chapter that Hooker continues the tradition that had been developed by Jewel, and more importantly by Whitgift, in that his main concern is the authority of the church in matters indifferent. While there are obviously many ways of reading Hooker, I will locate him in the debates on authority in the Church of England, which I discussed in detail in the previous chapter. What Hooker seems to offer is a change of rhetorical gear: while often polemical, Hooker's style differs from his contemporaries in that it is both more extensive – the *Laws of Ecclesiastical Polity* is after all a very big book – and usually more logical and reasoned.[35]

It is probably right to see Hooker as a founding figure of Anglicanism, but the 'Anglicanism' he represented was concerned first and foremost with the justification of the authority of law and order. In many ways, Hooker is perhaps the culmination of the theology of order, and in that sense he stands in marked continuity with the earlier conformist theology. To defend the polity of the Church of England as settled in 1559 seemed to Hooker to require a theory of natural law where God could be at work alongside his special revelation in scripture: divine authority was thus also at the basis of matters indifferent. While he would no doubt have agreed with the Reformers on many of their key points of doctrine – 'all the Reformed churches . . . are of our confession in doctrine'[36] – his aims were principally to defend a system of order theologically. While there is much of great interest in many different areas of his writings, especially in Hooker's discussions of sacraments and ceremonies in Book Five, I have chosen to focus on the *Ecclesiastical Polity* in terms of its underlying theme which concerns the question of authority and the careful analysis of different types of law and how these relate to the order, practices and ceremonies of the Church.

Richard Hooker's Context

Unlike virtually all of the theologians who have dominated this book so far, Hooker was never appointed to a bishopric or professorship, although he did spend a number of years as Master of the Temple in London, which gave him a prominent pulpit in an influential place. Born in or near Exeter in April 1554, he attended Corpus Christi College in Oxford in 1567, where John Jewel took him under his care. By 1577, he had become a Fellow and was appointed University Reader in Hebrew in 1579. He became a preacher at Paul's Cross where he marked himself out for his anti-Puritan sermons. After a brief period as incumbent of Drayton Beauchamp in Buckinghamshire, he was made Master of the Temple. He resigned to take up the living of Boscombe near Salisbury (where he was also subdean and precentor of the Cathedral) in 1591, and in 1595 he was presented by the Queen to the living of Bishopsbourne near Canterbury. He died on 2 November 1600, 'his body worn out, not with age, but study, and holy mortifications'.[37] The Preface and the first four books of the *Laws* were published in 1593, and Book Five in 1597. The last three books were assembled by John Gauden and published much later (Books Six and Eight in 1648 and Book Seven in 1662).

When Hooker was appointed Master of the Temple, Walter Travers (1548–1635) was working as lecturer. After education at Christ's College, Cambridge, he was elected to a Fellowship at Trinity College, Cambridge, but was forced out by Whitgift. He spent a number of years in Geneva where he got to know Beza. Cartwright arranged for the publication of his *Ecclesiasticae Disciplinae et Anglicanae Ecclesiae ab illa Aberrationis plena e verbo Dei et delucida Explicatio* (*A Full and Plain Declaration of Ecclesiastical Discipline we owe of the word of God, and of the declining of the church of England from the Same*) in 1574. For Travers, the Scriptures were normative in providing the model for ministry, which, he held, should take a Presbyterian form. Thus, according to Travers, 'I affirm that Christ hath left us so perfect a rule and discipline I understand and of that discipline which is common and general to all the church and perpetual for all times and so necessary that without it this whole society and company and Christian commonwealth cannot well be kept under the Prince and King Jesus Christ'.[38] This was that exercised by elders, who had had authority conferred on them by the people.[39] In a short book rich with biblical allusion from both Old and New Testaments, Travers attacks the offices of bishops and other dignitaries and presents a case for church reform.

After receiving Presbyterian ordination in Antwerp, Travers returned in 1580 to England having gained the significant position of chaplain to Lord Burghley, who secured for him the post at the Temple in 1581. When Hooker was appointed Master of the Temple in 1585 the legendary disputes between the two men began: 'What Mr Hooker delivered in the forenoon', Thomas Fuller famously wrote, 'Mr Travers confuted in the afternoon'.[40] However, given that much of their debate focused on Roman Catholicism,[41] Fuller's further assessment was somewhat misleading: 'the pulpit spake pure Canterbury in the morning and Geneva in the afternoon'.[42] MacCulloch claims that while Hooker 'might heartily dislike Puritans like Travers who did not give bishops the respect that they deserved . . . he was not going to be led out of the doctrinal consensus that he shared with moderate Puritanism . . . Fuller's celebrated dictum . . . could thus hardly be further from the truth'. Nevertheless, it has become an 'an essential cliché in the construction of the Anglican Hooker'.[43] Whitgift eventually banned Travers from preaching in 1586, and he devoted himself to producing a detailed book of discipline outlining principles of church reform. Under Burghley's influence he became Provost of Trinity College, Dublin in 1595, but resigned in 1598 spending the remainder of his life in relatively quiet retirement.

The Laws of Ecclesiastical Polity

The *Ecclesiastical Polity* was written chiefly to counter the contentions, complaints and arguments of Travers as well as those of Cartwright: indeed, each of the last seven books is given a heading that summarizes some part of their position, which the book that follows then attempts to counter. Before moving into specifics, however, Hooker roots the *Ecclesiastical Polity* in a detailed introduction in Book One, which provides an extended account of his method as well as the categorization of the different forms of law. What he offers is a defence of a divinely appointed law alongside that of Scripture which is capable of providing the rules for regulating in matters indifferent and is also fundamental in the task of understanding the content of

Scripture in the first place. The purpose of the Book is summarized towards its end:

> We have endeavoured in part to open, of what nature and force laws are, according unto their several kinds; the law which God with himself hath eternally set down to follow in his own works; the law which he hath made for his creatures to keep; the law which angels in heaven obey; the law whereunto by the light of reason men find themselves bound in that they are men; the law which they make by composition for multitude societies and politic societies to be guided by; the law which belongeth unto each nation; the law that concerneth the fellowship of all; and lastly the law which God hath supernaturally revealed.[44]

For Hooker, what is crucial is that there are whole spheres of law given by God for different purposes. Where Travers and Cartwright restrict law principally to the last kind, and tend to draw on the Old Testament for the regulation of society, Hooker provides an alternative source for the foundation of divine law. Thus, he can claim that even ecclesiastical laws come in different forms. This means that against those who would restrict the realm of law to Scripture alone he offers something quite different:

> seeing that our whole question concerneth the quality of ecclesiastical laws, let it not seem a labour superfluous that in the entrance thereunto all these several kinds of laws have been considered, inasmuch as they all concur in principles, they all have not their forcible operations therein, although not all in like apparent and manifest manner.[45]

Hooker outlines the different types of law at length. Hardly surprisingly, the methods inevitably make use of the humanistic philosophy of the period. Firstly, he speaks of the First Eternal Law, which is the form of law that applies to God. This implies a particularly kind of necessity: 'All things that are, have some operation not violent or casual. Neither doth anything ever begin to exercise the same, without some fore-conceived end . . . The being of God is a kind of law unto its working'.[46] Since only God is not subject to anything beyond himself, the Second Eternal Law applies to finite beings as they are subject to some divinely imposed law. He continues: 'All things . . . which they are as they ought to be'[47] are conformed to this type of law: 'God alone excepted, who actually and everlastingly is whatsoever he may be, and which cannot hereafter be that which now he is not; all other things besides are somewhat in possibility, which as yet they are not in act'.[48] This means that there is an unrealized potentiality in every finite creature, which, if it is to be fulfilled, requires guidance under laws. These laws, in turn, take different forms: first is the law of nature, which involves the survival and destiny of the physical realm. Under this form of law, nature's agents fulfil their destined end. The second form of law is something equivalent which applies to non-material bodies. This is the Celestial law, the ordering of heavenly bodies, which is the law of the angelic world, whose agents already know the outcome of their actions.[49]

The third form of law is the law of reason, 'which bindeth creatures reasonably in the world', a form of law that 'by reason they plainly perceive themselves to be most clearly bound'.[50] This form of law requires the exercise of the will and education in the form of knowledge required to decide upon the goodness of the purpose to be followed.[51] Freedom to choose is central to this aspect of law: 'To choose is to will one thing before another. And to will is to bend our souls to the having or doing of that which they see to be good'.[52] This means that when we wish to make a choice we need to do so in relation to universal axioms and natural justice.[53] This leads to the Golden rule, a universalizable system of justice.[54] The human conscience is entrusted with this guardianship of duties towards this form of law.

From the law of reason Hooker moves on to human law. It is reason that leads human beings to make laws which govern society. According to Hooker the foundations for these human laws of government rest first on what he calls the 'natural inclination' to desire sociable life and amiable fellowship; and secondly on the 'order expressly or secretly agreed upon touching the manner of their union of living together'. This second aspect is the 'Law of a commonweal'. This form of law comes about from the need to club together for the mutual provision of what we are unable to obtain for ourselves. Such laws, however, are never 'as they should be' because of human obstinacy and the depraved mind, which makes the human being little better than a 'wild beast'.[55] Nevertheless, laws can be framed to help the common good to be pursued even under such conditions. In addition, it is necessary in order to allow mutual grievances, injuries and wrongs to be righted. To do so, human beings give the 'common consent' to be ordered 'by some whom they should agree upon'. This led initially to the choice of a king, but it has resulted in different forms of government,[56] which can exercise law so that virtue is rewarded and vice is punished.[57]

Within the system of human laws, there are some laws that apply to all societies and all places, and others, which, while necessary, vary from place to place. Thus while it is always right to punish thieves, the precise form of punishment varies from society to society. 'In laws, that which is natural bindeth universally, that which is positive not so'.[58] Crucial for Hooker's argument, however, is that even those laws that human beings establish for the good order of their societies are rooted in the power 'which God hath over all'.[59] In turn, he claims that order is utterly central to the flourishing of society, which is ultimately based on consent. He qualifies this by suggesting that such consent is something given to a public society that persists through time – this means in effect that obedience depends on an act made to a corporation in the past: 'the act of a public society of men done five hundred years sithence standeth as theirs who presently are of the same societies, because corporations are immortal'.[60]

While positive laws vary from state to state, there are nevertheless many which are based on reason and demand duty and obedience. These are called 'mixedly' human[61] and establish a binding obligation. The 'mixed' law is where the positive and the rational combine to produce a human law that commands obedience (the laws against incest – 'the confusion of blood in marriage' – and polygamy are the examples used).[62] The manner of binding is all that is different in the mixed law: a rational law was upheld by conscience, but a mixed law is also a positive law and carries with it sanctions.[63] As well as the mixed law there is another form of law, which Hooker called the 'merely' human. These laws do not carry the same degree of necessity, but nevertheless reason teaches that they are 'fit and convenient'. The example used is that of the law of inheritance: while there needs to be some form of inheritance, its form is a matter of expedience. Whichever form is chosen no rational law is transgressed.[64] Finally, Hooker discusses a third type of law which he called the law of nations, which is established on human sociability, a quality which separates human beings from the beasts, and on the need to relate to other societies.[65]

The final type of law is the supernatural law whereby God is able to show human beings what they must long for to overcome the conditions of natural depravity. Human beings seek perfection and happiness, a possibility that is realized through the divine law that allows them access to achieve this state. This is the divine salvation that acts as the final goal of all human longings.[66] The Christian virtues of faith, hope and charity are based upon this divinely revealed supernatural law. Thus, Hooker claims, 'There is not in the world a syllable muttered with certain truth concerning any of these three, more than hath been supernaturally received from the mouth of the eternal God'.[67] At the same time, however, Scripture was not simply the repository of supernatural laws. Instead, it was 'fraught even with laws of nature'.[68] Although the 'principal intent of scripture is to deliver the laws of duties supernatural', it nonetheless abounds with other laws.[69]

Building on the lengthy discussion of the different types of law, the final sections of Book One set about exploring the key issues of the relationship of the laws founded upon a divinely grounded reason and things necessary to salvation. Before Scripture can be understood, Hooker claims that it is necessary to learn the methods for interpretation. Thus, he says:

> albeit Scripture do profess to contain in it all things that
> are necessary to salvation; yet the meaning cannot be
> simply of all things which are necessary, but all things that
> are necessary in some certain form; as all things which are
> necessary, and either could not at all or could not easily be
> known by the light of natural discourse; all things which are
> necessary to be known that we may be saved, but known
> with the presupposal of knowledge concerning certain
> principles whereof it receiveth us already persuaded, and then
> instructeth us in all the residue that are necessary.[70]

Scripture thus needs to be approached carefully using techniques that allow the reader to grasp what is necessary to salvation from the many other things to be found in the books of the Bible. This is illustrated in a crucial passage that helps clarify the relationship between the methods of interpretation and what is necessary to salvation. Scripture is not always plain but has to be 'collected' together:

> There hath been some doubt . . . whether containing in scripture do import express setting down in plain terms, or else comprehending in such sort that by reason we may from thence conclude all things which are necessary. Against the former of these two constructions instance hath sundry ways been given. For our belief in the Trinity . . . with such other principal points, the necessity whereof is by none denied, are in scripture nowhere to be found by express literal mention, only deduced they are out of scripture by collection.[71]

This implies that there needs to be an internal test for the use of Scripture. In a manner resembling the patristic principle of the 'rule of faith', which had been used by Whitgift in his debates with Cartwright, Hooker expresses a principle of interpretation: 'The main drift of the whole New Testament', he claims, 'is that which St John setteth down as the purpose of his history'.[72] It is therefore necessary to collect the sense of scripture, and at the same time to prove the variety of other laws at work. While there is an inevitable polarization between God's law and human law, to some extent at least this is overcome as reason itself is given a divine origin. Reason is required both to determine the meaning of scripture and to assist with the determination of matters indifferent. When in his Supplication to the Council made in 1585 during his time with Hooker at the Temple, Travers accused The Master of relying on his own reason,[73] Hooker responded:

> I alleged therefore that which might under no pretence in the world be disallowed, namely reason; not meaning thereby mine own reason as now it is reported, but true, sound, divine reason . . . reason proper to that science whereby the things of God are known; theological reason, which out of principles

in scripture that are plain, soundly deduceth more doubtful inferences in such sort that being heard they neither can be denied, nor any thing repugnant unto them received, but whatsoever was before otherwise by miscollecting gathered out of darker places, is thereby forced to yield itself, and the true consonant meaning of sentences not understood is brought to light. This is the reason which I intended.[74]

While Scripture was the source of all things necessary to salvation, it could be understood only through the application of sound reason. This meant that, while all law was ultimately established by God, there were sources of authority other than Scripture.

In one of the most telling passages in the whole of *The Laws*, Hooker concedes that his opponents are correct in maintaining that 'God must be glorified in all things'. Their error, however, is 'to think that the only law which God hath appointed unto men in that behalf is the sacred Scripture'. For Hooker there are other laws by which 'we set forth the glory of God as natural agents do'. There is a law written on the hearts of all people which shows what 'is good or evil'. This is the Law of Reason which

doth somewhat direct men how to honour God as their Creator; but how to glorify God in such sort as is required, to the end that he may be an everlasting saviour, this we are taught by divine law, which law both ascertaineth the truth and supplieth unto us the want of that other law. Proceed we further; let us place man in some public society with others, whether civil or spiritual; and in this case there is no remedy but we must add yet a further law. For although even here likewise the laws of nature and reason be of necessary use, yet somewhat over and besides them is necessary, namely human and positive law, together with that law which is of commerce between grand societies, the law of nations, and of nations Christian. For which cause the law of God hath likewise said, 'Let every soul be subject to the higher powers'. The public power of all societies is above every soul contained in the same societies. And the principal use of that power is to give laws unto all that are under it; which laws in such case we must obey, unless there be reason shewed which may necessarily enforce that the Law of Reason or of God doth enjoin the contrary. Because except our own private and but probable resolutions be by the law of public determinations overruled, we take away all possibility of sociable life in the world. A plainer example whereof than ourselves we cannot have. How cometh it to pass that we are at this present day so rent with mutual contentions, and that the Church is so much troubled about the polity of the Church? No doubt if men had been willing to learn how many laws their actions in this life are subject unto, and what the true force of each law is, all these controversies might have died the very day they were first brought forth.[75]

In other words, for Hooker, it was necessary to obey the many other laws established by God for the good order of the land which were required for all those matters on which Scripture was silent: unless this was done then the mutual contentions would continue. And in turn, it was also necessary to ensure that Scripture was understood in the light of reason and tradition. What emerges here is a defence of the lawfulness of those put in authority to establish law and order. In Book Three, Hooker clarifies the point, emphasizing the principle of 1 Corinthians 14 of doing 'all things in order and with seemliness' as the key interpretative principle.[76]

Having constructed his method, Hooker then moves on in Book Two to offer more detailed arguments in relation to the particular issues of contention. The proposition from his opponents that 'Scripture is the only rule of all things which in this life may be done by man' is subjected to discussion in the light of the principles of law. While Hooker did not fundamentally depart from the basic principles of the supremacy of Scripture, he nevertheless was clear that it was not self-authenticating: 'Wisdom hath diversely imparted her treasures unto the world. As her ways are of sundry kinds, so her manner of teaching is not merely of one kind'.[77] He repeats many of the arguments from the first book in differentiating between those thongs that are lawful and those that are expedient.[78] Again, as in Book One, the authority of Scripture was connected to the authority of Christian teachers: 'The Scripture could not teach us the things that are of God, unless we did credit men who have taught us that the words of scripture do signify those things'.[79] While this could perhaps be regarded as consonant with the *sola scriptura* of the Reformation, it undoubtedly pushes the idea to its limits. Indeed, Voak suggests, 'By implicitly asserting the principal religious authority of demonstrative reasoning, Hooker was not only moving away from the Reformed tradition, but also from the views on religious authority characteristic of the medieval western church'.[80]

In Book Three, Hooker goes on to discuss Church order, countering the proposition that in 'Scripture there must be of necessity contained a form of Church polity, the laws whereof may in no wise be altered'. Hooker stresses continuity with the past, even through the massive changes of the Reformation. Indeed, he went as far as to claim that even the Roman Catholic Church was part of the Christian family:

> Notwithstanding so far as lawfully we may, we have held and do hold fellowship with them. For even as the apostle doth say of Israel that they are in one respect our enemies but in another beloved of God; in like sort with Rome we dare not communicate concerning sundry her gross and grievous abominations, yet touching those main parts of Christian truth wherein they constantly still persist, we gladly acknowledge them to be of the family of Jesus Christ.[81]

Hooker is consequently keen to emphasize the diversity of the 'catholic church', which is 'divided into a number of distinct societies'.[82] These, he claims, embrace all people (with the sole exclusion of Muslims and Jews).

This discussion allows him to distinguish clearly between matters necessary to salvation and those things which are 'accessory' – a term he uses in preference to 'indifferent' – and to develop his earlier arguments on the understanding of Scripture. Things necessary to salvation are clearly expressed in the Articles as collections from Scripture:

> we teach that whatsoever is unto salvation termed necessary by way of excellency, whatsoever it standeth all men upon to know or do that they may be saved, whatsoever there is whereof it may truly be said, 'This not to believe is eternal

death and damnation,' or, 'This every soul that will live must duly observe;' of which sort the articles of Christian faith and the sacraments of the Church of Christ are: all such things if Scripture did not comprehend, the Church of God should not be able to measure out the length and the breadth of that way wherein for ever she is to walk, heretics and schismatics never ceasing some to abridge, some to enlarge, all to pervert and obscure the same. But as for those things that are accessory hereunto, those things that so belong to the way of salvation, as to alter them is no otherwise to change that way, than a path is changed by altering only the uppermost face thereof; which be it laid with gravel, or set with grass, or paved with stone, remaineth still the same path; in such things because discretion may teach the Church what is convenient, we hold not the Church further tied herein unto Scripture, than that against Scripture nothing be admitted in the Church, lest that path which ought always to be kept even, do thereby come to be overgrown with brambles and thorns.[83]

According to Hooker, there was an authority to change in matters accessory, since the precise form was not given in Scripture. Nevertheless – and here he is perhaps going further than his predecessors – the underlying path was the route to salvation even if the paving differed. Using a somewhat convoluted argument that rests on the way in which the Jews developed their rituals, he writes that order derives from the law of nature:

> The truth is they are rules and canons of that law which is written on all men's hearts; the church had for ever no less than now stood bound to observe them, whether the Apostles mentioned them or no.[84]

For Hooker, then, the foundation in these matters of church order is human reason rather than divine injunction. The precise form must be 'decent, tending towards edification'[85] and is not laid down in Scripture, as Travers claimed. Within this Catholic church, the clergy are understood as a necessary estate 'which hath been, and will be, as long as there is a church upon earth'.

This estate is marked by the distinction between bishops, who have existed since the time of the Apostles, and other ministers. [86] Indeed, as he was to say in Book Eight, 'Sound theology putteth a difference between of external regiment in the church and things necessary to salvation'.[87]

In Book Four, Hooker counters the claim that 'Our form of Church Polity is corrupted with popish orders, rites and ceremonies'. The arguments he uses are similar to those of Whitgift following the vestiarian controversy. He stresses the doctrine of the autonomy of each national church to decide on its own matters and, at the same time, emphasizes continuity with the past:

> The ceremonies which we have taken from such as were
> before us, are not things that belong to this or that sect, but
> they are the ancient rites and customs of the Church of
> Christ, whereof ourselves being a part, we have the selfsame
> interest in them which our fathers before us had, from whom
> the same are descended unto us.[88]

This discussion of rites and ceremonies is closely connected with the content of Book Five, which was published four years after the first four books in 1597 and which was significantly longer than the others. Probably because of its diverse content and discussions of a wide range of sacramental matters, it has been more widely read than the other books (although political theorists have shown more interest in Books One and Eight).[89] Book Five remained on the curriculum for prospective Anglican clergy until relatively recently.[90]

Book Five seeks to counter the claim of Hooker's opponents: 'Touching the several public duties of Christian Religion there is among us much superstition retained in them; and concerning persons which for performance of those duties are endued with the power of ecclesiastical order, our laws and proceedings according thereunto are many ways herein also corrupt'. Here again Hooker makes a clear distinction between mutability and immutability: the rites and ceremonies of the church are changeable, whereas doctrine remains the same. Echoing Article XXXIV, he asserts that the 'church hath authority to establish that for an order at one time which at another time it may abolish, and in both may do well'.[91] He had already made a similar claim in Book Three.

> The laws positive are not framed without regard had to
> the place and persons for which they are made. If therefore
> Almighty God in framing their laws had an eye unto the
> nature of that people, and to the country where they were
> to dwell; if these peculiar and proper considerations were
> respected in the making of their laws, and must be also
> regarded in the positive laws of all other nations besides:
> then seeing that nations are not all alike, surely the giving
> of one kind of positive laws unto one only people, without
> any liberty to alter them, is but slender proof, that therefore
> one kind should in like sort be given to serve everlastingly
> for all.[92]

The principle is straightforward: 'Laws touching matter of order are changeable, by the power of the church; articles concerning doctrine not so'.[93] The possibility of change, however, does not mean it is necessarily desirable. Hooker retains a strongly conservative streak. The church should be loath to change its principles 'unless some notable public inconvenience enforce the contrary'.[94]

In discussing the rites and ceremonies of the church, he touches on a huge range of topics, finding a theological defence for the content of the Book of Common Prayer. Somewhat acerbically MacCulloch writes, 'After reading Book V, one feels that if the parliamentary legislation of 1559 had prescribed that English clergy were to preach standing on their heads, then Hooker would have found a theological reason for justifying it'.[95] This is perhaps slightly harsh since in discussing the theology of the Prayer Book in the light of the Articles, Hooker shows a degree of creativity. This is especially true in his theology of the sacraments, particularly of the Eucharist. Although he explicitly denies the doctrine of the real presence in the sacrament,[96] he develops concepts such as 'participation' and deification,[97] which show an affinity with the theology of the Fathers. Grace is not simply imputed, but also infused:

Thus we participate Christ partly by imputation, as when those things which he did and suffered for us are imputed unto us for righteousness; partly by habitual and real infusion, as when grace is inwardly bestowed while we are on earth, and afterwards more fully both our souls and bodies made like unto his in glory. The first thing of his so infused into our hearts in this life is the Spirit of Christ, whereupon because the rest of what kind soever do all both necessarily depend and infallibly also ensue, therefore the Apostles term it sometime the seed of God, sometime the pledge of our heavenly inheritance, sometime the handsel or earnest of that which is to come.[98]

Even though we can offer nothing to him, Hooker claims, God has nevertheless 'deified our nature'. While God does not turn human nature into himself, 'yet by making it his own inseparable habitation, we cannot now conceive how God should without man either exercise divine power, or receive the glory of divine praise. For man is in both an associate of Deity'.[99] Hooker displays a particular eloquence in his understanding of the Eucharist. In words that take spiritual presence to a new level, he wrote:

they are things wonderful which he feeleth, great which he seeth and unheard of which he uttereth, whose soul is possessed of this Paschal Lamb and made joyful in the strength of this new wine, this bread hath in it more than the substance which our eyes behold, this cup hallowed with solemn benediction availeth to the endless life and welfare both of soul and body, in that it serveth as well for a medicine to heal our infirmities and purge our sins as for a sacrifice of thanksgiving; with touching it sanctifieth, it enlighteneth with belief, it truly conformeth us unto the image of Jesus Christ; what these elements are in themselves it skilleth not, it is enough that to me which take them they are the body and blood of Christ, his promise in witness hereof sufficeth, his word he knoweth which way to accomplish; why should any cogitation possess the mind of a faithful communicant but this, O my God thou art true, O my Soul thou art happy![100]

Hooker also tackles the controversial issue of ministry, where he emphasizes the importance of the task of the clergy (which they share with princes)[101] 'to honour God and save men'.[102] He emphasizes the 'power of separation' among ministers as an 'order consecrated unto the service of the Most High in things wherewith others may not meddle'.[103] The form of ministry inherited by the Church of England, of bishops, presbyters and deacons had its beginning 'from Christ and his blessed Apostles themselves'.[104] While the particular form might not be found in Scripture, Hooker is clear that the form ministry inherited by the Church of England is certainly very ancient.

Hooker continues the theme of ministry in the posthumously published Books Six (which counters the claim that Our laws are corrupt . . . in matter belonging to the power of ecclesiastical jurisdiction, in that we have not . . . certain lay elders) and Seven ('There ought not to be in the Church Bishops'). Here, Hooker argues against the equality of ministry, offering a sustained defence of bishops. Although he accepts the possibility of creating a ministry de novo,[105] he nevertheless argues strongly in favour of bishops. In Book Seven, he justifies the importance of bishops on the grounds that they have been around for a long time:

> A thousand five hundred years and upward the Church of Christ hath now continued under the sacred regiment of bishops. Neither for so long hath Christianity been ever planted in any kingdom throughout the world but with this kind of government alone; which to have been ordained of God, I am for mine own part even as resolutely persuaded, as that any other kind of government in the world whatsoever is of God.

Like Henry VIII, he accepts the legend of King Lucius and suggests that Bishops had come to England long before the time of St Augustine:

> In this realm of England, before Normans, yea before Saxons, there being Christians, the chief pastors of their souls were bishops. This order from about the first establishment of Christian religion, which was publicly begun through the

virtuous disposition of King Lucie not fully two hundred years after Christ, continued till the coming in of the Saxons.[106]

While episcopacy may not be of the essence of the church, it is nevertheless the most effective form of church government. Writing about apostolic times, Hooker claims:

> But forasmuch as the Apostles could not themselves be present in all churches . . . there did grow in short time amongst the governors of each church those emulations, strifes, and contentions, whereof there could be no sufficient remedy provided, except according unto the order of Jerusalem already begun, some one were endued with episcopal authority over the rest, which one being resident might keep them in order, and have preeminence or principality in those things wherein the equality of many agents was the cause of disorder and trouble. This one president or governor amongst the rest had his known authority established a long time before that settled difference of name and title took place, whereby such alone were named bishops. And therefore in the book of St. John's Revelation we find that they are entitled angels.[107]

In contrast, Hooker claimed, collegial government was a recipe for confusion: presbyters were to subject themselves to their bishops. To do the contrary was to 'oppose themselves against that which God himself ordained by his apostles'. While this did not mean that Bishops were exempt from corruption and the need for reform, Hooker's understanding placed their authority in 'an order descended from Christ to the apostles',[108] which moved him close to an understanding of apostolic succession that saw bishops as an 'ordinance of God'.[109]

Hooker's final Book aims to confute the statement that 'Unto no . . . prince . . . may be given such ecclesiastical dominion as by the laws of this land belongeth unto the supreme regent thereof'.[110] Here again Hooker returns to the theme of law and order as these are expressed in church and state. His central point is that the two realms are not separate but are so interrelated as to be effectively one. Indeed, in a famous statement he claims: 'There is not any man of the Church of England but the same man is also a member of the commonwealth; nor any man a member of the commonwealth which is not also of the Church of England'.[111] The idea of laws being made by general consent, which had been developed in Book One, implies that the correct legislative body for the Church is the Parliament.[112] In turn, bishops do not hold their authority directly from Christ, but have it granted to them from the spiritual community. This leads him to a defence of the Royal Supremacy.[113] The king, 'whose care is presumed to extend most indifferently over all', was regarded as the 'common parent'[114] who had the lawful supremacy of power 'to order and dispose of spiritual affairs'.[115] The sovereign will persist in the monarch's supreme legislating authority, whose duty is to ensure that good order is maintained in the church and the state. Drawing directly from his opponents, he asserts that the monarch is required to 'see that the laws . . . touching his worship, and touching all matters and orders of the Church, be executed and duly observed; to see that every ecclesiastical person do that office whereunto he is appointed'.[116] Within this framework of authority, the church exists as that politic society which maintains the Christian religion but always ultimately under the authority of the monarch:

> We are to hold it a thing most consonant with equity and reason, that no ecclesiastical law be made in a Christian commonwealth, without consent of the laity as the clergy, but least of all without consent of the highest power.[117]

Conclusion

All in all, the system established by Hooker suggests a complex interrelationship of Scripture and reason: in the determination of what counted as 'accessory' matters, Scripture first had to be 'collected' using a reason informed by the doctrinal truths of the Christian tradition. Underlying this exercise of authority was a social and political order that gave to the monarch the ultimate authority over all things: this was required because human beings were constrained by the conditions of their depravity to accept a common and impartial authority, lest individualism should take control and anarchy flourish. It was the duty of those in authority to legislate as best they could for the well-being of the commonwealth; and because the citizens of that commonwealth could do good only by obeying laws made for their benefit, then it was their duty to obey the proper legislating authority in all matters. The principle was almost that any law is better than none.

Such a defence of authority and obedience prefigured many of the debates that were to emerge in the seventeenth century. As the contested nature of his legacy reveals, Hooker proved particularly useful for a number of different versions of Anglican theology (and still does). The publication of the last three books at the Restoration reveals the usefulness of his anti-Puritan polemic for those seeking to establish the Church of England after the 1662 Act of Uniformity. This was in part because, as Lake suggests, rather than personifying or expressing 'existing "anglican" attitudes and values', Richard Hooker 'invented them'.[118] His views were distinct from what went before: they lack something of the polemical vigour and secure dogmatic rigidity of Whitgift, especially in relation to the issue of predestination that proved so divisive in the next generation (which is discussed in the next chapter). That said, one should not overestimate Hooker's novelty:[119] theologically at least, he stands clearly in the line of the Elizabethan conformists, even if his mode of argumentation was rather more subtle and philosophical: the 'Anglicanism' he invented was not quite as different from what went before as many of his successors might have wished.

Chapter 6

The Seventeenth Century

The Myths of 'Anglicanism'

In 1926, T. S. Eliot published an anonymous essay in the *Times Literary Supplement* with the short title, 'Lancelot Andrewes'.[1] He praises Andrewes (1555–1626), the great Bishop of Chichester, Ely and Winchester, for his style and humanist rationality: he is to be read alongside Richard Hooker, George Herbert and Jeremy Taylor as the representative of intellectually credible religion and as the first 'great preacher of the English Catholick Church' quite distinct from the protestant polemicists of the previous generation. His 'intellect and sensibility were in harmony', and his prose, together with Hooker's, 'came to complete the structure of the English Church as the philosophy of the thirteenth century crowns the Catholic Church . . . . If the Church of Elizabeth is worthy of Shakespeare and Jonson, that is because of Hooker and Andrewes'. Although Eliot's understanding has many merits, and while Andrewes was deeply influential on Eliot's poetry,[2] his interpretation nevertheless creates an idealized and intellectualized picture of a pure literary 'Anglicanism' far removed from bitter theological controversies of the time. Andrewes's elegant and learned personal prayer books together with his majestic sermons, however, should not blind us to the polemical context of seventeenth-century theology. What this chapter demonstrates is that Andrewes and his Laudian heirs sought to create a somewhat different form of Anglicanism from what had gone before: while such an Anglicanism turned out to be normative in the years that followed, at least in some parts of the Church of England and beyond, it was something of a deviation from the predominant style of theology in the early sixteenth century.

For Eliot, and for many others since, the seventeenth century has been singled out as the high point of Anglican theology.

R. W. Church, for instance, claimed in a sermon that Andrewes marked a 'step in the unfolding of the theology of the Reformed Church of England . . . . Andrewes claimed for the English Church its full interest and membership in the Church universal'.[3] He 'fought both Romanist and Puritan with such weapons as he found in his hand'.[4] Andrewes, it seemed, represented the Anglican position between puritan and Roman Catholic. Similarly, in a lecture of 1897, Walter Frere, one of the early members of the Community of the Resurrection and later Bishop of Truro, gave a lecture on 'Lancelot Andrewes as a Representative of Anglican Principles',[5] where he regarded Andrewes as the successor to Jewel in defining the *via media* position of the English Church.[6]

Such an approach influenced Paul Elmer More and F. L. Cross who gave the simple title *Anglicanism* to their compendium of writings from the religious literature of the seventeenth century, although they did not confine their affections to Andrewes.[7] The title implies that the elegant writing of the seventeenth century exemplified by such men as Jeremy Taylor, William Laud and Andrewes was more authentically 'Anglican' than the polemical works of the Reformers and their heirs in Tudor England. Such writers, most of whom held high office in the Church, were in general defenders of the King, were anti-Calvinist in their theology and stressed the importance of order and dignity in worship: in hindsight, their theology can be characterized 'Anglican' only if the term is to be equated with a form of churchmanship that was also dubbed 'Anglo-Catholicism' in the mid-nineteenth century and that was quite distinct from the protestant emphasis of the previous century. Whether such theology – which has been called 'avant-garde conformity'[8] – was typical of the seventeenth century has been much debated, but what is important to note is that it is an influential but highly contested version of Anglicanism.[9] Later churchmen, as will become clear in the next chapter, created a myth of certain varieties of seventeenth-century theology as something of a high point of Anglicanism. It is also worth noting, however, that the tradition of myth-making was far from new. Immediately after his death, the myth of Andrewes developed very rapidly: indeed, it can be seen as beginning as early as 1629 with the first publication of Lancelot Andrewes's works by William Laud and William Buckeridge.[10]

As so often, it was the nineteenth century that formulated such idealized versions of history. As I have already noted in Chapter 2, among Anglo-Catholics there was a downplaying of the importance of the Reformation and a strong emphasis on the continuity with the pre-Reformation church, especially that of the first few centuries. This historiography can be illustrated using the example of two massive publishing projects, both of which were the outcome of a particular understanding of the Church of England that was formulated in the 1830s. The leaders of the Oxford Movement (or the Tractarians) set about proving the continuity of the Church of England with its pre-Reformation past: to do so, they stressed the patristic period, particularly of the undivided church up to the Council of Chalcedon (451 AD). From 1838, the three leading figures of the Oxford Movement, John Henry Newman, John Keble and Edward Bouverie Pusey, along with many other associated figures, published translations of texts in a series called the *Library of the Fathers*. The full title of the series reveals their intentions: *A Library of the Fathers, anterior to the division of the East and West. Translated by members of the English Church*.[11] The Oxford Movement had tried to ground its theology of the undivided Church through the doctrine of the so-called 'apostolical succession', which held that the bishops received their authority in terms of succession from the early church. It was through this episcopal link that the tradition was handed on until the present day. One of their prime motivations in reviving the study of the Fathers was to try to understand as much as possible about the past in which this authority was first demonstrated and in which the church forged its definitive teaching.[12] Some of the early Tracts of the Oxford Movement had been translations of some of the most important writings of the Fathers, and by the late 1830s, these early initiatives had been developed into a systematic publishing project.

The idea of producing the *Library of the Fathers* took shape in August 1836 at a meeting between Pusey and Newman. Pusey wrote to Newman the following month that he would seek to find a publisher and also try to ensure that there was interest across the country as well as in America, where, he felt, it might be a great help to the 'soundness of doctrine'.[13] In his prospectus for the *Library*, Pusey claimed 'the circumstance that the Anglican branch of the Church Catholic is founded upon Holy Scripture and the agreement of the Universal Church, and that therefore the knowledge of Christian antiquity is necessary in order to understand and maintain her doctrines, and especially her creeds and her liturgy'.[14] Pusey, like other figures associated with the Oxford Movement, held to a branch theory of the church which claimed that the Church of England was the local branch of the one holy catholic and apostolic church rooted in the early church. This meant that on the basis of a full knowledge of the writings of what he called 'Catholic antiquity, which is disparaged by Romanists in order to make way for the later Councils', Pusey sought to rediscover the essential characteristics of the Church of England as the true inheritor of the Church of the Fathers. On such a model, the Church of England was quite distinct from other churches, especially those that had emerged from the Continental Reformation. In the Preface to the first volume, a translation of St Augustine's *Confessions*, he stressed the importance of understanding the Fathers as interpreters of Scripture, something which had been emphasized by the Canons of the Church of 1571. As a body, the Fathers bore witness to what was known as the Vincentian Canon: what had been taught at all times, everywhere and by all.[15]

Eventually, the *Library of the Fathers* project received the support of large numbers of subscribers: as early as 1838 when the first volume, which was dedicated to the Archbishop of Canterbury, was published, there were 800 names and by 1853 there were 31 bishops among the 3700 subscribers. The project was welcomed by many from across the Church divides including Edward Bickersteth, one of the leading Evangelical scholars of the period, who wrote to Pusey in 1836: 'Few things could be more seasonable, or more beneficial to the Church of England, to which, I feel more and more, it is a real privilege, in these days of disunion and division, to be united'.[16] Eventually, the *Library* amounted to 48 volumes when it was completed in 1885. The massive scale of the publication of translations of the Fathers said a great deal about the essence of Anglicanism for Keble, Pusey and Newman. The implicit assumption, however, was what Peter Nockles called 'patristic fundamentalism'[17] which saw that doctrinal development and the revelation of Christian truth simply stopped in the fifth century. It comes as little surprise that there was an alternative historical model put forward by some who held the Reformation in higher esteem than the Oxford Movement. As I have discussed in Chapter 2, the *Library of the Fathers* provoked direct competition in the Parker Society editions of the Reformers, produced by more protestant-minded scholars whose understanding of the Church of England was quite different.

'Anglo-Catholic' Theology

At the same time as the Tractarians sponsored a systematic translation of the writings of the early church, so they also made efforts to come to terms with something of the more recent historical legacy of the Church of England in which they were working. Given their distancing of their own church from the Reformation, they would need to find a more congenial set of documents than those of the Reformers, which has begun to be republished in Parker Society editions. In their efforts to present an alternative model of the Church of England, the Tractarians consequently placed great stress on the writings of the high churchmen of the seventeenth century, who have been somewhat loosely called the 'Caroline Divines' (although some, including Andrewes, were active well before the reign of Charles I).[18] Thus, alongside the *Library of the Fathers*, the leading figures of the Oxford Movement and a number of their associates – admittedly with very different degrees of enthusiasm – began to produce a second lengthy series, the *Library of Anglo-Catholic Theology* which was published from 1841 to 1863.[19] Building upon Keble's edition of Richard Hooker, the *Library of Anglo-Catholic Theology* series focused on the publication of new editions chiefly of the seventeenth-century Anglican divines. As a complement to the *Library of the Fathers*, the series located the essence of Anglican theology in the revived sacramentalism of the Caroline high churchmen, many of whom were vigorously opposed to the dominant Calvinism of their contemporaries and to some of the forms of Protestantism of the earlier period of the English Reformation.

The scheme was the brainchild of H. N. Evans, a Hampstead doctor and first treasurer and secretary of the committee, who sought to establish a 'society for reprinting some of our standard writers in divinity which have become so scarce as to be out of the reach of those who have not access to large libraries'.[20] Newman wrote to Evans on 10 December 1839 expressing his willingness to subscribe to a series of writings which should be 'selected by a Committee composed of persons of sound principles', among whom he included himself. Newman's curate William Copeland (1804–1885) was superintending editor of what Pusey called this body of 'Anglican theology'[21] from 1840 to 1843, even if a series without the Reformers presented what amounted to a very particular brand of theology as the true heart of 'Anglicanism'. Newman, it should be noted, had earlier expounded a number of seventeenth-century divines in his *Lectures on the Prophetical Office*, while recognizing that their Anglicanism (or Anglo-Catholicism)[22] was perhaps both unrepresentative and impracticable:

> It cannot be denied there is force in these considerations; it still remains to be tried whether what is called Anglicanism, the religion of Andrewes, Laud, Hammond, Butler, and Wilson, is capable of being professed, acted on, and maintained on a large sphere of action and through a sufficient period, or whether it be a mere modification or transition-state either of Romanism or of popular Protantism, according as we view it.[23]

Among the leaders of the Oxford Movement, however, there was less than unbridled enthusiasm for the series. Pusey wrote to Newman on 8 January 1841 doubting that 'any of us are sufficiently acquainted with our divines to be able to fix definitively upon the list of what it would be advisable to publish; for simply to say that the works of certain *authors* only would be published, would be nothing; since one might have Catholic and unCatholic works from the same writer'.[24] Pusey, who claimed a 'great ignorance' of the Divines, also feared that the 'AngloCatholic [sic] Library will look very meagre, and very sadly compared to the Gallo-Catholic library' of devotional works which was being mooted by Isaac Williams.[25] 'Perhaps', he went on, 'the name AngloCatholic Library is too high-sounding'.[26] Newman responded a few days later noting his own lack of enthusiasm for the project: 'As to

the AngloCatholic Library, with you I never have been for it'.[27]
Nevertheless, he felt the need to respond to the Parker Society,
which was about to produce its first volume. He had urged
Copeland to make a list of authors that included Andrewes,
Bramhall, Laud and Bull. Newman concluded to Pusey: 'I feel,
what you say, about the absurdity of calling it AngloCatholic
Library'. While Newman and Pusey were on far less secure ground
in their understanding of the English Divines than they were
with the Fathers, they nevertheless sponsored the series that made
'Anglo-Catholicism' – which in 1837 was Newman's synonym
for Anglicanism – into a familiar term associated with a highly
selective list of authors drawn from the seventeenth century. As
More and Cross's recently republished volume bears witness, their
half-hearted revisioning of Anglicanism has had a powerful effect.

James I and the Calvinist Orthodoxy[28]

It is not simply from the ideological perspective of the nineteenth
century, however, that the seventeenth century is controversial.
Among recent historians, it has been one of the most hotly
contested periods in the theology of the Church of England,
and there seems to be little sign that the controversy over its
interpretation will become any less heated. The first forty years
of the century, with which this chapter deals, is a period where
theological debate and discussion have been regarded by subsequent
historians to be of special importance. The basic outline of the
historical controversy is shaped by those who have challenged
the so-called 'Anglican' interpretations of the history of the late
sixteenth and early seventeenth centuries, which have regarded
religious policy as dominated by the persistence of the Elizabethan
via media.[29] These *via media* understandings of Anglicanism are
regarded as distortions of the truth. Instead, the revisionists hold
that the dominant religious approach for most of the period
was Calvinist. This means that puritanism was not necessarily
the novelty: while this Calvinist supremacy was challenged by a
few unrepresentative figures in the late Elizabethan and Jacobean
Church, it was subjected to a major revision particularly under the
influence of William Laud at the end of James's reign and under

Charles I. It was anti-Calvinism (or Arminianism) that marked the major change of direction.[30] There were, as Conrad Russell said in one of the first revisionist works, 'rival claimants to the title of orthodox, and therefore between rival criteria of orthodoxy'.[31]

In this chapter, I shall endeavour to navigate through this difficult terrain, but with a particular focus on the development of 'Anglican theology': while it seems to me that the balance of the historical scholarship points in the direction of Laudianism as marking a novel departure from the earlier Calvinist consensus, which implied a distancing from the Reformation, its chief importance rests in its appropriation by the next generation who re-established the Church of England after the Commonwealth. This forms the subject of the next Chapter; in turn, Laudianism became the basis for the Victorian appropriation of the seventeenth century with which I began this chapter. While the divisions that had characterized the theology and church life of the later sixteenth century continued after the accession of the Stuarts, what is crucial to note is that eventually under Charles I and his Archbishop, William Laud, the political intelligence that was required to hold the church together withered away under the impact of parliamentary politics: the country and its church were divided and the allegiance to the monarch, which had proved so central to the Elizabethan Settlement, was thrown into question as different forces competed for power. In all this, the church played an important yet highly contested role. As Felicity Heal writes about the end of the sixteenth century: 'The next half-century was to show that even in England the Reformation had taught men of conscience that the king did not have binding control over their religious behaviour'.[32] Since it would be far too ambitious to attempt a thorough account of the history of the church and its theology in the period up to the Civil War, I will simply outline a few salient features of this period as they relate to 'Anglican theology'.

On the accession of James I in 1603, there were evidently some important questions which would have to be addressed as he came to establish his authority over the English Church: after all, the new King's experience of ecclesiastical government was of the Scottish Church, which had established a different polity from that of the Church of England. And yet, James remained an implacable opponent of Presbyterianism. In ecclesiastical affairs, he displayed a balance which meant that something of a middle way could be steered to ensure the maximum degree of conformity possible from both moderate puritans and even some Roman Catholics. As he searched for appropriate suitors for his children, he displayed an even-handedness with a catholic for Prince Henry (who resisted the idea) and later for Charles, and a Calvinist, the Elector Palatine Frederick, for his daughter Elizabeth. All in all, James I was, as he put it in a speech before both Houses of Parliament in 1607, 'ever for the medium in everything. Between foolish rashness and extreme length there is a middle way'.[33] Throughout his reign, he ensured a breadth of views and regularly heard sermons from a variety of viewpoints.[34] This proved an eminently sensible policy. As Fincham and Lake write, 'In his management of ecclesiastical affairs, James I combined a detailed grasp of abstract theory with a native political shrewdness'.[35]

Shortly after he came to the throne, James I convened a meeting of divines and politicians in response to the so-called Millenary Petition which expressed a number of puritan hopes for church reform. This was held for three days at his palace at Hampton Court in January 1604 and, according to Shriver, became 'one of the most significant events in the political and religious history of England'.[36] While the different participants had different hopes, it would seem that James wanted to ensure as much conformity as possible by ensuring that puritans were brought to heel.[37] James followed the pattern set by the divines of the previous century in regarding some of the more hotly contested issues as matters indifferent, while at the same time seeking to ensure conformity to the ecclesiastical settlement. There was no sense in which religion could be seen to be contending with the King's majesty.[38] He had a strong track record in emphasizing his divine right, publishing a short book in 1598 on *The True Law of Free Monarchies*, where he claimed that 'Kings are called Gods by the prophetical King *David*, because they sit upon God his throne in the earth, and have the count of their administration to give unto him'.[39]

The Conference was dominated by Bishop Richard Bancroft (1544–1610) of London (and soon afterwards elevated to Canterbury), Robert Cecil and four puritans whose leading spokesman was John Reynolds, president of Corpus Christi

College, Oxford. The Royal Proclamation set the terms for the conference: 'Our purpose and resolution ever was, and now is to preserve the estate as well Ecclesiastical as Politic, in such form as we have found it established by the Laws here, reforming only the abuses which we shall apparently find proved'.[40] Such abuses were listed in the various demands for relatively moderate reforms over such issues as a proper preaching ministry in every parish, the exercise of clerical pluralities, and impropriated tithes. Reynolds' further call for a reform of the episcopacy which would share their functions with a synod – the archbishops a national synod, the bishops a provincial synod and the archdeacons a diocesan – was rejected (even if in the very long term it became close to the final form of the Church of England's contemporary synodical system).[41] Seeking concessions from the puritans, James made various promises (including a 'learned and painful minister'[42] in every parish, modest reform of the Prayer Book, an extension of the catechism, and revision of the sixteenth Article of Religion so that the words 'we may depart from grace given' might be suitably qualified with the words 'yet neither totally nor finally', and even the inclusion of the Lambeth Articles into the Thirty-Nine) but firmly resisted any change to the system of episcopacy: his motto was 'no bishop, no King'. He went on: 'When I mean to live under a presbytery, I will go to Scotland again. But while I am in England, I will have bishops'.[43] While his tolerance of more radical puritanism was low – 'cherish no man more than a good pastor; hate no man more than a proud puritan'[44] – his political astuteness meant that the bishops were asked to deal gently with those who did not conform. The Conference met with a degree of success. As Shriver puts it: 'if one accepts the sober belief that politics is the art of the possible, the Church settlement of 1604 and the puritan policy of James I seems to have worked quite well'.[45] At the same time, James also conceded to a new translation of the Bible to be undertaken by 54 scholars of different persuasions including Andrewes and Reynolds, which appeared in 1611. Unlike the Geneva Bible, it was to contain no marginal notes which gave it a greater degree of doctrinal neutrality.

The implementation of James's desire to ensure a preaching ministry in every parish floundered chiefly because of the problem of finance: one-third of benefices were worth less than £5 per annum, and 90 per cent less than £26. Incomes were particularly low because large proportions of the tithe income of the church had been given over to lay 'impropriators' after the Reformation, which provided a significant amount of the revenue for the Oxford and Cambridge Colleges. Despite the King's wishes, it proved impossible for the church to regain control of what had become an important source of income to many influential laity: parliament refused to increase clerical incomes and declined to expand the coercive power of the ecclesiastical courts against the power of the civil courts. Failure to modify the system of clerical income meant that the old method of episcopal visitation continued to be used to improve the functioning of the clergy. The visitation returns provide a good snapshot of ecclesiastical life in the early Stuart years.[46] Ecclesiastical finance and an impoverished clergy remained a matter of constant dispute until well into the nineteenth century: indeed the lack of a well-financed and educated clergy may well have had an important effect on the development of Anglican theology beyond the narrow confines of a clerical and academic elite.

In the summer of 1604, Convocation agreed 44 new canons that were added to the 97 existing canons. Many of these had been formulated in the Tudor reigns but finally received ratification. The canons compelled subscription to the Thirty-Nine Articles and the Prayer Book (§36) and acknowledgement of the Crown's 'ancient jurisdiction over the state ecclesiastical'. While a number of canons made concessions to some of the moderate puritan demands for a resident preaching ministry (§45) and sought to clamp down on the excessive granting of marriage licences (§62), they remained uncompromising over some controversial issues including the use of vestments (§§14, 58, 74) and holy tables (§82) and the making of the sign of the cross at baptism (§30).[47] In the end, the vast majority of moderate puritans agreed to obey the canons. A temporary toleration of those with tender consciences was allowed until November 30, provided that they were obedient to the King. Indeed, in a moment of rare charity, the Proclamation enjoined 'all Archbishops, Bishops, and other Ecclesiastical persons to do their uttermost endeavours by conferences, agreements, persuasions, and by all other ways of love and gentleness to reclaim all that be in the Ministry, to the obedience of our Church

Laws'.[48] Although in practice there were very few concessions made, eventually fewer than ninety clergy were deprived: bishops exercised a relatively tolerant policy towards those clergy who posed no great threat to the stability of the church provided that they subscribed to the Thirty-Nine Articles.

Most bishops shared the King's commitment to the preaching ministry and had no great liking for a maximum interpretation of the revived ceremonial implied by the ornaments rubric.[49] Some deprived clergy went on to find alternative positions.[50] James sought to rule a national church by ensuring as much conformity as possible by alienating the smallest number. His policy also displays a degree of breadth in preferments to the episcopal bench. The men who occupied the most important positions of leadership in the church were from very different viewpoints. These included George Abbot (1562–1633), a definite Calvinist, who succeeded Bancroft as Archbishop in 1611 (and who shared much with him),[51] and Lancelot Andrewes at Chichester (1605), Ely (1607) and Winchester (1609), who was enjoined to silence on the controversial subject of predestination.[52] James's famous speech to both houses of Parliament on 23 March 1610 summarizes his approach:

> I never found, that blood and too much severity did good
> in matters of religion; for, besides it being a sure Rule in
> Divinity, That God never loves to plant his Church by
> Violence and Bloodshed, natural Reason may even persuade
> us, and daily Experience proves it true, That when Men are
> severely persecuted for Religion, the Gallantness of many
> Men's Spirits, and the Wilfulness of their Humours, rather
> than the Justness of the Cause, makes them to take a Pride
> boldly to endure any Torments, or Death itself, to gain
> thereby the Reputation of Martyrdom, though but in a false
> Shadow.[53]

Doctrinal Disputes

While James had managed to maintain a cautious breadth of acceptable theology between the excluded extremes, the Church nonetheless began to show signs of division. In a period of international tension, particularly in the run up to the thirty years' war, the Church of England was certainly not isolated from theological developments on the Continent, and it participated in one of the major disputes over the seemingly rather arcane subject of predestination.[54] It is important to stress that the Church of England regarded itself as part of the Reformed family: the vast majority of clergy and laity, from both conformist and puritan backgrounds, were Calvinists.[55] Indeed, there was little challenging of the sort of doctrine contained in the Lambeth Articles of 1595, even if it was not added to the Thirty-Nine Articles.[56] As Nicholas Tyacke has observed, detailed analysis of sermons as well as the theses presented at the University faculties represent this Calvinist dominance, although there were some exceptions (including the French Huguenot, Peter Baro, Lady Margaret Professor at Cambridge, who preached against the Articles in 1596, and John Overall, Regius Professor and afterwards Bishop of Norwich).[57] Despite these opponents, however, the acceptance of a moderate Calvinism by most factions (as represented in Article 17) helped to quell too much division within the Church of England.[58]

The theological dispute that shook the church is frequently summarized in terms of a conflict between Calvinists and Arminians. The main doctrinal focus was over the related doctrines of election and predestination, which go far further back into the Reformation and the early church. Arminianism, which was named after Jacobus Arminius (1560–1609), believed against the Calvinists that the elect could fall from grace.[59] In 1610, a Remonstrance of five points was presented to the Dutch States General. The key issues against the Calvinist opponents were that election was conditional; that Christ died for all; that human beings could co-operate with God's grace; that the grace of God was not irresistible and that true believers might fall away from God totally and finally. This meant that there was a significant sphere for free will which was compatible with divine sovereignty.

George Abbot and James I had opposed the appointment of the Arminian Conradus Vorsitus in 1611 as successor to Arminius at the University of Leiden. The controversies led to the summoning of a Synod at Dordrecht (Dort) in 1618–19 where Calvinists from Holland and other parts of Europe debated the finer points of doctrine. James I sent George Carleton, Bishop of Llandaff and then Chichester, cousin of Sir Dudley Carleton, British Ambassador, to lead an English delegation, which also comprised a number of Cambridge theologians who had opposed the pro-Arminian views espoused by John Overall and Baro in the 1590s. The King's choice emphasized the Calvinist credentials of the English Church, although he was keen to make sure that his delegation urged the Synod to avoid too much harshness in its condemnation of the Remonstrance. Carleton, however, acting under instructions from Abbot, adhered to the rigid Calvinism which asserted that Christ died only for the elect. While it is still a matter of some contention,[60] the vast majority of members of the Church of England adopted a Calvinist approach, although there were other bishops, including John Overall and Lancelot Andrewes, who would have been far closer to the Remonstrant line.[61] The Synod firmly upheld a strongly Calvinist line, emphasizing that faith is a gift of God given to some but not to others, that God had elected some before the foundation of the world and that atonement was made only for those elect.[62] The British delegates supported the Synod's canons, even if they refused to call them the doctrines of the Reformed church. Despite Carleton's efforts, however, there was no official ratification of the Synod in England, although a formal presentation edition was accepted by James I and Abbot and a doctorate was conferred by Oxford University on Festus Hommius, the secretary to the Synod.[63]

Arminianism, Laudianism and Carolinism

James I's policy of allowing a degree of diversity, however, meant that even if Calvinism was the dominant theology of the Church of England, it was certainly not the only form of theology that could be found. As important in the later years of James I and in the reign of his son and heir – and in the longer term more important for Anglicanism as it evolved in the eighteenth and nineteenth centuries[64] – was the gradual development of Arminianism, which came to be associated with William Laud, Charles I's Archbishop of Canterbury from 1633. While such an 'Arminian' theology was in part concerned with the thorny issues of grace and predestination, it involved something far broader than seemingly obscure points of doctrine, which Peter Lake has called the 'Laudian Style'.[65] It was a 'coherent, distinctive and polemically aggressive vision of the Church, the divine presence in the world and the appropriate ritual response to that presence'.[66] Some historians, however, have been keen to emphasize the driving force of the religious changes of the 1630s in the King's 'highly personal notion of sacramental Kingship', which has been called 'Carolinism', which presented 'a very weird aberration from the first hundred years of the early reformed Church of England'.[67] This meant that it was the King's own expression of power rather than doctrine that was paramount in religious policy.

In turn, 'Laudianism' was associated with the Archbishop's defence of the Royal Supremacy coupled with a high sacramentalism and defence of the divine right of the episcopate. As Laud put it in a sermon in 1626, 'First, the magistrate, and his power and justice. And resist either of these, and ye resist "the power, and the ordinance of God"'.[68] Others, however, have stressed 'anti-Calvinism' as the central motivation behind the Laudian changes.[69] Others still have claimed to see the Caroline Church as maintaining something of the *via media* of its Elizabethan precursor.[70] In a period when theology and politics were extraordinarily enmeshed, it is a risky business for the non-specialist to be too certain about the theology of the period. Nevertheless, it seems most plausible to regard the changes under Laud and his circle as a serious effort at a sort of modest 'Counter Reformation', which aimed to move away from the Calvinist doctrinal consensus of the early Stuart years, which was also coupled with a relative latitude in uniformity and practice. In its place Laud sought to return the church to more rigorous obedience to the Elizabethan injunctions that had been reasserted in 1604 and also to promote causes – especially the reorientation and railing of altars – which would be highly likely to provoke serious opposition.

The story of the rise of Arminianism can be narrated briefly: shortly after the Synod of Dort, Abbot's influence had waned, partly because of his opposition to the Spanish marriage match for Prince Charles. By the 1620s, a number of 'anti-Calvinists' had been promoted, adding to Andrewes and Richard Neile, who was Bishop of Durham from 1617–28. At Durham, Neile moved the communion table into an altarwise position and, in about 1620, rebuilt a stone table. He also appointed John Cosin, one of the leading figures in the Restoration church, as prebendary of his cathedral. A circle began to form around Neile (the so-called Durham House Group), which included John Buckeridge (Bishop of Rochester from 1611), John Howson (Bishop of Oxford from 1619) and Laud, who had been appointed to the relatively minor see of St David's in 1621, as well as Richard Montagu ((1577–1641) Archdeacon of Hereford from 1617, and from 1627, Bishop of Chichester). This meant that even before the accession of Charles, there was support for the anti-Calvinist line. As Hugh Trevor-Roper wrote, 'by 1620 [the Arminian] innovations had become quietly established'.[71]

It was Richard Montagu who proved one of the most controversial figures of the time. He was, as Tyacke writes, 'the stalking horse for a court-based faction of leading clergy, who sought not merely to counteract the effects of Dort but fundamentally to alter the doctrinal stance of the English Church'.[72] His polemic *A New Gagg for an Old Goose* (1624),[73] while not explicitly Arminian, emphasized the importance of a vigorous form of anti-Calvinism. Montagu demonstrated similarities between the Church of England and that of Rome in a book which eventually gained royal approval after Abbot failed in his efforts at censure. The royal favourite George Villiers, who became Duke of Buckingham in 1623, under the influence of Laud, his chaplain, threw his support behind Montagu. For some, especially a number of prominent puritan MPs, the sort of position represented by Montagu was a kind of crypto-papism. A meeting summoned by Buckingham at York House, his London residence, in 1626 between a group of Arminians and a number of Calvinists settled nothing. Shortly afterwards some members of parliament felt that the very teaching of the Church of England was under threat, claiming a 'conspiracy to alter the doctrine of the Church of England'.[74] Some thought it necessary to embark on an authoritative explanation of the Thirty-Nine Articles. A Bill to incorporate the significantly more Calvinist Irish Articles (which included the Lambeth Articles) into English law failed chiefly because Parliament was dissolved. Despite the fact that efforts had been made to impeach Montagu, he received preferment to the bishopric of Chichester. In 1626,

Charles I, who had succeeded his father in February 1625, issued a Proclamation to stifle 'any new inventions, or opinions concerning Religion'.[75] The controversies, however, refused to go away. By 1629, Francis Rous, one of the most prominent of the puritan MPs, summarized the popular perception of Arminianism:

> I desire that we may consider the increase of Arminianism, an error that maketh the grace of God lackey it after the will of man, that maketh the sheep to keep the shepherd, that maketh mortal seed of an immortal God. Yea, I desire that we may look into the belly and bowels of this Trojan horse, to see if there be not men in it ready to open the gates to Romish tyranny and Spanish monarchy.[76]

Laud's Theology

The role of the Duke of Buckingham and Laud cannot be underestimated. Laud's most extensive theological work took the form of a polemical encounter with a Jesuit, which was written shortly after he had been appointed to St David's. The context was the conversion of the mother of George Villiers to Roman Catholicism. After fears of the Duke's own conversion, the Conference between Laud and John Fisher, the Jesuit, took place on 24 May 1622. Although initially private, the Conference, together with various other responses to Fisher and other Catholics, was published in 1624. While far from original, the Conference amounts to a straightforward application of a justification of the independent authority of the Church of England: what is important to note is that the context is neither Arminian not Calvinist, but the fear of Catholicism. It is for this reason that Laud was keen to emphasize that since no one part of the church was exempt from error, each church was free to make its own decisions in obedience to the rule of Scripture: 'I admit no ordinary rule left now in the Church, of divine and infallible verity, and so of faith, but the Scripture'.[77] There could be no arbiter save that of Scripture: 'For what need is there of another, since this is most infallible; and the same which the ancient Church of Christ admitted'.[78] Virtually the whole of the Conference with Fisher is concerned with the possibility of error in the application of this rule of faith. Indeed, Laud claims that all institutions of the church can err, including a general council:[79] 'if a General Council will go out of the Church's way, it may easily go without the Church's truth'.[80] While Laud held to a doctrine of 'indefectibility' in the sense that the church taken as a whole could not err, the Catholic Church could not be identified with any particular institution: it was always far greater and more expansive.

On this basis, Laud develops a theory of the autonomy of the local church which he regards as a provisional – yet a necessary – stopgap until such time as wider councils can be convened: when a General Council 'cannot be had, the church must pray that it may, and expect till it may; or else reform itself *per partes*, by national or provincial synods'.[81] Indeed, it was crucial that if the wider church refused to reform itself, then the particular church had the duty to do so:

> Was it not lawful for Judah to reform herself, when Israel would not join? Sure it was, or else the prophet deceives me? . . . Besides, to reform what is amiss in doctrine or manners, is as lawful for a particular Church, as it is to publish and promulgate any thing that is catholic in either. . . . If she erred in fact, confess her error.[82]

Sometimes Laud uses rather more graphic language: 'Should we have suffered this gangrene to endanger life and all, rather than be cured in time by a physician of a weaker knowledge and a less able hand?'[83] In short, he went on:

> when the universal church will not, or for the iniquities of the times cannot, obtain and settle a free General Council, it is lawful, nay sometimes necessary, to reform gross abuses by a national, or a provincial.[84]

To justify his claim about the need for national and provincial reform Laud draws on the schoolman Albertus Magnus,[85] as well as the Parisian conciliarist Jean Gerson (1363–1429), who 'will not deny but that the Church may be reformed in parts; and that this is necessary, and that to effect it, Provincial Councils may suffice; and in some things, Diocesan'.[86] Provincial councils, Laud claims, have the duty to 'decree in causes of faith, and in cases of reformation, where corruptions have crept into the sacraments of Christ'.[87] Laud develops this idea further by claiming that the authority of the 'patriarch' of Rome is essentially the same as that of the other patriarchs, and there is no appeal beyond the patriarch who is 'supreme in his own patriarchate'.[88] Laud understands the authority of the archbishop of Canterbury as that of a patriarch: 'Now, the Britons having a primate of their own (which is greater than a metropolitan,) yea, a patriarch, if you will, he could not be appealed from to Rome, by S. Gregory's own doctrine'.[89]

While Laud conceded that the Bishop of Rome had authority in Rome, it was impossible for his jurisdiction to be exercised over the whole church because this threatened the sovereignty of the local king:

> Suppose [the Church] is a Kingdom; yet the Church militant remaining one, is spread in many earthly kingdoms, and cannot well be ordered like any one particular kingdom. And therefore, though in one particular kingdom there be many visible judges and one supreme, yet it follows not that in the universal militant Church there must be one supreme. For how will he enter to execute his office, if the kings of those kingdoms will not give him leave?[90]

At the same time, however, Laud's 'conciliarism' – like its Tudor forebears – emphasizes the unity of Church and State ('for both are but one Jerusalem'):[91] the church was the spiritual arm of this one commonwealth. While its ultimate authority might rest in Scripture, its temporal sovereign over all matters indifferent was the king. This understanding was to prove central to the religious policy of the 1630s.

While Laudianism was in part a 'revival of patristic and scholastic doctrines of the Church',[92] and Laudians, including Laud himself, were impressive scholars, it also displayed a revived love of order, with an implied sacramentalism that stressed the 'beauty of holiness'. One of the most important aspects of English theology, as Laud put it in a speech to the Star Chamber in 1637, was 'the external decent worship of God'.[93] At the same time, however, Laud stressed the doctrine of obedience, preaching on the importance of order and hierarchy rather than 'parity', at the opening of Parliament in February 1626.[94] Charles I similarly stressed the importance of order and of the unity between Church and State. He wrote to Abbot, Archbishop of Canterbury, in 1626:

> We have observed that the Church and the State are so nearly united and knit together, that though they may seem two bodies, yet indeed in some relation they may be accounted but as one, inasmuch as they both are made up of the same men, which are differenced only in relation to Spiritual or Civil ends. This nearness makes the Church call in the help of the State, to succour and support her, whensoever she is pressed beyond her strength: And the same nearness makes the State call in for the service of the Church, both to teach that duty which her Members know not, and to exhort them to, and to encourage them in that duty they know.[95]

This meant that Arminianism, with its emphasis on free will, was not necessarily in conflict with a strong doctrine of obedience. John Selden (1584–1654), one of the greatest minds of the period and the greatest of the early historians of tithes (a deeply controversial subject at the time), noted the irony of the situation:

> The Puritans who will allow no free-will at all, but God does all, yet will allow the subject his liberty to do or not to do, notwithstanding the king, the god upon earth. The Arminians, who hold we have free-will, yet say, when we come to the king there must be all obedience, and no liberty must be stood for.[96]

Laudianism

By 1628, Laud had been translated to the Diocese of London: he pursued a policy that sought to silence Calvinist preaching at St Paul's Cross – later exercised against Bishop John Davenant of

Salisbury in 1630 – and to ensure uniformity and conformity. While some sought to ban Sabbath-day activities, Laud, who replaced Abbot at Canterbury in 1633 and who 'deserves to rank among the greatest archbishops of Canterbury since the Reformation'[97] (although one of the least successful), revived the *Declaration of Sports*, which had allowed for sports and other recreations to be pursued on Sundays. The *Declaration* was to be read out in church, which provoked a number of bishops and other clergy into acts of defiance. Also in 1633 the issue of the position of altars returned to the centre of controversy.[98] St Gregory's church, next to St Paul's in London, was being rebuilt and was to have its altar placed against the east end of the church and fenced off. When an appeal by five parishioners to have it returned to the middle of the church appeared to be succeeding, Charles I intervened, referring the matter to the Privy Council, in which Neile (by this stage Archbishop of York) and Laud sat. Other bishops, including Matthew Wren (Norwich), and William Piers (Bath and Wells) encouraged similar moves. The railing of altars also implied that communion was to be received kneeling, which again provoked the puritan opposition.

The 1630s saw a degree of sometimes barbarous persecution of opponents of Laud's policy, which led to a number of more outspoken critics (including William Prynne, Henry Burton and John Bastwick) being found guilty of libel and having their ears cut off. Prynne was branded of both cheeks with the letters 'S. L.' for 'Seditious Libeler', which he called the 'Stigmata of Laud'.[99] The charges against Laud had concerned his support for the doctrine of episcopacy as *jure divino*, which, while hardly novel after Richard Bancroft's famous sermon of 1589,[100] had returned to the centre of controversy.[101] What Laud maintained was that, even though bishops were part of the divine law, the exercise of the power was 'derived wholly from the Crown', as he put it at his trial a few years later. He continued: 'for the exercise of this power under his Majesty, I have not used it to the contempt, but to the preservation, not the destruction of his people'.[102] A high doctrine of episcopacy like an Arminian doctrine of grace did not necessarily conflict with the King's sovereignty. In his reply to Prynne in the Star Chamber, Laud asserted: 'our being Bishops, *Jure divino*, by Divine Right, takes nothing from the Kings Right or power over us. For though our Office be from God and Christ immediately, yet may we not exercise that power, either of Order or Jurisdiction, but as God hath appointed us, that is, not in his Majesties, or any Christian Kings Kingdomes, but by and under the power of the King given us so to do'.[103] For Laud, then, bishops were the king's agents.

Laud's 'Anglicanism' was not marked by a wholesale doctrinal reform, or even a complete reshaping of liturgy: indeed, there was little in the official policy of the 1630s that differed from what had gone before. And yet, James I's caution in the exercise of policy was not continued under Laud: where most puritans had been happy to continue to support James and his bishops, even if they might have had some reservations about a number of the canons of 1604, by the end of the 1630s many of the moderate puritans had been alienated by what to some appeared a popish plot.[104] It was the efforts to impose a new set of canons and a modified version of the English prayer book on the Scots that revealed some of the major flaws in the King's religious policy, at least when applied to his northern Kingdom. The Scottish Canons of 1636 would have enforced a communion table at the 'upper end of the chancel or church'[105] and a new Prayer Book. When this was used for the first time in St Giles' Cathedral in Edinburgh in the summer of 1637, it provoked a riot. It was essentially a revised version of the 1552 Prayer Book, but with revisions that made it rather more like the 1549 Prayer Book in that it contained the prayer of oblation immediately after the Prayer of Consecration and the prayer of humble access immediately before reception. It also had prayers for the saints in the Prayer for the Church Militant. So controversial did the attempt to impose the book become, however, that shortly afterwards in 1638 the General Assembly of the Scottish Church drew up a National Covenant: the spread of Laud's 'Anglicanism' into Scotland was quickly and violently resisted.

Soon afterwards, the settlement of the English Church was decisively challenged in the resistance to the new canons that had been produced by Convocation in 1640.[106] While these again did nothing to assert anything novel in doctrine or church order, they nevertheless proved highly controversial. In particular, the so-called 'et cetera' oath that would have forced all clergy never to 'alter the government of this church by archbishops, bishops, deans and archdeacons, *et cetera*' proved particularly controversial as it was regarded by some as allowing for the possibility of government by other clergy – even the pope himself.[107] However, in the end, it was Laud, as Davies writes, who was the real casualty of the oath.[108] The years that followed saw warfare, the Commonwealth and the Protectorate, in which religion loomed large. Laud himself suffered the martyr's death in 1645, which was followed four years later by the execution of the King.

Efforts to reform the national church, however, proved impossible. A substantial number of theologians, most of whom represented different shades of Presbyterianism, together with a smattering of independents, met at Westminster from 1643. Initially, they were charged with reforming the Thirty-Nine Articles but were later asked to compose a Confession. This was completed in 1646 and contains a solidly Reformed expression of Faith. Article XXV, for instance, claims that the 'The Catholick or Universal Church which is invisible, consists of the whole number of the Elect, that have been, are, or shall be gathered into one, under Christ the Head thereof; and is, the Spouse, the body, the fulness of him that filleth all in all'. A few years later, the Westminster Assembly produced the *Directory for the Public Worship of God*, which was intended to provide directions for worship across the country to replace the Book of Common Prayer, although it was never adopted with much enthusiasm.[109] While Richard Baxter, one of the most prominent Presbyterians, commented that 'the Christian world, since the days of the apostles, had never had a Synod of more excellent divines (taking one thing with another) than this synod and the synod of Dort',[110] others were more deeply critical. John Milton, for instance, in his somewhat bitter poem, 'On the New Forcers of Conscience under the Long Parliament', thought it was characterized by 'plots and packings worse than Trent'.[111] His much-cited view of Presbyterianism was less than flattering. The poem concludes: 'When they shall read this clearly in your charge:/ New *Presbyter* is but old Priest writ large'.[112]

Conformity and uniformity could not be imposed in the highly volatile situation of Civil War and the Commonwealth and Protectorate that followed. Instead, there was a proliferation of sects, which meant that it was a degree of religious tolerance rather than either theocracy or uniformity that won the day in what one of the leading puritans called 'changeable and uncomposed times'.[113] The Westminster Assembly spent much of its time improving the quality of the ministry, a task that was followed by the work of the National Committee of Triers and local Committees of Ejectors. Cromwell claimed that 'there hath not been such a service to England since the Christian religion was professed in England'. He noted a marked improvement in the quality of ministry: only those would be admitted to office who 'could give a very good testimony of the grace of God in him'.[114]

This short period of religious liberty and toleration experienced during the Commonwealth and Protectorate was to have a profound effect on the nature of Anglican theology as it developed after the restoration of monarchy in 1660. Despite the collapse of the Church of England from 1640 to 1642, it was a distinct strand of 'Anglicanism' that survived underground and took on a more distinctive character as it differentiated itself from the other forms and expressions of Christianity. The Episcopate came to take on a particularly central role, but this was coupled with a particular emphasis on the sort of theology represented by the Laudians and other supporters of the King. As I will discuss in the next chapter, 'Anglicanism' emerged as a response to this somewhat unexpected experiment in religious toleration. 'In Cromwell's England', writes Judith Maltby, 'it was the suppression of [the liturgy, the calendar, and episcopacy] . . . that paradoxically helped to create a self-conscious "Anglicanism"'.[115]

Chapter 7

1662, Latitudinarianism and the Invention of Anglicanism

Jeremy Taylor's Booklist

It is not implausible to suggest that Anglicanism began in the year 1660. At the beginning of that momentous year after the collapse of the previous regime following the death of Oliver Cromwell, there was a degree of excitement in Britain and Ireland about the imminent return of the King. On 13 January, the eminent theologian and spiritual writer, Jeremy Taylor (1613–67), who was soon to be elevated to the Irish bishopric of Down and Connor, recommended a number of books to some Irish friends which he thought should form the basis for a reliable library of what could be considered Anglican theology.[1] At least in Taylor's eyes, Anglican theology – in the sense of the theology of the church that was soon likely to be re-established after a particularly difficult period – had achieved some sort of literary canon beyond the Book of Common Prayer and the Bible, which would serve to define its style and limits.

In the letter to his friends, Taylor listed 66 books under five headings: liturgy; church government; doctrine and polemics (by far the longest); ecclesiastical history and 'scholastic divinity'. The books listed represent some of the most important writers of the period but also reveal his understanding of what is important in Anglicanism: his list shows a resemblance to the authors later republished in the *Library of Anglo-Catholic Theology*. Under liturgy, for instance, he includes his own 1642 book on the liturgy as well as Henry Hammond's, *A Vindication of the Ancient Liturgie*. His selection of polemical works lists the standard high church anti-Catholic writing of the time, including Bramhall, Overall and Andrewes, but also contains the Lutheran John Gerhard's *loci communes.* This entry comes with a word of warning: 'you must pare away his two Lutheran spots viz of consubstantiation and ubiquity'. Similarly, he writes of the French Reformed minister, Daniel Chamier, that he 'is a very good writer but you must abate his Calvinism'.[2] Taylor also selects sermons by Andrewes, Anthony Farindon, preacher under Charles I at St George's, Windsor, and Robert Sanderson. A few years later, it should perhaps be noted, Jeremy Taylor's own classic works on *Holy Living* and *Holy Dying* would have been included in any such list along with those of his own works he had already selected (including his life of Christ, *The Great Exemplar*). Finally, Taylor instructs his correspondents to follow up this reading by moving to the 'fathers of the first 300 years at least, they are few and not very voluminous and they are the surest guides'.[3] For Taylor, then, the key texts are not drawn from the Reformers but from a highly selective group of churchmen, many of them associated with King Charles I and Archbishop Laud. As with the Oxford Movement in the nineteenth century, these writers were to be used to amplify the teachings of the Fathers of the Church.

This brief discussion demonstrates that in the 1660s, the Churches of England and Ireland were forced to focus on the question of identity: after all, regime change offers a good incentive to think about such matters, and when the church was so closely tied to the regime as the Church of England, some difficult questions could hardly be avoided. This meant some heart-searching for many in positions of authority in church and state after the Restoration of the monarch. This was a decisive period in the formation of Anglicanism as a denomination when it ceased simply to claim to be identical to the English church, even if there were continued struggles over what counted for orthodoxy. However, things were not settled at the time of the Restoration. The chief question was whether the Church of England would become comprehensive and incorporate as wide a range of views as possible or whether there would be efforts to return to something approaching the situation immediately before the outbreak of the Civil War but in a very different context. The brief, if limited, success of Presbyterianism and independency during the Commonwealth and the sheer diversity of different sects that emerged through the period demonstrated the simple truth that the old model of one episcopal church co-extensive with the one state was not the only option. Even if some clung on to the Book of Common Prayer through the Interregnum, the idea and institution of episcopacy and the church it represented had been decisively challenged: the execution of William Laud, Archbishop of Canterbury, in 1645 was a particularly salutary reminder of this fact.

The Restoration Settlement

In 1660, however, it was not clear precisely what would happen to the churches of the British Isles on the Restoration of the Stuarts. 'Anglicanism' with its bishops and uniformity was not the only option on offer. The new King, Charles II, it seems, had a genuine and strong desire to re-establish the Church of England by making it as broad as possible. It was to embrace what was called at the time 'comprehension' so that it might be able to contain moderates of all views. In what would have been a revolutionary departure from the earlier settlement, it was possible that members of the Church of England might only have had to agree on certain fundamentals, while on non-essentials there could be a variety of practices and interpretations. In his famous Declaration of Breda of 4 April 1660, which was read to both Houses of Parliament shortly before his return on 29 May, Charles II expressed his desire to allow a degree of breadth in the future Church:

> Because the passion and uncharitableness of the times have produced several opinions in religion, by which men are engaged in parties and animosities against each other (which, when they shall hereafter unite in a freedom of conversation, will be composed or better understood), we do declare a liberty to tender consciences, and that no man shall be disquieted or called in question for differences of opinion in matter of religion, which do not disturb the peace of the kingdom.[4]

Such a 'liberty to tender consciences' was certainly not one of the hallmarks of his father's approach to the Church of England or the other churches of his realm, even if it was more typical of his grandfather's. In 1660, it thus looked quite feasible that things would change in the Church of England and there would not simply be a return to the old order which had proved so divisive in the late 1630s. This meant that given the King's apparently progressive views, as I. M. Green wrote, '[t]he Restoration should have seen the emergence of a new form of church government'.[5] But despite the apparently promising situation of 1660, in practice quite the opposite happened.

Even before Breda, a number of supporters of episcopacy showed that they were prepared to make significant concessions to some of the demands of the puritans for a reformed ministry. Thus, John Gauden (1599/1600?–1662), a chaplain to the King and shortly to be appointed Bishop of Exeter and later Worcester, showed himself to be a supporter of Archbishop James Ussher's idea of 'Ignatian' or 'primitive episcopacy', which had been influential in Ireland before the Civil War.[6] Such a view of episcopacy would have made bishops far less princely rulers of massive dioceses and more pastoral overseers of small groups of clergy.[7] Gauden, who had written a defence of episcopacy against Presbyterianism, *Hiera dakrya, ecclesiae Anglicanae suspira* (1659), nevertheless preached a conciliatory sermon *Slight Healers of Publique Hurts* at St Paul's in February 1660 in thanksgiving for the restoration of 'secluded members' to the House of Commons. In a lengthy subtitle, he called his sermon 'a door of hope thereby opened to the fulness and freedom of future Parliaments: the most probable means under God for healing the hurts, and recovering the health of these three Brittish kingdoms'.[8] Through the course of the extensive text, he made demands for significant church reform. Churches should be governed, he claimed,

> not by the *Dominion* and the *pomp, luxury* and *tyranny* of *Bishops*, nor yet by the *factious* and *refractory humours* of *Presbyters*, much less by the *schismatick saucinesse* of people, who cast off both *Bishops* and *Presbyters*; but by the *fatherly gravity*, prudence and Eminence of godly and Reverend *Bishops*; by the brotherly *assistance*, and *son-like subordination* of sober and *orderly Presbyters*, by the *service* and *obsequiousness* of *humble* and *diligent Deacons*; and by the meek submission

of Christian people to the Care, Monition, Counsel, and respective *Superiority* of every order; as sheep to their Chief *Shepherds*, and their *Assistants*, or *Attendants*.[9]

After Charles's return, there were a number of efforts to put the Breda Declaration into practice. Most important was the Worcester House Declaration[10] of 25 October 1660, in which leading theologians of different opinions participated. These included Gauden and Richard Baxter, one of the leading puritans (or 'reconcilers' as they would have preferred to have been called).[11] The Royal Declaration, which was presented to the House of Lords on 9 November, went a long way to satisfy the demands of the Puritans and aimed to 'gratify the private consciences of those who are aggrieved with the use of some ceremonies'[12] provided there was some degree of unity in fundamentals. The old thorny issues of the wearing of the surplice, the sign of the cross at Baptism, bowing at the holy name and kneeling at Communion, which came up in many of the earlier religious struggles over the nature of the Church of England from Elizabethan times, were not to be considered matters requiring a uniformity of practice. Charles thus declared: 'No Man shall be compelled to bow at the Name of Jesus, or suffer in any Degree for not doing it; without reproaching those who out of their Devotion continue that ancient Ceremony of the Church'. Similarly, 'For the Use of the Surplice, We are contented that all Men be left to their Liberty to do as they shall think fit, without suffering in the least Degree for wearing or not wearing it'. There was the promise of many other concessions. It was, for instance, to be possible for those being ordained and inducted into ecclesiastical offices to do so without taking the oath of canonical obedience to a bishop, provided the oaths of allegiance and supremacy were sworn. Reforms were also proposed to modify the exercise of episcopacy or oversight by bishops of lower clergy and parishes. These included the creation of a number of suffragan or assistant bishops. This might have made it far more acceptable to those who had adopted the more locally based, accountable and less hierarchical Presbyterian system. Toleration of non-essentials within the boundaries of the one church obviously displayed huge concessions to the Puritans. Indeed, the Worcester House Declaration and Charles's declaration before the House of Lords can be considered 'a remarkable step in meeting Puritan objections and aspirations'.[13] Had such concessions been adopted, it might have changed the face of the Church of England for ever: there might have been a comprehensive church instead of a 'denominational' Anglicanism, at least of the kind presented by Jeremy Taylor to his friends.

And yet on 28 November 1660, Parliament failed to accept the declaration and to enact a statute to put it into practice: the vote was lost by 183 to 157 votes in the House of Commons.[14] In effect, this meant that it would only be a matter of time before Puritan opinion would be driven out altogether from the Church of England. Of course, given the dismemberment of the church in the Commonwealth and Protectorate when episcopacy had been abolished, this would mean that the policy would have the effect of going much further even than the policy of the 1630s. Thus, while for the most part, as I demonstrated in Chapter 6, the Church of England had managed to *contain* Puritanism before the Civil War (despite much conflict and bitterness), the uneasy truce could no longer be maintained after the experiments in alternative polities in the Commonwealth.[15] The November 1660 parliamentary defeat of the Declaration can be seen as the beginning of the end of the comprehensive national church. It might thus be regarded, at least symbolically – and undoubtedly only in hindsight – as the setting in stone of a denomination called 'Anglicanism' set against alternative models of church polity and order.

The defeat in the Commons meant that the discussions in the months immediately after the Worcester House Declaration, most importantly the Savoy Conference of 1661 which met to examine the revision of the Book of Common Prayer, were not held in the same spirit of trust and reconciliation. Richard Baxter, who was the leading inspiration behind the production of a more reformed prayer book,[16] and who was one of the key representatives of the twelve Puritans, noted that 'we spoke to the deaf'.[17] Bishop Gilbert Sheldon of London (and afterwards Archbishop of Canterbury), who had ensured that Baxter and another Presbyterian were barred from sitting in Convocation, was able to dictate the terms of the Conference, which met in his house. In the end, there was little agreement between the parties except for a declaration that there was agreement on fundamentals. Assessing the outcome of the Conference, Baxter wrote in his autobiography: 'We were all agreed on the ends, for the Church's welfare, Unity and Peace, and His Majesty's Happiness and Contentment, but after all our debates, were disagreed of the means. And this was the end of that Assembly and Commission'.[18] Where the Church of England had earlier managed to embrace loyal churchmen of widely divergent opinions, even when they were locked in conflict over the nature of that church, things had changed after 28 November 1660: there was simply no more room at the inn for very many puritans.

This attitude of exclusion reached its climax in the Act for the Uniformity of Public Prayers, which was, according to John Spurr, 'the product of parliamentary horse-trading rather than theological self-definition'.[19] The Act received Royal Assent on 19 May 1662 and was to be implemented by St Bartholomew's Day, 24 August of the same year.[20] From that day, all licensed ministers in parishes and elsewhere had to submit to episcopal ordination, and all clergy had to take an oath of 'unfeigned assent and consent to all and everything contained and prescribed in' the (modestly) revised Prayer Book, which was appended to the statute. Similarly, all preachers had to assent to the Thirty-Nine Articles in order 'for the ministers of the church to be of sound religion'. The Act of Uniformity clearly reveals that a comprehensiveness that might have included moderate puritans in the Church of England had proved impossible in the complex situation of the early 1660s. Thus, while the Act 'did not create a breach within English Protestantism, for that had been growing over the preceding two decades, . . . it did prevent the union of moderate Presbyterians with the established church and set the legal boundaries within which a Restoration Anglicanism would be elaborated'.[21] For many, the Act was shocking, especially after such high hopes had been kindled by the Breda Declaration. Some expressed deep anxiety, including the diarist Samuel Pepys, whose own minister at St Olave's, Hart Street in the City of London, was deprived of his living. Pepys wrote in his diary of 22 June 1662 that the 'true spirit of the nation . . . will have liberty of conscience in spite of this act of uniformity, or they will die. . . . I confess I do think that the Bishops will never be able to carry it so high as they do'.

On 17 August, the week before the implementation of the Act, he lamented: 'I hear most of the Presbyters took their leaves today. And the city is most dissatisfied with it. I pray God keep peace among us and make the Bishops careful of bringing in their room, or else all will fly a-pieces'.[22] In the event, the country did not 'fly-a-pieces' or erupt into further bloodshed. Instead, non-conformity grew as a significant if only semi-tolerated force, which meant that a counter-current of English protestant dissent grew alongside 'Anglicanism' as the established religion.

After the imposition of the Act, some 936 incumbents (or by some estimates significantly more) were deprived of their ecclesiastical livings. In the following few years, a number of relatively harsh laws (the so-called Clarendon Code, named after the Lord Chancellor, the Earl of Clarendon) were introduced to proscribe public worship and advancement by those who dissented from the Act. And, as if to rub in the point, the cult of King Charles the Martyr, the only saint to be canonized by Act of Parliament,[23] was encouraged: 30 January was to be kept as a fast day, and by 1675, a statue had been erected at Charing Cross. Despite the official policy of repression, however, there were still a number of further efforts at comprehension right through to the 1680s, all of which proved equally unsuccessful.[24] There remained the constant fear that too much comprehension would simply result in a church embracing schism within itself, which would lead to the sort of anarchy that emerged from the 1630s and which flourished in the Commonwealth. As one anonymous Member of Parliament put it, 'A Church that grows numerous by taking in Dissenters, may be no stronger than an Army that fills up its Company with Mutineers'.[25] In the end, comprehension within the Church of England proved more threatening than the creation of dissent alongside the Church. By the 1680s, however, there had increasingly been legal acceptance of dissenters outside the Church of England, a situation that was finally enshrined in the 1689 Act of Toleration. The fear of schism – and of warfare – were both real and determinative. Whatever the reasons, however, the struggle for the identity of the Church of England was decisively altered by the rejection of the Worcester House Declaration and the 1662 Act of Uniformity. There could simply be no going back. The irony of 1662 was noted by Norman Sykes:

The Restoration Church Settlement, for better and for worse, marked the parting of the ways in England. A 'comprehension' might have reduced the Independents and Baptists to a comparatively insignificant minority, and delayed the advent of toleration. Instead, the failure of comprehension and the victory of toleration (partial and restricted though it was) opened a great door and was effectual in the future history and development of the English religious tradition.[26]

It was precisely this failure of reconciliation and comprehension after the Commonwealth that helped forge Anglican identity. The fact that after 1662 – and more decisively after the Act of Toleration in 1689 – there was no comprehensive protestant church comprising virtually all Englishmen and women apart from the more radical sectarians meant that the Church of England had to take on the status of being one church among others. As one writer comments, 'At the Restoration [the Worcester House Declaration] marked the high water-mark of mutual concessions. At the Revolution the last Bill for comprehension would look back nostalgically to Worcester House as the one real hope of union between Churchmen and Dissenters'. [27] With the failure of comprehension especially after 1689 what the Church of England was and what it was not, who was in and who was not in, became increasingly important questions since they were tied up with questions of political power. This meant that since it failed to embrace everybody within its ranks, whether it liked it or not, the Church of England had become something like a denomination. It is thus fair to conclude that the Church of England could no longer plausibly maintain its earlier claim to be the universal religious expression of the English people. While privileged and established, its hold on the nation had changed: 'in 1689', as Judith Maltby writes, 'a *national* church was finally replaced by the more pragmatic idea of an *established* church'.[28] Similarly, John Spurr noted that the Toleration Act was a product of a parliament that 'understood Anglicanism as a badge of political and ideological trustworthiness; widening the terms of communion meant widening access to office; but a toleration would simply allow freedom of worship, while restricting political power to safe hands. The cost to the church of England was incalculable'.[29] While this judgement might perhaps be a little overstated, it is nevertheless undeniable that the Church of England was simple one privileged member of a family of denominations. This meant that the unity of church and state maintained by Richard Hooker – 'there is not any man of the Church of England but the same man is also a member of the commonwealth; nor any man a member of the commonwealth which is not also of the Church of England'[30] – had finally broken down. Or, as Norman Sykes put it somewhat more provocatively and somewhat tastelessly in the mid-twentieth century: 'For better and for worse the Tudor theory of the identity of Church and State had been finally shattered; and the future pattern of English religious life was never to approach the ideal of ein Reich, ein Volk, eine Kirche'.[31]

This discussion of the Restoration has helped explain some of the complexities I outlined at the beginning of the chapter: the relative comprehensiveness of the Elizabethan and early Stuart churches which embraced a significant amount of disagreement and debate (and where most puritans remained loyal to the Church of England) mutated after 1660 into an Anglicanism established on a notion of absolute uniformity to the Book of Common Prayer. Where Elizabethan and Jacobean uniformity was contested from within, however, after 1662, dissent was driven out and different churches began to coexist. This meant that at least from the time of the Restoration onwards, the particular identity of Anglicanism as a church – and at this point this meant little more than the Churches of England and Ireland – had to be defined as one church within the wider economy of churches. Jeremy Taylor's 1660 booklist may even have unwittingly been the starting point of Anglican self-definition, which has been a process that has continued ever since. The fundamental question, however, remains that of the relationship between the church before 1662 and that which developed afterwards, especially as it was the post-1662 church that was responsible for the expansion of Anglicanism overseas. In expounding Anglican theology it soon becomes clear that there is a contested and often extremely volatile relationship between the Church of England of the Reformation and the Elizabethan Settlement, and what came later. Indeed, as I have shown through the course of this book, later discussions about the 'Anglican' identity of the Church of England in the hundred and thirty or so years after the break with Rome until the Act of Uniformity were frequently attempts to impose a particular ideology or narrative of identity on the church of the past. In the process they could easily distort history almost beyond recognition.

Restoration, Comprehensiveness and the Via Media

Despite the failure of comprehension and the Act of Uniformity, however, the Church of England still retained a vision of itself as a 'comprehensive' church, which steered a middle way between Rome, on the one hand, and the dissenters on the other. While there is an obvious similarity with what went before in the sense that many earlier theologians sought to exclude the more radical branches of puritanism and Roman Catholicism,[32] the post-1662 situation gave a different flavour to comprehensiveness. 'Anglicanism' could accommodate far less than beforehand, and had begun to define itself far more as an 'episcopal' church centred on ordered worship. Doctrinal latitude went hand in hand with liturgical uniformity. The somewhat hackneyed understanding of the Church of England as a *via media* thus needs serious qualification. In the pre-Restoration church, it was developed by a number of 'avant-garde conformists', including Richard Hooker. There was, as might be expected in the climate of humanistic learning in which the leading theologians and churchmen were educated, a strongly Aristotelian background to the idea of a *via media*.

The Aristotelian golden mean, which steers between excess and deficiency, was regarded as the balanced solution to ethical problems, which naturally led to an emphasis on measuring everything in terms of the middle way. The earliest proponent of such a theology seems to have been Richard Montagu, Bishop of Chichester, who, as has been discussed in the previous chapter, was one of the strongest supporters of Charles I and William Laud. In 1624, he noted in a letter to the young John Cosin, at the time recently appointed to a prebendary of Durham (and to be its Bishop at the Restoration), that God should raise up leaders in the Church of England to fill 'in the gapp against Puritanisme and Popery, the Scilla and Charybdis of antient piety'.[33] The English church was portrayed as a ship sailing in the dangerous narrows of the clear water between extremes on either side.[34] Nevertheless, references to the *via media*, however, are infrequent, and it does not seem to have been associated with 'Anglicanism' as a particular ideology. A notable and interesting exception, however, comes from an outsider, Thomas Harrab, a Roman Catholic polemicist, who seems first to have developed the idea in 1616 of what he called 'Anglianisme',[35] which was disparagingly likened to the 'Turkisme of the Turks'.[36] In an analysis of the four different schismatic versions of Christianity, Anglianisme, he believed, stood between Calvinism and his own religion because it 'retaineth yet some ceremonies of ancient Religion, although daily decreasing'.[37] According to Harrab, this middle way derived from Elizabeth I who believed, he felt, 'that Calvin's Religion was too leane, and the Catholike Religion too fat, because the one had many ceremonies, the other none'.[38] He concluded:

> the religion of England, is composed of Catholike religion, of Lutheranisme, and Calvinisme, and yet approacheth no one of them, but differeth much from every one of them, singled out by themselves. Divers ceremonies thou seest in this Religion, and divers rejected, so that this is plainly the fourth brother with halfe a beard.[39]

In later developments of this sort of model, much has been made of the so-called *via media*. This sees Anglicanism as a kind of 'bridge church' between protestants and Roman Catholics, which is something that would certainly have surprised the solidly protestant theologians of Elizabethan England, even if there is possibly an element of truth with regard to Elizabeth I's own religion.

Latitudinarians

After the Restoration, the understanding of the Church of England as a *via media* was noted by Simon Patrick (1626–1707), at the time vicar of St Paul's, Covent Garden, and later appointed Bishop of Chichester and then Ely following the accession of William and Mary. For Patrick, however, such a mean was no longer Aristotelian but was based upon an openness to the new learning which would allow the Church to keep up with developments in scholarship. In a letter to an 'Oxford friend' published in 1662,[40] Patrick reveals an attitude quite different from Montagu and the Laudians: the context of the letter was his failure to be appointed as Master of Queens' College, Cambridge, when a Royalist sympathizer was appointed by the King. In the letter, he defines a 'new sect of Latitude-men', while at the same time maintaining a degree of distance from them.[41] He notes a new breadth and undogmatic character among this group which distanced them from both Presbyterians and Roman Catholics. They stood for a new form of thought which sought an alliance between faith and reason. In a purple passage he claimed that the 'latitude men' in the Church of England stood as a 'virtuous mediocrity' between what he calls 'the meretricious gaudiness of the Church of *Rome* and the squalid sluttery of fanatick conventicles'. He goes on:

Devotion is so overclad by the Papists that she is oppressed and stifled with the multitudes of her own garments. . . . Some of our modern Reformers to make amends have stripped her stark naked, till she is become in a manner cold and dead. The Church of England only hath dressed her as befits an honorable and virtuous matron.[42]

The method of the latitudinarians, however, made use of a new philosophy 'which they think is much ancienter than *Aristotle*'. While Patrick thought he was too old to learn such Platonic novelties, he was sympathetic with the new sect on the grounds that it 'was a great bug-beare to Presbyterians as a Crosse and a Surplisse'.[43] '*New philosophy*', he claimed, 'will bring in *new Divinity*; and freedom in the one will make men desire a liberty in the other'.[44] He goes on to show that the Church has nothing to fear from true philosophy and counsels: 'let her old loving Nurse, the *Platonick Philosophy* be admitted again into her family'.[45] This alone would give the Church the weapons to keep up with the progress in scientific knowledge: 'True Philosophy can never hurt sound Divinity'.[46]

Such Platonism was represented in Cambridge by a group of men who were labelled 'Cambridge Platonists' in the nineteenth century, who included Benjamin Whichcote, Provost of King's College, and Ralph Cudworth, Master of Christ's.[47] Their philosophy was based on a sense of the fallibility of the human mind which meant that certainty was always qualified. In one of his aphorisms, for instance, Whichcote could write:

> Our Fallibility and the Shortness of our Knowledge should
> make us peaceable and gentle: because I may be Mistaken,
> I must not be dogmatical and confident, peremptory and
> imperious. I will not break the certain Laws of Charity, for a
> doubtful Doctrine or of uncertain Truth.[48]

Cudworth similarly emphasized that the truth of the Gospel was something that rested beyond mere words and was to be experienced in the life of the believer. 'The Gospel', he wrote, 'cannot save us; no more than that Physician's Bill could cure the ignorant Patient of his disease, who, when it was commended to him, took the Paper only and put it up in his pocket, but never drank the Potion that was prescribed by it'.[49] This revived Platonism was influential in many figures who went on to prominent positions in the Church of England. While always a minority alongside the more dogmatic conformists, the Cambridge Platonists nevertheless continued to exert an influence on a number of later figures, including S. T. Coleridge, and F. D. Maurice, two of the most prominent English theological writers of the nineteenth century.[50]

In their own time, the Platonists were influential on a number of figures later associated with Latitudinarianism,[51] who had made a name for themselves in some of the most prominent London pulpits.[52] These included Simon Patrick but also a number of other bishops who rose to prominence after 1688, including Edward Fowler, Bishop of Gloucester, who had produced a book *The Principles and Practices of certain moderate divines of the Church of England (greatly mis-understood), truly represented and defended*,[53] which took as its motto a passage from St Paul's letter to the Philippians: 'Let your moderation be known unto all men'. He presented a strongly practical Gospel:

None have with more strength of reason demonstrated, that the grand designe of the Gospel is to make men good: not to intoxicate their brains with notions, not furnish their heads with a systeme of opinions; but to reform men's lives and to purifie their natures: which noble principle together with the former, doth utterly overthrow that *Latitudinarianism* they are accused of.[54]

The principle adopted by such latitudinarians is that of being as open as possible. In religion, there was a proper place for disputation:

Amicable disputes sometimes, merely in order to the finding out of Truth, can have no other than a good effect: and moreover, they add to the pleasure of Conversation. And therefore let the Professors of Christianity labour for the true spirit and temper of Christians; and it will be as well with the Christian World, as if we were all of the same mind. I mean, let us not magisterially impose upon one another, and be so charitable as to believe well of Dissenters from us that live good lives, are of modest and peaceable deportment, and hold no Opinions, that directly oppose the design of the Christian Religion, and of making men like to God; and then we shall see, that there will be little reason to desire an Infallible Judge of Controversie, to make us all of one Opinion.[55]

Edward Stillingfleet, later to be Bishop of Worcester, had used the same biblical motto in his *Irenicum* of 1660. Arguing against the divine right of any particular form of church government, he felt that uniformity of practice was not something that could be attained because of 'the different perswasions of mens minds'.[56] Such an understanding was reflected in the works of other prominent churchmen including Gilbert Burnet, Bishop of Salisbury, and two archbishops of Canterbury, Thomas Tenison and John Tillotson: among them there was a keenness for critical enquiry and for an accommodation of religion to the new science. They were also keen to ensure that the ideal of a national church which might even include dissenters at least remained a possibility: eirenicism and comprehension remained their abiding interest.[57]

It should be noted, however, that such a model was far from universally held: many 'high church' figures were deeply suspicious of latitudinarianism and the toleration that came out of it. With the promotion of latitudinarians to bishoprics after 1689, there was a real sense to those who were anxious of the watering down of the claims of the established Church, of the 'church in danger', even if others felt such challenges were overblown. One Whig (or 'low') churchman wrote in 1696: 'The Church of England is always represented, as at this time, in greater danger than it ever was'.[58] Although the Archbishop of Canterbury (Sancroft) and seven other bishops refused to swear the oath of allegiance to the Crown and became non-jurors, together with about 400 clergy, their influence soon waned even if Thomas Ken and William Law became prominent writers. The 'high churchmen' who remained in the church continued to hold to the church principles that had been honed in the seventeenth century and resisted those who sought toleration and latitude, which led to real division in the early 1700s.[59] There was an increasing polarization between high church and low church, even if such titles were always fluid and ill-defined.[60] However, what is clear is that for many more conservative churchmen, the latitudinarians were failing to protect the church. One writer claimed at the end of the seventeenth century:

> there seems to be an universal Conspiracy amongst a sort of Men, under the Style of Deists, Socinians, Latitudinarians, Deniers of Mysteries, and pretending Explainers of them, to undermine and overthrow the Catholick Faith. There seems too much reason to fear, there is no Order, Degree, not Place among us, wholly free from the Infection.[61]

A few years later, Henry Sacheverell preached a sermon on 5 November 1709 attacking Toleration as the seed of dissent, while his adversary Benjamin Hoadly was accused of anti-monarchism. Latitudinarianism, which developed a sense of comprehensiveness within the Church of England as well as an openness to those outside, was one competing vision of the church in the late seventeenth and early eighteenth centuries. Built as it was upon the principle of human fallibility, it was always open to the accusation of a denial of the singularity of the truth. Indeed, the high churchmen who retained a sense of continuity with their Laudian predecessors were only too willing to dismiss toleration as a denial of the very substance of the Church. Both, however, were – perhaps unwittingly – reshaping the Church of England as a denomination: the low churchmen had begun to see the church as one voluntary group among others, while the high churchmen had continued to stress the distinctiveness of the Church of England over and against those outside. The idea of a *national* church was something that was becoming increasingly difficult to maintain.

Much theological debate in the years that have followed has been shaped by a resistance to Latitudinarianism. Since the eighteenth century, there have been frequent cries of 'church in danger', and many efforts to distinguish 'real' Christianity from the nominal and lukewarm religion that appeared to many subsequent writers to characterize the eighteenth century. This was, of course, one of the main aspects of the Evangelical Revival, which began later in that century, with its emphasis on personal conversion and practical rather than conventional religion. This is tellingly illustrated by the full title of William Wilberforce's *A Practical View of the Prevailing Religious Systems in Higher and Middle Classes in this Country contrasted with Real Christianity*.[62] What precisely constituted 'real' Christianity, however, was evidently open to question. And this brings me full circle to where I began this book: Evangelicalism as it developed became embroiled in the controversies of the past, and many of its divisions and distinctive emphases mirrored the conflicts that had divided those of earlier generations. Although many figures of the early Evangelical revival, including John Wesley, can be regarded as high churchmen and were influenced by the seventeenth century writers including Jeremy Taylor, as the movement progressed and came to maturity within the Church of England, so it came to present a particular model of what constituted the authentic identity of the Church of England. As I discussed in Chapter 3, it gradually came to be focused on an appreciation of a history in which the Reformation played a significant and decisive role. While obviously a gross simplification, it is fair to say that what emerged from the Evangelical revival represents a reshaping of a tradition back towards the sixteenth century and away from the seventeenth. The writings of the Reformers and the example of the Marian martyrs developed into a paradigm for what the Church of England ought to be when shorn of its Laudian and high church accretions.

On the other hand, however, there were those who responded to the seventeenth and eighteenth centuries not by returning to the Reformation, but by doing their best to retain the high church identity of the Church of England. While there were many precursors in the High Churchmen of the eighteenth and early nineteenth centuries,[63] the most prominent nineteenth-century defenders of the high church tradition, and certainly those with the longest after-effect were those associated with the Oxford Movement, whom I have discussed through the course of this book as they sought a distinct historical identity for the Church of England. For the Tractarians, 'real' Christianity was rooted in a past that was quite distinct from that of Rome but also from Protestantism. For John Henry Newman – at least before his conversion to Rome – the Church of England was not to be equated with Protestantism but stood between the Reformation and Romanism. In his 1837 *Lectures on the Prophetical Office of the Church*, he outlined his understanding of where precisely the Church of England stood:

> though it is not likely that Roman Catholics will ever again become formidable in England, yet they may be in a position to make their voice heard, and in proportion as they are able, the Via Media will do important service of the following kind. In the controversy which will ensue, Rome will not fail to preach far and wide the tenet which it never conceals, that there is no salvation external to its communion. On the other hand, Protestantism, as it exists among us, will not be behindhand in consigning to external ruin all who are adherents of Roman doctrine. What a prospect is this! two widely spread and powerful parties dealing forth solemn anathemas upon each other, in the name of the Lord.[64]

Against such extremes the Church of England was to maintain a vision of the truth in what he called 'characteristic calmness and caution'. However, while it was 'clear and decided in its view', it gave 'no encouragement to lukewarmness and liberalism', and withheld 'all absolute anathemas on errors of opinion, except where the primitive Church sanctions the use of them'. By rooting his understanding of the Church in the theology of the Fathers, Newman was able to locate an essential core of Anglicanism which contained 'the practical exercise of our faith' but which was a long way removed from the eclectic principle of comprehensiveness or the tolerance of latitudinarianism. This, he felt, would lead to 'a recognised theology' based not on 'invention, nor originality, nor sagacity, nor even learning in our divines', but on 'a peculiarly sound judgement, patient thought, discrimination, a comprehensive mind, an abstinence from all private fancies and caprices and personal tastes – in a word, divine wisdom'.[65] Such wisdom, Newman held, had been demonstrated perhaps most clearly by Bishop Thomas Wilson, the reforming bishop of Sodor and Man in the eighteenth century, whose writings were comprehensively republished in seven volumes of the *Library of Anglo-Catholic Theology*. Thus, Newman wrote: 'Until we can produce diocese, or place of education, or populous town, or colonial department, or the like, administered on our distinctive principles, as the diocese of Sodor and Man in the days of Bishop Wilson, doubtless we have not as much to urge in our behalf as we might have'.[66] As he moved from the Church of England, so Newman came to believe that another Bishop Wilson would be unlikely, and, more importantly, that the Church of England lacked a clear understanding of truth. Indeed, he gradually became convinced that there was no solution to the situation of the Church of England as he had described it in the 1830s: it appeared to lack a definitive doctrinal base and authoritative voice. He wrote in the *Via Media*:

It may be argued that the Church of England, as established by law, and existing in fact, has never represented a doctrine at all or been the development of a principle, has never had an intellectual basis; that it has been but a name, or a department of the state, or a political party, in which religious opinion was an accident, and therefore has been various. In consequence, it has been but the theatre of contending religionists, that is, of Papists and Latitudinarians, softened externally, or modified into inconsistency by their birth and education, or restrained by their interests and their religious engagements.[67]

Newman became dissatisfied with a church that appeared to offer no dogmatic certainty and that, in his opinion, was little more than a department of state. On such a model, latitudinarianism had much to answer for.

Conclusion

The contending models of Anglican theology rooted in the sixteenth, seventeenth and eighteenth centuries that I have presented in some detail through the course of this book by a close engagement with history continue to shape contemporary debate in Anglicanism, but the circumstances have changed beyond all recognition: Anglican theology is no longer equated with the theology of the Church of England. This presents a number of serious and sometimes intractable problems, since theologies developed in the very particular political and social circumstances of England (and to a certain extent in Ireland) take on a quite different shape when applied to new circumstances with distinct political and constitutional histories. Nevertheless, they still continue to exert a great influence over the many independent churches of the Anglican Communion. The development of non-English Anglican theology forms the subject of my next chapter. Its possible future – or futures – will be addressed in the concluding chapter

Chapter 8
Theology and the Anglican Communion

Most of this book has been concerned with the construction of Anglican theology and identity as they emerged partly under the influence of the extraordinary period of publishing enterprise in Victorian England. Competing versions of Anglicanism developed out of very particular ways of reading the past. The different chapters have revealed various interpretations of what constitutes Anglican theology. While the models I have presented are far from comprehensive, they should nevertheless give the impression that Anglican theology is both highly complex and highly contested. There are definite gaps in my coverage, particularly the eighteenth century, which many have argued was a much more interesting period in English Church history,[1] not least because of the Evangelical revival, and I could no doubt have devoted more space to the Great Tew Circle[2] or some of the great poets such as John Donne or George Herbert. Nevertheless, I hope that what I have covered will give a picture of competing versions of what constitutes the Anglican tradition and Anglican theology. For contemporary Anglicans, however, the biggest gap is that because the discussion has been essentially historical, there has been very little discussion of Anglican theology outside England (with the occasional foray into Ireland). A different kind of book on Anglican theology might have begun with the present worldwide denomination and worked backwards, although such a method would have been too ambitious for a book of this size.[3] However, given that the churches of the Anglican Communion now make up the third largest Christian grouping with a stated membership of approximately 80 million, in which the Church of England is one church among many others, the focus on England is obviously a deficiency that needs to be addressed. This final chapter outlines the theology of the Anglican Communion, which is a network of churches, most of which – though not all – owe their existence to the Church of England and which have developed over the last two hundred years or so.[4] After a discussion of the origins of what can be termed 'Anglican Communion theology', I conclude with a discussion of the quest for an authentic Anglican theology into the present.

'The Anglican Way'

By way of contrast to my earlier chapters on the development of Anglican theology, which have begun in the nineteenth century, I shall focus on one recent and more international initiative in identity formation, which, as with my previous chapter, concerns the production of a bibliography for those interested in Anglicanism. Over the years, the modest international bodies of the Anglican Communion – variously called the 'instruments of communion' or 'instruments of unity'[5] – have commissioned various reports to help explain what Anglicanism is and how Anglican churches are supposed to relate to one another. Over three hundred years from the time when Jeremy Taylor produced his booklist for his Irish friends, the so-called 'Primates' of the Anglican Communion[6] meeting in Brazil in 1983 set up a working group called 'Theological Education in the Anglican Communion' (TEAC). Its aim was to monitor the styles and content of educational programmes for both clergy and laity across the constituent churches throughout the world. Part of its charge was that of 'understanding and describing our unique ethos and contribution to the wider Church'. To this end, and perhaps rather optimistically, it has sought to chart some agreed expectations for Anglican theological education and formation across the world and to produce a basic curriculum for what might count as 'The Anglican Way'.[7]

In its work on 'The Anglican Way', TEAC has produced a number of more or less useful documents and flow charts about what a curriculum might look like as well as lists of books that, it suggests, all institutions offering Anglican theological education in English ought to have in their libraries. These lists are very informative.

What is most striking about them is that there is nothing at all on the English Reformation or the Elizabethan Settlement or the seventeenth century – and no works that might be regarded as theological classics, such as John Jewel's *Apology* (although there is one recent book of selections of 'Anglican' spiritual writers).[8] There is a lack of historical consciousness, which makes the sort of approach I have adopted in this book virtually redundant. While no doubt many of the books on Anglicanism that are listed contain sections on the religious changes of the sixteenth and seventeenth centuries and discussions of the theology that developed, the main focus of the books chosen is on the international denominational identity of contemporary Anglicanism. In fact, the first book listed is the Report of the Lambeth Conference of 1998,[9] which does at least have the advantage of making explicit some of the most divisive aspects of the relationships between the different churches of recent years. Yet, there is no primary source or even a text book on the English Reformation; neither is there anything on the Book of Common Prayer or the Thirty-Nine Articles, which were undeniably formative in the teaching and identity of the Church of England and later of its many progeny. It is very hard to imagine a similar body initiated by the Lutheran World Federation failing to offer some sort of basic guidance to the German Reformation and the theology of Luther and the Augsburg Confession, which, for Lutherans, offers 'a pure exposition of the Word of God'.[10] In relation to the chapters above, the TEAC booklists are a very long way from the Parker Society or the *Library of Anglo-Catholic Theology*.

While it would be rash to conjecture about the reasons for the absence of books on the English Reformation or the later Divines in a bibliography on 'The Anglican Way', and while it is probably unfair to be overly critical of what is intended as a very pragmatic set of suggestions, the booklist is symptomatic of a reading of Anglican identity which has been particularly influential at least since the mid-nineteenth century. Many Anglicans have been unsure about where to look for norms and sources of theology and they have been wary of using history. Where Lutherans can be secure that they should at least look to Luther and the Augsburg Confession, even if they might disagree profoundly about interpretation, Anglicans have frequently been rather less certain about what constitutes their key identity – and for many contemporary Anglicans, none of the nineteenth-century interpretations of the past seems entirely adequate, especially when these have often been experienced along with the colonial expansion of the British Empire with which Anglicanism was often associated. What has emerged as the most commonly expressed feature of denominational identity has been a kind of latitudinarianism shorn of its Whiggish association with a tolerant state. Admittedly unconsciously and without reference to their writings, many supporters of Anglican diversity and comprehensiveness have developed something similar to the model of the Church of England developed by the low churchmen after the post-1662 settlement. The absence of a single model of what constitutes Anglicanism means that there has been a great deal of talk of 'comprehensiveness' and unity in diversity[11] and a widespread acceptance of an ecclesiology of *koinonia* which is often seen as related to the unity in diversity in the Godhead.[12]

Comprehensiveness

Some fairly recent writers on Anglicanism have been deeply critical of such theologies of comprehensiveness and have sought a solid doctrinal underpinning for Anglican theology. For instance, Stephen Sykes, one of the more prolific writers on Anglican identity in recent years, has been sometimes an outspoken opponent of such a theology. He has attacked the notion as little more than a woolly minded fudge that allows for incompatible ideas to be held together in an incoherent muddle. Indeed, he offers a similar charge to that which was levelled against comprehension in the seventeenth century. In an early book that expresses an often acerbic mood,[13] he was deeply critical of theologies of comprehensiveness as lacking doctrinal clarity. In a particularly strident passage, he commented:

> Coined at a time when internal party strife was at its most acute, [comprehensiveness] apparently offered a non-partisan refuge for that large body of central Anglicans who properly speaking belonged to no party . . . Theologically speaking, however, the effect of the proposal has been disastrous. It

must be stated bluntly that it has served as an open invitation to intellectual laziness and self-deception.[14]

Sykes detected incoherence in various writers, particularly those, such as Michael Ramsey, who had been influenced by F. D. Maurice, one of the leading theologians of Victorian England, who, Sykes misleadingly held, had first formulated a theology of comprehensiveness with his opposition to 'system-building'. According to Sykes, comprehensiveness was to prove 'a marvellous excuse to those who believe they can afford to be condescending about the outstanding theological contribution of theologians from other communions and smugly tolerant of second-rate theological competence of their own'. Similarly, he felt, 'the failure to be frank about the issues between the parties in the Church of England has led to an ultimately illusory self-projection as a Church without any specific doctrinal or confessional standpoint'.[15] Similarly Paul Avis, another recent prolific writer on Anglicanism, notes: 'The notion of a tacit consensus residing in a common ethos is a post factum accommodation to the demise of doctrinal accord within the Church'.[16] Here, he echoes what Hensley Henson wrote rather less diplomatically in the early twentieth century during a period of particularly strong partisan strife in the Church of England: 'Our duty is to save the Church of England from the strange transformation at the hands of its own members, which, if it proceed much further, will leave it nothing Anglican but the name'.[17]

Sykes gives a number of examples of what he feels to be incoherent comprehensiveness, including the 1938 Church of England Doctrine Commission Report,[18] which tried to define the content and limits of Church of England – occasionally conflated with Anglican – doctrine. The Report adopted the model of comprehensiveness based upon an understanding of the church as only partially in possession of the truth:

> our aim is not to compose a new *Summa Theologiae*, but to promote unity and mutual appreciation in the Church of England, partly by the interpretation of one school of thought, and partly by pointing to the fulness of a truth diversely apprehended in different quarters.

If this Report is to render the service for which it is designed, the purpose and method of its composition must be borne in mind. As we have already indicated, it is in no sense the outline of a systematic theology; that is something in one way more, but in another less ambitious than what we have attempted. For a systematic theology proceeds from premises regarded as assured, and from these builds up its fabric by continuous reasoning. There are systems of Catholic Theology and of Protestant Theology .... But there is not, and the majority of us do not desire that there should be, a system of distinctively Anglican theology. The Anglican Churches have received and hold the faith of Catholic Christendom, but they have exhibited a rich variety in methods both of approach and of interpretation. They are the heirs of the Reformation as well as the heirs of the Catholic tradition; and then hold together in a single fellowship of worship and witness those whose chief attachment is to each of these, and also those whose attitude to the distinctively Christian tradition is most deeply affected by the tradition of a free and liberal culture which is historically the bequest of the Greek Spirit and was recovered for Western Europe at the Renaissance.[19]

On Sykes' account, what emerges in this quotation is less of a *via media* than an eight-lane motorway that takes in both hard shoulders along with the main carriageway. Sykes felt this sort of theology to be little more than a kind of special pleading for toleration rather than a serious attempt to understand the truth of Christian doctrine.

An influential definition of comprehensiveness, which, according to Sykes, was equally problematic, was given at the 1968 Lambeth Conference, which was held during Ramsey's time as Archbishop of Canterbury. In discussing the nature of comprehensiveness in the Anglican Communion, the authors of the Report noted:

Comprehensiveness demands agreement on fundamentals, while tolerating disagreement on matters in which Christians may differ without feeling the necessity of breaking communion. In the mind of the Anglican, comprehensiveness is not compromise. Nor is it to bargain one truth for another. It is not a sophisticated word for syncretism. Rather it implies that the apprehension of truth is a growing thing: we only gradually succeed in 'knowing the truth'. [20]

While this looks remarkably close to some seventeenth-century models of comprehension, especially those with a strong platonic background, where fallibility implies humility and openness, Sykes understands it quite differently. Since he evidently does not share much in common with the Latitudinarians, he regards such a theology as an evasion of the responsibility for clarity and doctrinal truth: 'Lots of contradictory things may be said to be complementary by those with a vested interest in refusing to think straight'.[21] He consequently regards contemporary theologies of comprehensiveness as far removed from the theology of the Elizabethan Settlement, which was extremely clear about the limits of diversity. Comprehensiveness, he claims, is principally a nineteenth-century development:

> The exacerbation of the conflict between evangelical and anglo-catholic in the nineteenth century gave rise, again understandably, to the theory of complementarity of both viewpoints to a greater truth. It was a theory with an irresistible attraction for bishops endeavouring to achieve a *modus vivendi* between warring groups in their dioceses.[22]

Sykes felt that such an understanding of truth was a denial of the responsibility to make coherent truth-claims for Christianity. Apologists for comprehensiveness, he held, thought that somehow what would emerge from this strange melting pot of partially understood truths would be a finely balanced meal of the finest delicacy instead of a vile concoction of badly mixed ingredients. To counter this tendency towards woolly thought, Sykes was determined to produce an Anglican systematic theology, since, on his view, there *was* such a thing as Anglicanism, with distinct and definable characteristics and it was not simply a hybrid of catholic and protestant elements. Thus, against any tendency towards modesty and understatedness, Sykes called for an unashamed Anglicanism, even if he failed to produce the promised Anglican dogmatics.[23]

Theologies of Fallibility

Sykes, as I have noted, reserves particular venom for F. D. Maurice and Michael Ramsey, Archbishop of Canterbury through the 1960s, who had been deeply influenced by Maurice. Both are accused (correctly) of resisting systems, and by implication of a lack of coherent theological thinking. Yet to some extent, Sykes misses the point. Maurice resisted systems precisely because he saw them as reducing Christianity to a controllable and bounded structure that was focused on itself, rather than pointing beyond itself to God, who simply could not be contained by any system. Maurice was not a theorist of complementarity but upheld a deeper truth which he identified with the church catholic which could be possessed by no group or party ('system') within the church. The different systems in the church, the 'Protestant, Romish, English', he wrote, 'seem to me to bear witness of a *Divine Order*; each to be a miserable, partial, human substitute for it'.[24] Truth was thus not a blend of competitors, but a goal or a quest to which all aspired:

> Our church has no right to call herself better than other churches in any respect, in many she must acknowledge herself to be worse. But our position, we may fairly affirm, for it is not a boast but a confession, is one of singular advantage . . . [O]ur faith is not formed by a union of Protestant systems with the Romish system, nor of certain elements taken from the one and of certain elements taken from the others. So far as it is represented in our liturgy and our articles, it is the faith of a church and has nothing to do with any system at all. That peculiar character which God has given us, enables us, if we do not slight the mercy, to understand the difference between a Church and a System.[25]

Although the man who refuses to belong to a party or a system in the church might be accused of 'Eclecticism or Syncretism' (or even comprehensiveness, although Maurice does not use the term), he 'will understand that that he who endeavours to substitute a Church for systems, must regard with most dread and suspicion the attempt at a complete, all-comprehending system'.[26] The church was bigger than any one expression. Indeed, the church did not 'comprehend' all existing systems but instead criticized them all.

Similarly, writing nearly a century later, Michael Ramsey was aware of the ambiguous nature of truth in the church. 'The Church', he wrote, 'is a scene of continual dying; yet it is the place where the sovereignty of God is known and uttered, and where God is reconciling the world to Himself'.[27] For Ramsey, life in the Church is a recognition of both the triumph and glory of the church, but also of the provisionality and partiality of all concrete expressions of Christianity. Within any church, there was always the need to be aware of the temptation to make one's own partial truth into a system. The Church was thus to bear witness, not to the perfection of those who share in it,

> but to the Gospel of God by which alone, in which alone, in one universal family, mankind can be made perfect. It is not something Roman or Greek or Anglican; rather does it declare to men their utter dependence upon Christ by setting forth the universal Church in which all that is Anglican or Roman or Greek or partial or local in any way must share in an agonizing death to its pride.[28]

The Gospel guarded against the temptation towards idolatry by forcing upon us a dying to self through the repeated rehearsal of the drama of the death and resurrection of Christ. Although this process could never be complete, it nevertheless served to deliver us 'from partial rationalisms', into an

> orthodoxy which no individual and no group can possess . . . As he receives the Catholic Sacrament and recites the Catholic creed, the Christian is learning that no single movement nor partial experience within Christendom can

claim his final obedience, and that a local Church can claim his loyalty only by leading him beyond itself to the universal family which it represents.[29]

Similar themes can be detected in the writings of the present Archbishop of Canterbury, Rowan Williams. Like Maurice and Ramsey, he too is resistant to the enticements of systems, and is deeply aware of the need for a careful critique of the ways in which power is expressed within all groups in the Church. The task of theology, he once wrote in an essay on Ramsey, is to disclose 'the kind of ideological bondage that threatens to take over a Church-based or a Church-focused theology'.[30] Similarly, in an early programmatic essay, he wrote of the need to expose the 'destructive longing for final clarity, totality of vision, which brings forth the monsters of religious and political idolatry'.[31] What he termed 'Catholic Orthodoxy' presents 'a challenge to the shrinking of a tradition to the dimension of one person's or one group's need, for comfort and control'.[32] On such a model there could be no simple clarity and no straightforward system: 'To be introduced into relation with [Jesus Christ]', Williams wrote, 'is to encounter what is not exhaustible in word or system . . . it is to step into faith (rather than definitive enlightenment)'. Faith rests not so much in a submission to a system but far more on the acceptance of 'the questioning story of a crucified and resurrected Lord' which disturbs all securities.[33] It was a similar theology of fallibility, which developed in an unplanned and somewhat accidental way, which was to become the dominant theology of the Anglican Communion.

Lambeth 1867

It was the practical issue of comprehensiveness that gave rise to the theology of the Anglican Communion. As the Communion expanded through the nineteenth century, the limits of diversity needed to be defined both within and between the churches of the Anglican Communion: how far could there be international regulation between the newly independent churches in different parts of the world? It was the Colenso affair that proved to be one of the major impetuses behind the calling of the first Lambeth Conference by Archbishop Charles Longley in 1867. In 1853, John William Colenso (1814–83),[34] a Cornishman, was appointed first bishop in the new diocese of Natal, a crown colony composed of Zulus, Dutch and British settlers.[35] As he set about translating the Bible into Zulu, as well as lecturing and preaching, he became convinced that African customs were not to be simply dismissed as empty superstitions but had to be understood sympathetically. It was the duty of the missionary bishop, he held, to search out parallels and similarities between Christianity and the native religions. Indeed, Colenso claimed, God's forgiveness extended to everyone, Christian and non-Christian alike. In a commentary on St Paul's letter to the Romans, he expressed his ideas on the universality of redemption.[36] God's love, he felt, was for all – his mercy was available for everybody regardless:

> [God] himself, the Father of Spirits, is everywhere
> enlightening and quickening the spirits of men. Every good
> thought, which has ever stirred within a heathen's mind, is
> a token of that work which God's good spirit is working
> within him, as one of the great human family, redeemed by
> the Love of God in Christ Jesus, and related all to the Second
> Adam by a second spiritual birth, (of which Baptism is the
> express sign and seal to the Christian).[37]

If that was not enough to upset the apple cart, Colenso also maintained a relatively tolerant attitude towards polygamous converts. On practical grounds, he recognized that all the wives needed to be cared for.[38] These views were enough to provoke the high church bishop of Cape Town, Robert Gray, into accusations of heresy and to a complete estrangement between Colenso and the Dean of his Cathedral at Pietermaritzburg. A long court case was pursued through the English courts.

Similar controversies were emerging elsewhere. In England, a book called *Essays and Reviews* that contained seven contributions by Oxford scholars caused a similar furore.[39] Some of the essays, especially Benjamin Jowett's on 'The Interpretation of Scripture', which was the longest and probably the most influential in the volume,[40] were the first full-scale popular discussions of a critical way of reading the Bible in the Church of England. Jowett, who at the time was Regius Professor of Greek at Oxford and shortly afterwards became Master of Balliol College, Oxford, was one of the leading scholars of his day, which meant that his views carried weight. While he recognized in his essay that the interpretation of Scripture required "'a vision and faculty divine'", he nevertheless held that 'in the externals of interpretation, that is to say, the meaning of words, the connexion of sentences, the settlement of the text, the evidence of facts, the same rules apply to the Old and New Testaments as to other books'.[41] While this was obviously a highly contested statement in 1860, Jowett was secure in his faith that God's truth was to be discovered both within and outside the Christian tradition. 'The education of the human mind', he wrote, 'may be traced as clearly from the book of Genesis to the Epistles of St Paul, as from Homer to Plato and Aristotle'.[42] Jowett was clear about the purpose of the book. He wrote to A. P. Stanley, Dean of Westminster, that the object of the essayists was to liberate the truth,

> to say what we think freely within the limits of the Church of England . . . We do not wish anything rash, or irritating to the public or the University, but we are determined not to submit to this abominable system of terrorism, which prevents the statement of the plainest facts, and makes true theology or theological education impossible.[43]

A typical conservative response to *Essays and Reviews* came from Henry Parry Liddon, Pusey's future biographer. On 31 March 1860, shortly after the book's publication, he wrote to John Keble, expressing his anxiety about the spread of what he called 'Rationalism'.[44] Liddon brought the book to the attention of the Bishop of Salisbury, in whose diocese one of the suspect contributors held a living: 'What [the bishop] will do, I don't know. He insists much upon the necessity of large consideration for others, as a condition of holding things at all together. Of course, it becomes a question of limits'.[45] It was this 'question of limits' that had been pressed by the Colenso and *Essays and Reviews* controversies that became a central concern both within and between the churches of the Anglican Communion.

After some persuasion from bishops in North America and New Zealand (churches which had become independent from the British Crown), Charles Longley, Archbishop of Canterbury, invited the bishops of the Anglican Communion to participate in a conference to be held at Lambeth Palace, his London residence. The Conference lasted only three days. A few commentators felt this brevity was strange, given that some bishops had sailed from the other side of the world to take part. *The Times* leader writer, for instance, thought that it was 'incongruous to have dragged a Bishop all the way from Honolulu or New Zealand in order to take a seventy-fifth part in a three days' consultation'.[46] Longley approached the Conference with great caution. Given that such a gathering was unprecedented, nobody – least of all the archbishop – knew quite what to expect (and some, including Archbishop William Thomson of York, even refused to attend since they were unclear what sort of authority such a conference could possibly claim over an established church under the sovereignty of the Queen). However, others had high expectations that the Conference might come to a clear decision about the acceptability of certain beliefs and help to create a central decision-making authority over the whole of the Communion.

Robert Gray naturally spent some time agitating among his fellow bishops for a declaration that Colenso's views could find no place in the Anglican Communion. Nevertheless, Archbishop Longley was clear that a definitive settlement of the Colenso issue would be to overstep the authority of the Conference. He consequently refused to put a resolution approving the excommunication and deposition of Colenso onto the agenda. This incensed many bishops, which meant that during the debate itself strong resolutions opposing Colenso were brought forward. These were discussed at length, even though Colenso had very few supporters beyond the redoubtable Connop Thirlwall, Bishop of St David's. Under the influence of the American bishops, what eventually emerged was a statement 'that this conference accepts and adopts the wise decision of the convocation of Canterbury as to the appointment of another bishop to Natal'. This satisfied neither side, since there was no condemnation of Colenso's opinions. Consequently, as the bishops were leaving after the conference, Gray organized a stronger petition, which was signed by about two thirds of those present, which declared their 'acceptance of the sentence pronounced upon Dr Colenso by the metropolitan of South Africa, with his suffragans, as being spiritually a valid sentence'. But formally at least, the bishops did not definitively rule on the Colenso case – spiritual authority was very different from legal authority, which still rested with the Privy Council. What was most important is that the Conference did not make a hard and fast decision, which would have had the effect of dividing the Communion. For this reason, according to Alan Stephenson (somewhat overstating the case), Longley 'deserves an important place among the heroes of Anglicanism'.[47] In terms of the future development of the Anglican Communion, what is central is that a degree of comprehension survived, despite the hostility to Colenso.[48]

Although the idea of Anglicanism as a balance between those who disagreed with one another was not considered a virtue by many bishops in 1867, this is what emerged by default. Thus, through his skilful (or possibly incompetent) chairmanship, Longley ensured that breadth was maintained and there were no exclusions. The way in which the provinces were developing, even as early as 1867, gave effective control to the independent national churches rather than to the Archbishop of Canterbury or the Church of England. This was particularly obvious in the American and Scottish churches, which were totally free from the influence of the British Crown. This meant that as things stood there could be no legal mechanism to solve disputes, since canons could not transcend national boundaries. Consequently, while resolutions could be adopted by Lambeth Conferences, there was no central power to put them into practice. Again the Colenso case is illuminating. Even though a new bishop for Natal (William Kenneth Macrorie) was consecrated, Colenso remained in place thanks to the ruling of the Privy Council, and until Colenso's death in 1883 there were parallel jurisdictions. After a lengthy and complex legal process between the two churches, a new bishop of Natal (A. H. Baynes) was eventually consecrated in 1893 after Macrorie's resignation in 1891. Nevertheless some churches chose to remain 'Church of England' and outside the Church of the Province of South Africa.

Many of the bishops in 1867 sought a definitive closure to the Colenso crisis: what seemed to them to be required was an independent form of ecclesiastical sovereignty exercised by the bishops in council, as inheritors of the authority of the apostles themselves. While many churches adopted synodical structures, sometimes with significant lay participation (as in the USA), what was fundamental was that the church had to possess its own source of authority rooted in the primitive church if it was to withstand the assaults of an increasingly infidel state. For high churchmen, there was a need to return to a more primitive form of the church which was identified with the teachings of the undivided church of the first five centuries or so. If bishops were to exercise authority they too would need to return to a model of 'Primitive episcopacy', which would yield a quite different style of church independent of the state and guided by a synod. The reluctance – and canonical impossibility – of the archbishops of Canterbury to exercise authority over the different churches of the Anglican Communion meant that the hopes of those who sought a strong centralized authority exercised by bishops on the primitive model were bound to be thwarted. Instead, what emerged was a theology of the Anglican Communion, which was about as doctrinally and structurally weak as was possible.

William Reed Huntington: The National Church and the Anglican Communion

It was the 1888 Lambeth Conference that was to shape the identity of the Anglican Communion decisively. What emerged was not a strong doctrinal Anglicanism rooted in English formularies, but an extraordinarily inclusive denominational identity, exercised through highly decentralized churches. This meant that under the influence of the American Church as well as the reluctance of the archbishops of Canterbury to expand their claims, Anglicanism had ceased to be explicitly English by 1888. Instead, it had mutated into a loose collection of churches, which, although they shared much common history, had begun to go their own separate ways.

Crucial in the shaping of the early theology of the Anglican Communion was William Reed Huntington (1838–1909),[49] Rector of All Saints' Church, Worcester, Massachusetts (1862–83), and then of Grace Church, New York (from 1883), and one of the leading theological voices in the American Episcopal Church in the last three decades of the nineteenth century. Huntington, who was a principal inspiration behind the revision of the American Prayer Book, had been deeply influenced by the work of F. D. Maurice (1805–72)[50] and other defenders of a broad national church. Where Anglo-Catholics upheld the church as a divinely constituted sacred society, Maurice regarded the church as coterminous with the world, but pointing that world to its true goals. In a famous passage, Maurice wrote:

> The world contains the elements of which the Church is composed. In the Church, these elements are penetrated by a uniting, reconciling power. The Church is, therefore, human society in its normal state; the World, that same society irregular and abnormal. The world is the Church without God; the Church is the world restored to its relation with God, taken back by him into the state for which he created it.[51]

Maurice's conception of the Church was of something akin to the family and the nation, but expressing the most universal expression of the filial and fraternal principle which were found only in part in these other social forms: the Church was 'that spiritual constitution of which the nation and the family are the lower and subordinate parts'.[52] Instead of original sin, Maurice claimed an original unity rooted in the unity of the Triune God: 'unity among men rests upon a yet more powerful and perfect unity'.[53] The Church existed to provide an integrating centre for all people against the tendencies to fragmentation in the modern world: 'The Church exists to maintain the order of the nation and the order of the family, which this selfish practice and selfish maxim are constantly threatening'.[54] Maurice here stands in continuity with the earlier stress on decency and good order and social stability that had characterized so much of the ecclesiological thought after the Reformation.

However, where Maurice was working in the increasingly plural society of Victorian England, Huntington wrote in the very different context of a society torn apart by a disastrous Civil War, which remains one of the bloodiest wars in the whole of human history. In a bitterly divided society, Huntington was engaged in promoting church unity through what he called the 'Anglican principle', which was not to be equated with anything distinctively English, but which would allow the church to become 'the reconciler of a divided household'.[55] The word 'Anglican' was thus used as a synonym for catholicity rather than Englishness. For Huntington, the creation of an American Catholic Church was central for it to fulfil its national vocation.[56] Like Maurice, he too moved through the different stages of family and nation towards the Church.

Huntington begins *The Church-Idea* by describing the division, which 'best expresses the state of mind in which Christendom finds itself to-day. . . . Unrest is everywhere. The party of the Curia and the party of the Reformation, the party of orthodoxy and the party of liberalism, are all alike agitated by the consciousness that a spirit of change is in the air'.[57] It was in this period of rapid change and theological controversy that he sought to redefine Catholicity by going back to basics:

> Clearly we have come upon a time for the study of first principles, a time to go down and look after the foundations upon which our customary beliefs are built. The more searching the analysis, the more lasting will the synthesis be sure to be. [58]

This analysis leads him to develop the 'Anglican principle', which moves beyond any tendency to sectarianism or provincialism: 'Anglicanism stands, as Wellington's squares of infantry stood at Waterloo, firm, patient, dogged, if we must call it so, but true, – true as steel'.[59] This led him to ask: 'What are the essential, the absolutely essential features of the Anglican position?' His answers were both radical and provocative. Thus, in a famous passage, he develops an understanding of Anglicanism shorn of its Englishness:

> When it is proposed to make Anglicanism the basis of a
> Church of the Reconciliation, it is above all things necessary

to determine what Anglicanism pure and simple is. The word
brings up before the eyes of some a flutter of surplices, a vision
of village spires and cathedral towers, a somewhat stiff and
stately company of deans, prebendaries, and choristers, and
that is about all. But we greatly mistake if we imagine that
the Anglican principle has no substantial existence apart from
these accessories. Indeed, it is only when we have stripped
Anglicanism of the picturesque costume which English life
has thrown around it, that we can fairly study its anatomy, or
understand its possibilities of power and adaptation.

The Anglican principle and the Anglican system are two
very different things. The writer does not favor attempting
to foist the whole Anglican system upon America; while
yet he believes that the Anglican principle is America's best
hope. At no time since the Reformation has the Church
of England been in actual fact the spiritual home of the
nation. A majority of the people of Great Britain are to-day
without her pale. Could a system which has failed to secure
comprehensiveness on its native soil, hope for any larger
measure of success in a strange land?[60]

The growing awareness of the special vocation of the American
church was in part established on a dismissal of Englishness, which
perhaps unwittingly resembles the anti-Britishness of the founding
myths of the American republic.[61]

Huntington moves on to describe what he calls the 'true Anglican
position'. This, he claims, 'like the City of God in the Apocalypse,
may be said to lie foursquare'. He thus describes the fundamental
principles of Anglicanism under four points using the analogy of a
'quadrilateral' derived both from Augustine as well as the four great
fortress cities of Mantua, Verona, Peschiera and Legnano, which
had become famous during the Austro-Prussian War of 1866.

Honestly to accept that position is to accept, –

1st. The Holy Scriptures as the Word of God.
2nd. The Primitive Creeds as the Rule of Faith.
3rd. The two Sacraments ordained by Christ himself.
4th. The Episcopate as the key-stone of Governmental
Unity.

These four points, like the four famous fortresses of
Lombardy, make the Quadrilateral of pure Anglicanism.
Within them the Church of the Reconciliation may stand
secure. Because the English State-Church has muffled these
first principles in a cloud of non-essentials, and has said to
the people of the land, "Take all this or nothing," she mourns
to-day the loss of half her children. Only by avoiding the like
fatal error can the American branch of the Anglican Church
hope to save herself from becoming in effect, whatever
she may be in name, a sect. Only by a wise discrimination
between what can and what cannot be conceded for the sake
of unity, is unity attainable.[62]

In a manner highly reminiscent of Maurice, Huntington thus
sees the Church as an agent of reconciliation. His four points
are straightforward and uncontroversial, the first three providing a
simple description of the identity of the church rooted in history.
Although the fourth stresses the visible unity of the church founded
on the episcopate, Huntington does not limit his understanding of
episcopacy solely to the form inherited by his own church.

Huntington thereby sought to move the Episcopal Church
onto a higher level: its denominational identity was to be found
not in a vague recollection of Englishness but in the identity of the
primitive Catholic Church itself. In such a church Englishness did
not feature except as a nostalgic recollection which was no longer
relevant. Episcopalianism was thus less Anglican than *national* as
it sought to embrace all those protestant Christians who were
prepared to adopt the minimal definition of what constituted the
Church. Thus, even if it might not in practice become the sole
national church and would remain one denomination among
many, it could at least aspire to this ideal. Towards the end of *The
Church Idea* he spoke candidly of the danger of Episcopalianism
becoming little more than a respectable sect denying all claim to
catholicity. To counter all such tendencies, Huntington held up a
very different vision of the Church:

If we aim at something nobler than this, if we would have our
Communion become national in very truth, . . . then let us
press our reasonable claims to be the reconciler of a divided

household, not in a spirit of arrogance (which ill befits those whose best possessions have come to them by inheritance), but with affectionate earnestness and an intelligent zeal.[63]

Huntington continued to develop his ideas of a national church through the remainder of his life. In a course of lectures entitled *A National Church*, for instance, he emphasizes the importance of the Americanization of the Church as central for it to fulfil its national vocation.[64] While he might have hoped for an ultimate 'federation of the world', he held that at present 'the Sovereign Commander of all the world has use for nations',[65] in which the national church would continue to play a crucial role, even if it was a 'temporary expedient, . . . forced upon us by the necessities of the present, and destined in due time, . . . to merge in the larger *ecclesia* in which are to be gathered all the nations of the earth'.[66] In the period following the declaration of Papal Infallibility in 1870, Huntington held that the national church was especially important in providing an alternative ideal from that of the infallibilist:[67] the national church offered something quite different from the absolutism of what he called 'Vaticanism'.

Recognizing that 'in this world of dimmed eyes and wayward wills, absolutism has a charm all its own', he nevertheless sought a model of ecclesiastical authority based on consent and open to the future.[68] 'Would you be a good Catholic?', he asks, and answers:'Be a good Nationalist first'.[69] This meant that an American Catholic Church would have to do its best not simply to mimic its English antecedent:

> The English ivy is a beautiful plant, and nothing is one-half so becoming to church walls; but unfortunately the English ivy does not flourish in all climates, and to insist that it shall be "Ivy or nothing" in a land where the woodbine and other fairly presentable vines are indigenous is a mistake.[70]

While the Churches of America obviously owed a great deal to England, Huntington urged his audience not to be drawn to 'the fools' paradise of those who fancy that American Christianity in its entirety can be Anglified'.[71] Instead, such Christianity should be as diverse as American society. Consequently, Huntington asks: 'Why should it be any greater hardship to dwell in the same Church with a man who dotes upon candles and incense, than to dwell in the same town as him?'[72] Now that the Episcopal church had come of age, he claimed, it needed to move towards a new vision of national inclusivity. Thus, he concluded:

> Surely an American Catholic Church worthy of the name ought to have godlier words for those whom it is her duty to gather and include, than the cold, hard, stolid *Non possumus* of absolutism, or sharp apothegm, This people which knoweth not the rubrics is accursed.[73]

On such a model, Anglicanism offered the different nations the possibility of a theology rooted in context: theologically this meant an inevitable distancing from the English social and political context. The non-English version of Anglican theology developed by Huntington presents an enormous challenge to the Anglican theologies I have outlined in this book, all of which can scarcely be disentangled from their English social and political context. Indeed, it may be the case that despite family resemblances, the Anglican theology of the Anglican Communion that emerged from Huntington's theology is quite different from the competing models of Anglican theology developed in the Church of England.

The Chicago-Lambeth Quadrilateral

Huntington's four points were taken as constitutive of the identity of the church catholic at the General Convention of the American Episcopal Church held at Chicago in 1886: again the aim of the Convention was to promote national unity and reconciliation. There was, however, little sense of catholicity between the different national churches contained in the quadrilateral: it was, after all, concerned more with national unity than with global communion. For the General Convention, as for Huntington, the point of the quadrilateral was to promote an inclusive national church on the Maurician model, which the scattered denominations might be invited to join. To this was added an understanding of the primitive or 'historic' episcopate which was seen as the best way of representing this unity. The Anglican Principle of a national unified church for all people was expressed in the broader resolution adopted at Chicago which was addressed 'especially to our fellow-Christians of the different Communions in this land, who, in their several spheres, have contended for the religion of Christ'.[74] The entry requirement into the church was simply baptism, while in 'all things of human ordering or human choice, relating to modes of worship and discipline, or to traditional customs, this Church is ready in the spirit of love and humility to forego all preferences of her own'. Unity was to be established by a return to the undivided church of the past. Before affirming the quadrilateral, the Convention asserted

that the Christian unity can be restored only by the return of all Christian communions to the principles of unity exemplified by the undivided Catholic Church during the first ages of its existence; which principles we believe to be the substantial deposit of Christian Faith and Order committed by Christ and his Apostles to the Church unto the end of the world, and therefore incapable of compromise or surrender by those who have been ordained to be its stewards and trustees for the common and equal benefit of all men.

As inherent parts of this sacred deposit, and therefore as essential to the restoration of unity among the divided branches of Christendom, we account the following, to wit:

1. The Holy Scriptures of the Old and New Testaments as the revealed Word of God.
2. The Nicene Creed as the sufficient statement of the Christian Faith.
3. The two Sacraments – Baptism and the Supper of the Lord – ministered with unfailing use of Christ's words of institution and of the elements ordained by Him.
4. The Historic Episcopate, locally adapted in the methods of its administration to the varying needs of the nations and peoples called of God into the unity of His Church.

Furthermore, Deeply grieved by the sad divisions which affect the Christian Church in our own land, we hereby declare our desire and readiness, so soon as there shall be any authorized response to this Declaration, to enter into brotherly conference with all or any Christian Bodies seeking the restoration of the organic unity of the Church, with a view to the earnest study of the conditions under which so priceless a blessing might happily be brought to pass.[75]

The Chicago Quadrilateral was aimed principally at reconciliation at home and as an invitation to other denominations to unite, rather than as a mechanism for defining any international Anglican principle.

At the Anglican Communion level, however, the pressing question was what sort of unity a church established on the basis of national independence could adopt at a transnational level. The question of unity was addressed at the 1888 Lambeth Conference over which Edward White Benson (1829–96) presided. The bishops adopted a slightly revised version of the Chicago Quadrilateral as the basis 'on which approach may be by God's blessing made towards Home Reunion'. A crucial difference, however, was that instead of simply seeing the four points as inherent parts of the deposit of faith and order, the Lambeth Resolution[76] regarded the four points as 'articles', presumably akin to the Thirty-Nine Articles, and therefore as *constitutive* of Anglicanism and the wider catholic faith.[77] Huntington's 'Anglican Principle' thereby became less of a clamour for reconciliation and more a description of those churches which could be accepted as members of the Anglican Communion. This meant that for the first time an international definition of what constituted Anglicanism was given, but with the perhaps surprising absence of anything distinctively English including the Prayer Book or any doctrinal formulary. Furthermore, the basis in Home Reunion was soon forgotten. Thus, instead of serving the project of ecumenical reconciliation and as an invitation to move beyond denomination through applying what were effectively four widely accepted criteria for catholicity, the Lambeth Quadrilateral served the opposite purpose of creating a definition of worldwide Anglicanism as a particular denomination but shorn of most of its distinctive identifying features.

Such an understanding certainly suited Archbishop Benson. His own vision of Christian unity did not imply uniformity (which, he held, was the failing of what he called 'Roman Unity'),[78] but instead it had to be sensitive to its cultural setting. Its focus was consequently on its future fulfilment in the final consummation:

> If we wish to prepare a future for our people and our children, we must make provision for an active, realised unity in the Church. . . . But we must avoid a common fancy. We cannot recur to the past for unity. External unity has not existed yet, except superficially. *Unity is not the first scene, but the last triumph of Christianity and man.* Christ himself could not *create* unity in His Church. He could pray for it, and his prayer most movingly teaches us to work for it. On earth it is not a gift, but a growth. If any vision of it is granted us we must work both in and towards what we have seen that 'although it tarry, it may be for an appointed time,' but rather still that 'it may come and *not* tarry'.[79]

The unity of the Church, according to Benson, could thus never be a completely undifferentiated unity imposed from above, but had to respond to local circumstances. A failure to be responsive to the cultural conditions and

> to seek to build up a like Church, stone by stone as it were, spiritually, out of the utterly different characters, experiences, sentiments of another race, is to repeat without excuse the error of the great Boniface, in making not a Teutonic but an Italian Church in Germany. It is to contradict the wise axioms with which Gregory tried to save Augustine from the error.[80]

The crucial question for the Anglican Communion was consequently over precisely how it could function as a catholic church without at the same time adopting the alternative model of a centrally imposed uniformity. Benson, like Maurice and other Platonists before him, was clear that true unity resided with God and was always a hope rather than a reality.

The Focus on Bishops

Given that most other protestant denominations would have had little difficulty with the first three articles, the Lambeth Quadrilateral ended up in practice by placing the distinctive identity of Anglicanism in 'The Historic Episcopate, locally adapted in the methods of its administration to the varying needs of the nations and peoples called of God into the Unity of His Church'. This in effect meant that the Anglo-Catholic theology of the 'apostolical succession' – which is how 'historic episcopate' has usually been understood[81] – was elevated into an article of faith for Anglicans. This was noted by William Perry, Bishop of Iowa:

> Our longings for union must not lead us to the surrender of the great trust committed to us as an integral part of the Church Catholic of CHRIST. Concessions involving disloyalty to revealed truths, to Apostolic practice, and to primitive belief, are out of the question. It is not to be expected that the great and overwhelming majority of Christians now living on the earth should abandon the form of Church government which has been theirs 'from the Apostles' time,' and which they believe to be *jure divino*, with a view of comprehending in their Communion a few most excellent and devoted Christian bodies or individuals who practically recognize no visible Church, who deny the existence of the threefold ministry, who refuse to admit the claims of the Historic Episcopate, and who will not concede the grace of Holy Orders. Thus abandoning the Church's vantage ground, we might, indeed, add to our numbers a small gain, but we should lose the greater possibilities which may GOD, in His good time, enable us to realize in the reunion of Christendom, the bringing together of all Christian men and peoples in the unity of God's Church.[82]

Episcopacy, which, as has been shown, was regarded by most earlier Anglicans as the best means of ensuring good order, but not as an absolutely necessary feature of a true church,[83] was elevated into *the* criterion for Catholic identity. This also had the effect that while the Lambeth Conference may not ever have been able to claim legal authority, the fact that its bishops have been invested with a supernatural authority means that it has taken on a quasi-conciliar structure and has sometimes been seen to be teaching 'authoritatively' rather than simply acting as an advisory body.

The Lambeth Quadrilateral has continued to function as the chief standard of Anglican Communion identity. In the famous Lambeth 'Appeal to All Christian People' of 1920, the fourth article was adopted as a principle for reunion on the basis of 'a ministry acknowledged by every part of the Church as possessing not only the inward call of the Spirit but also the commission of Christ and the authority of the whole body'.[84] Similarly, the Committee on the Unity of the Church, which was set up in response to various proposals for reunion of the churches, particular those of South India, reported to the 1930 Lambeth Conference that the episcopate 'occupies a position which is, in point of historical development, analogous to that of the canons of scripture and the creeds. . . . The Historic Episcopate as we understand it goes behind the perversions of history to the original conception of the apostolic ministry'.[85] Since then, most attempts at reunion have foundered over the question of episcopacy. A good example is the Meissen Agreement of 1988 between the British Anglican Churches and the Evangelical Church of Germany (EKD) – while there is a mutual recognition that both are true churches, there is nevertheless a refusal to allow an interchangeability of ministries on the grounds that the German churches lack 'the historic episcopate'.[86]

What has emerged from the loose principles enunciated in the Lambeth Quadrilateral in 1888, which have continued to shape Anglican Communion theology and ecclesiology, is a strong doctrine of provincial autonomy with very little holding the church together beyond the most minimal of definitions. As the historian Norman Sykes said:

> The validity of the Anglican position depends upon the recognition of the right of national churches to fashion their own doctrine, discipline, and organisation, and of the right of the laity to participate in the definition of matters of faith and order.[87]

This legacy has had a profound effect on shaping the identity of Anglican theology, and it rests behind the lack of a broader English historical consciousness displayed in the TEAC bibliography with which I started this chapter, which has been replicated in most Anglican documents. In the light of the models of Anglican theology discussed earlier in the course of this book, however, it is questionable whether the Quadrilateral is sufficiently focused to function as the basis for Anglican theology, especially when the constituent churches of the Anglican Communion have been increasingly in conflict with one another. One of the resolutions of the Lambeth Conference of 1920 was strong on assertion but failed to ask how truth and love were to be discerned:

> The Churches represented [in the Anglican Communion] are indeed independent, but independent with the Christian freedom which recognises the restraints of truth and love. They are not free to deny the truth. They are not free to deny the fellowship.[88]

Principally because of a series of serious controversies in the Communion, a number of church leaders have consequently sought to find a more definitive set of agreed formularies across the Anglican Communion as the basis for solving theological disputes. These have emerged chiefly in response to disagreements over homosexual practice and the priesthood. The quest for common Anglican statements and methods has dominated much of the discussion in recent years. This has led to the production of a draft Anglican Covenant, which will be discussed at length in the concluding chapter.[89] While virtually all Anglicans would no doubt acknowledge the supremacy of Scripture, and probably nearly all would maintain the importance of the Prayer Book and its many heirs and successors across the world, the methods of interpretation of the Bible and the liturgical and doctrinal inheritance stemming from the Prayer Book have become widely divergent. Furthermore, as will become clear in the next chapter, it is not obvious who or what could define the essential core of Anglicanism. The question of authority continues to be a major problem, just as it had been in the Reformation. While some might clamour for a teaching office – something like an Anglican

Magisterium as an equivalent to the papacy – few are likely to agree on how this might be constituted. In this context too, the word 'Anglican' is once again problematic: for most of its life, it simply meant 'English'.[90] Yet, a theology that emerged in the context of an English national church where authority was exercised by the civil rulers is very different from the sort of theology that developed in non-English churches where Anglicanism was one denomination among others and where the civil powers had only a very limited authority in matters ecclesiastical. Anglican identity, to say the least, is in a period of flux.

Chapter 9

Conclusion

Anglican Theology Today

Anglican theology today seems to be characterized by a sense of déjà vu: some of the mid-Victorian debates that led to the production of the texts of Anglican identity, which I have discussed through the course of this book, are reflected in the controversies within and between the different churches of the Anglican Communion. For those with eyes to see, there is an odd clash between half-articulated and sometimes updated versions of Reformed, Anglo-Catholic and Latitudinarian identities. These identities are frequently rooted in missionary and colonial history as well as liturgical identity. A good recent example comes from Henry Luke Orombi, the outspoken Archbishop of Uganda. He has focused on the Word of Scripture as interpreted according to the Reformation formularies in his definition of what counts as authentic Anglicanism: 'The basis of our commitment to Anglicanism', he writes, 'is that it provides a wider forum for holding each other accountable to Scripture, which is the seed of faith and the foundation of the Church in Uganda'. He goes on: 'For the Ugandan church to compromise God's call of obedience to the Scriptures would be the undoing of more than 125 years of Christianity through which African life and society have been transformed'. There is a sense that there can be no compromises for a particular version of Anglican identity, which makes comprehension a troublesome concept. Indeed, with reference to the contemporary problems being experienced in the Anglican Communion, he boldly asserts:

> We would not be facing the crisis in the Anglican
> Communion if we had upheld the basic Reformation
> convictions about Holy Scripture: its primacy, clarity,

sufficiency, and unity. Part of the genius of the Reformation was its insistence that the Word of God and the liturgy be in the language of the people – that the Bible could be read and understood by the simplest plowboy. The insistence from some Anglican circles (mostly in the Western world) on esoteric interpretations of Scripture borders on incipient Gnosticism that has no place in historic or global Anglicanism.

The ultimate authority in Anglicanism rests in Scripture, interpreted as the 'power of the Word of God precisely as the *Word of God* – written to bring transformation in our lives, our families, our communities, and our culture'.[1] No doubt the divisions over biblical interpretation derive in part from a range of post-colonial problems, including the 'coming of age' of the massive African churches and what Orombi called the end of the 'long season of British hegemony'.[2] While the issues emerging from post-colonialism have only recently begun to be seriously investigated, there is evidence of an obvious power struggle both between the global south and the north as well as between conservatives and liberals within many of the 'northern' churches, some of which masquerades as questions of biblical interpretation (about which much could be written).[3] The antagonism towards the American Episcopal Church displayed by many of the growing churches in the Global South, as well as some critics from within, has at least some of its origins in a post-colonial reaction to what is often understood to be the economic and social imperialism of American liberal values. There are obvious similarities between the sort of outcry against rationalism demonstrated by Orombi and some of the recent attacks that have been made against what is perceived to be the inexorable march of secular liberalism, particularly in the American church (by, for example, Ephraim Radner and Philip Turner).[4] The simple point, however, is that the notion of Anglicanism as resting on a fixed and easily demonstrable truth challenges the theology of Anglican comprehensiveness as well as the implicit national church ideology of the Lambeth Quadrilateral.

At the same time, the primary focus of Anglicanism in most parts of the world is unlikely to be on the international institution, as it might be in the more obviously global communion of Roman

Conclusion

Catholicism. Instead, the stress on national and provincial autonomy means that Anglicans are more likely to focus on the local, which can be conceived in different ways – for example, the national (or 'provincial') church, the diocese or even the parish church. Because of the way in which the different churches developed, the stress on the local means that there is a variety of Anglican 'games' or 'languages' with family resemblances but also with many different nuances in doctrine, style and practice. In the days of the British Empire, there was an obvious connection between most forms of Anglicanism and England, which remained the source of both religious and political leaders. But as the different churches became self-governing provinces in their own right in the nineteenth and twentieth centuries, so Anglicanism grew to be something far less 'English'. Instead of being a singular phenomenon or a unique global brand, Anglicanism, with its huge diversity of contemporary forms, is much more akin to locally produced and – more importantly – locally designed goods aimed primarily at the domestic market. Unlike Coca-Cola or McDonalds, which are much the same everywhere, Anglicanism is made up of a variety of local brands that usually bear family resemblances with one another, but unlike Coca-Cola, there is no secret formula protected in a head office. Furthermore, as I showed in Chapter 2, *rejection* of an international communion was fundamental to the origin of the English Reformation, even if new models of international communion developed, especially in northern Europe, exemplified, for instance, by the Synod of Dort of 1618–19.

The understanding of 'provincial autonomy' is further complicated when the traditional 'centre' of Anglicanism – which is most obviously embodied in the Archbishop of Canterbury, and the inevitable connection with the English Crown, which still appoints him – is identified with the ambiguous historical legacy of the colonial church. Indeed, the very idea of a 'global' church raises enormous questions of power and authority. The question is simple: in the post-colonial Anglican Communion, where is the centre of global power?[5] There is a complex combination of issues stemming from post-colonialism and anti-globalization, which can be detected in some of the recent Anglican squabbles. Once again, theology is responding to a complex set of social and political issues.

The Move Towards an Anglican Covenant

The crisis that has engendered intense debate and division within the Anglican Communion has been provoked principally by the question of homosexual practice and its compatibility with the Christian faith.[6] Although the question of homosexuality found its way onto the agenda at the Lambeth Conferences of 1978 and 1988, the issue did not provoke serious disagreement. Both Conferences affirmed 'heterosexuality as the scriptural norm' but also recognized the need to 'take seriously both the teaching of Scripture and the results of scientific and medical research'.[7] However, the issue of homosexuality led to deep division at the Lambeth Conference of 1998. Although it is not clear why homosexuality should have become such an important and divisive subject, especially in parts of Africa at this time, Kevin Ward has suggested that it may have something to do with making a stand against what seem to be the inexorable forces of modernization in which the mainline denominations are often one of the main carriers – ironically, perhaps, rather than being an attack on the Enlightenment, it is a product of a changing understanding of what it is to be human:[8] 'Homophobia', Ward claims, 'is as much a western intrusion as is homosexual identity'.[9] The emphasis on homosexuality is perhaps an export of the tensions of the North American churches across the globe – and is evidence for a strange form of the globalization of specifically American moral questions. Thus, Ward writes:

> The fact that the conflict has focussed so fiercely on homosexuality is itself an indication of the ways in which what is essentially a conflict within western secular society has spilled over to the rest of the world, itself coming to terms with modernity and the increasing dominance of secularity and its discontents.[10]

This is ironic given that the Chicago-Lambeth Quadrilateral of 1888 was originally designed to unite all Christians after the bloodshed of the American Civil War. Yet that society still remains divided between north and south and conservative and liberal.

Such divisions still continue to make an impact on the Anglican Communion.

The preparatory papers for the 1998 Lambeth Conference had suggested that the time was not yet ripe for a full discussion or decision about homosexuality – in the same way that the first Lambeth Conference deliberately avoided the divisive issue of Bishop Colenso in 1867, so in 1998, it was recognized by many that any decision over homosexuality would be too divisive. The result was an impressive compromise:

> We have prayed, studied and discussed these issues, and
> we are unable to reach a common mind on the scriptural,
> theological, historical, and scientific questions that are
> raised. There is much that we do not yet understand.
> We request the Primates and the Anglican Consultative
> Council to establish a means of monitoring work done in
> the Communion on these issues and to share statements
> and resources among us. The challenge to our Church is
> to maintain its unity while we seek, under the guidance
> of the Holy Spirit, to discern the way of Christ for the
> world today with respect to human sexuality. To do so will
> require sacrifice, trust, and charity towards one another,
> remembering that ultimately the identity of each person is
> defined in Christ.
> … Our sexual affections can no more define who we
> are than can our class, race or nationality. At the deepest
> ontological level, therefore, there is no such thing as 'an
> homosexual' or 'an heterosexual'; there are human beings,
> male and female, called to redeemed humanity in Christ,
> endowed with a complex variety of emotional potentialities
> and threatened by a complex variety of forms of alienation.[11]

Nevertheless, things changed very quickly in the course of the 1998 debate. What emerged was a significantly amended resolution which made it much tougher and less ambiguous than the draft. There was overwhelming support for the final resolution. The key parts of the final amended text are as follows (italics indicate amendments):

This Conference: …

(c) recognizes that there are among us persons who experience themselves as having a homosexual orientation. Many of these are members of the Church and are seeking the pastoral care, moral direction of the Church, and God's transforming power for the living of their lives and the ordering of relationships, *and we commit ourselves to listen to the experience of homosexual people. [A24]* We wish to assure them that they are loved by God and that all baptized, believing and faithful persons, regardless of sexual orientation, are full members of the Body of Christ;

(d) *while rejecting homosexual practice as incompatible with Scripture, [A36]* calls on all our people to minister pastorally and sensitively to all irrespective of sexual orientation and to condemn *irrational fear of homosexuals [A27]*, violence within marriage and any trivialization and commercialization of sex;

(e) cannot advise the legitimizing or blessing of same-sex-unions, nor the ordination of those involved in such unions;

Section (d) was the most far-reaching. If one accepts the authoritative voice of the Bishops, which is implied by the emphasis of the 'historic episcopate' of the Lambeth Quadrilateral, then the short amended subclause that regards 'homosexual practice as incompatible with Scripture' rules out the legitimacy of all forms of homosexual practice, at least for all those Anglicans who regard Scripture as the basis for moral norms. Lambeth 1998 reaffirmed 'in agreement with the Lambeth Quadrilateral, and in solidarity with the Lambeth Conference of 1888' that 'Holy Scriptures contain "all things necessary to salvation" and are for us the "rule and ultimate standard" of faith and practice'. The overwhelming majority of the bishops in the Anglican Communion had thus ruled that something was incompatible with Scripture.[12] Possibly because of this Scriptural underpinning, Resolution 1.10 was treated very differently from Lambeth Resolutions of the past. In many quarters, it came to be regarded as a magisterial teaching of the Anglican Communion, and yet what was left unclarified was the precise status of the resolutions of the Lambeth Conference in relation to the independent churches. The Lambeth Conference had always claimed to be nothing more than advisory, and its rulings were always open to future change (as happened, for instance, on polygamy and contraception).[13] But Resolution 1.10 was not treated in this way – instead, it was elevated into something like a test of soundness or orthodoxy. Homosexuality was and always would be contrary to Scripture.

Intra-Communion matters were changed decisively in 2003, when the Diocese of New Hampshire elected Gene Robinson, a divorcee in a same-sex relationship, as bishop. His election was confirmed at a meeting of the General Convention in Minneapolis the following August, which conservative critics saw as marking the decision by the Episcopal Church to become another denomination and 'to find its primary identity as a liberal but liturgical option within the spectrum of Protestant denominations that make up America's religious kaleidoscope'.[14] In May 2003, shortly after Robinson's election, matters were complicated still further when the Canadian Diocese of New Westminster authorized rites for same-sex blessings. In England, the Bishop of Oxford nominated Jeffrey John, an openly homosexual priest, although not practising, as suffragan Bishop of Reading, who was forced to stand down. A number of bishops from Africa and Asia began to intervene in other churches across the Atlantic. This meant that there was an urgent need to examine the nature and theological basis of the relationships between the provinces.

The Anglican Covenant

The Archbishop of Canterbury summoned the Primates to an emergency meeting at Lambeth in October 2003. They reaffirmed Resolution 1.10, including the need to listen to homosexuals and to one another, but also noted that the Diocese of New Westminster and the Episcopal Church had acted before the Communion was of one mind. At Lambeth 1998 (and coming out of the earlier *Virginia Report* on inter-Anglican relations),[15] there had been a suggestion that the Archbishop of Canterbury establish a Commission to consider his role in conflict resolution. This now seemed more pressing, which meant a commission was appointed whose remit included 'urgent and deep theological and legal reflection on the way in which the dangers we have identified at this meeting will have to be addressed'.[16] The Lambeth Commission on Communion, which was chaired by Archbishop Robin Eames of Ireland, produced *The Windsor Report* in October 2004.[17] It is a lengthy document that seeks to clarify the nature of communion and authority in the Anglican Communion, especially the constraints, restraints and discipline necessary to ensure that the greatest degree of communion between provinces can be maintained. It called for 'Communion-wide dimensions of theological discourse' (§41) as well as for formal mechanisms to promote inter-provincial conversation and consultation. At the same time, it concluded that the Diocese of New Westminster, the General Synod of the Anglican Church of Canada and the Episcopal Church had 'acted in ways incompatible with the Communion principle of interdependence, and our fellowship together has suffered immensely as a result of these developments' (§121). Where the *Virginia Report* was virtually silent about sanctions, *The Windsor Report* noted that there had to be some legal recognition of the rights of other provinces to constrain unilateral action if there was to be a future for the Communion (§§113–20).

The Windsor Report suggested that one way forward would be the adoption of what it called a 'common Anglican Covenant' which would 'make explicit and forceful the loyalty and bonds of affection which govern the relationships between the churches of the Communion', which would require some form of canon law to ensure its effectiveness (§118). A provisional and fairly lengthy draft was drawn up in Appendix Two. It affirmed the basic principles of the Chicago-Lambeth Quadrilateral, together with some ideas about the requirements for forms of restraint or what it called 'mutual reciprocity and forbearance'.[18] This was to be policed by what was called a 'Council of Advice', acting as an extension of the office of the Archbishop of Canterbury.[19] The recommendations of *The Windsor Report* were broadly endorsed by the 2005 Primates' meeting in Dromantine, Northern Ireland.

Tension remained high. That summer, the Council of Anglican Provinces of Africa (CAPA) issued a statement (*The Road to Lambeth*)[20] that they would 'definitely not attend any Lambeth

Conference to which the violators of the Lambeth Resolution are also invited as participants or observers' (although this was not unanimously received). At the meeting of the Primates in Dar-Es-Salaam in February 2007, eight Primates refused to receive communion at a service at which Katherine Jefferts-Schori, the recently elected Presiding Bishop of The Episcopal Church, was present. The Primates in Tanzania were also able to consider a first draft of a Covenant which had been written with remarkable efficiency.[21] It was a more developed version than that included in *The Windsor Report* and more historically aware about the nature and development of Anglicanism. What is most significant, perhaps, is that the first use of the word 'covenant' is as a verb (§1), a feature that has been retained in subsequent drafts. The sense of voluntary commitment is the key point of the document – it amounts to a pledge by the individual churches, firstly, to a set of definitions about the nature of Anglicanism and, secondly, and more crucially, to a method for solving disputes.

Models of Catholicity

For some Anglicans, however, such a voluntary method will never be sufficient to hold the Communion together. For many more conservative bishops, it is clear that the best way forward is to define Anglicanism more rigidly and prescriptively and ensure that churches subscribe to a set of doctrinal and theological propositions. In the light of the tensions following 1998, a number of bishops boycotted the 2008 Lambeth Conference, choosing instead to attend the Global Anglican Future Conference (GAFCON) in Jerusalem, which was held shortly beforehand. In his opening address at the Conference, Peter Akinola, Primate of Nigeria, spoke of 'setting participants free from [the] spiritual bondage which T[he] E[piscopal] C[hurch] and its Allies champion. Having survived the inhuman physical slavery of the 19th century, the political slavery called colonialism of the 20th century, the developing world economic enslavement, we cannot, we dare not allow ourselves and the millions we represent be kept in [a] religious and spiritual dungeon'.[22] After the meeting, a Declaration was issued which suggested that the only solution was either to make use of the existing instruments of communion to expel the errant churches or to set up a network of 'orthodox' churches. The Fellowship of Confessing Anglicans, which was established at the Conference, is clearly a call for some sort of clearly defined group, either inside or outside the wider Anglican Communion founded on subscription to a set of teachings based upon a particular way of reading the Bible, which 'is to be translated, read, preached, taught and obeyed in its plain and canonical sense, respectful of the church's historic and consensual reading'. They went on: 'We reject the authority of those churches and leaders who have denied the orthodox faith in word or deed'.[23] The GAFCON bishops called for a new structure to control membership through a far tighter definition of Anglicanism.

A very different model of catholicity was tried at the Lambeth Conference a few weeks later. Rowan Williams sought to encourage a deep sense of listening named after a Zulu method of conflict resolution called 'Indaba'. The principle was that decisions were to emerge as participants voluntarily agreed to certain constraints on unilateral action. The autonomy of each province was thereby constrained by some sense of spatial catholicity. Coming together in deep listening was not simply about tolerating difference, but about exploring and understanding that difference, and drawing it into one's own decision-making structures. Throughout the Lambeth Conference, Williams spent much time wrestling with the issue of what sort of conditions were required for deep listening to take place. In a memorable analogy, he likened the role of the bishop to that of the linguist, 'listening for the nuances, listening for the hidden music in what someone says or does, listening sometimes for what's beneath the surface as well as what is immediately in front of us'.[24] On the basis of such listening, there might be a real progress 'beyond peaceful diversity' towards a deeper sense of 'Christian unity'. This was not to be founded on simple toleration but on something far deeper – on the unity that adheres in Jesus Christ. This required a covenantal commitment: 'every association of Christian individuals and groups makes some sort of "covenant" for the sake of mutual recognition, mutual gratitude and mutual learning'.[25] Catholicity, on this model, is rooted in Christ and expressed by all who seek to relate – or to covenant – to one another in order to listen to what Christ is saying through those who are different. In this way, he claimed, the Anglican Communion might become 'more of a "catholic" church in the proper sense, a church, that is, which understands its ministry and service and sacraments as united and interdependent throughout the world'. Instead of a loose federation of autonomous churches, it would grow into a set of churches interrelated to one another and rooted and unified in a common endeavour to listen to one another and to Christ. The 2008 Lambeth Conference can be seen as pioneering a way of being catholic through a voluntary commitment to a non-coercive form of mutually shared authority. It is this model that underpins the Anglican Covenant.

Conclusion

Further drafts of a Covenant have been produced since the 2008 Lambeth Conference which attempt to formulate the agreed basics of Anglicanism,[26] which are significantly more extensive than the four points of the Lambeth Quadrilateral, and which extend to doctrinal and liturgical principles (parts one to three of the final draft). While they are unlikely to satisfy those in the GAFCON movement who clamour for a dogmatic and moral fixity to Anglicanism, the principle of communion adopted nevertheless moves far beyond provincial autonomy, as it seeks to relate the local to the universal. Since churches cannot be limited purely to their own context,[27] under the Covenant there is a voluntary commitment from all churches to listen to others before acting. In turn, there is also a recognition of the need for mediation and 'dispute resolution',[28] which has been conspicuously absent in the past few years. When resolution cannot be had, a joint committee of the Primates and the Anglican Consultative Council (the Standing Committee) will be established to make recommendations to churches whose actions cause controversy. This does not affect the legal autonomy of each church, unless of course it changes its own canons to give the Committee legal recognition. Each church thus retains the right and ability to act without recourse to other churches. The only sanction is for churches no longer to be invited to the inter-Anglican bodies, which would not necessarily affect 'communion' between them. In practice, 'expelled' Anglican churches might well remain in communion with other Anglican churches including the Church of England. There may well be tough decisions and splits ahead, since the Covenant will work only if sufficient people want the Anglican Communion to remain a vital and living vision of the holy Catholic Church. This requires an attitude of discipline, obedience, respect and tolerance as well as a readiness to listen and learn. As I write, the Covenant is being debated by a number of churches including the Church of England, although only a handful have as yet adopted it. All in all, the Covenant is a kind of 'tepid constitutionalism',[29] a rather belated adoption of a mechanism for ecclesial coherence across a set of churches which failed to adopt any of the models of Anglican identity which held sway in the early years of the Church of England.

Although there are, of course, many other aspects to Anglican theology which I could have mentioned and which may well prove to be of importance into the future, my presentation of Anglican Theology finishes with these efforts to provide a structure for the Anglican Communion. This means that there will be gaps, not least of which is the absence of any discussion of the various ecumenical reports or discussions which have been produced in recent years and which have moved towards a limited degree of rapprochement with other churches.[30] My approach has of necessity been limited to a more historical presentation, which derives from pre-ecumenical times, and, although I do not have time to defend it, it is usually the case that ecumenical statements draw on very specific models of Anglican theology. Nevertheless, I hope that the detailed presentations of Anglican theology through the course of this book have revealed something of the theological style and culture of the Church of England and of the Anglican Communion. All I can say by way of conclusion is that I hope I have succeeded in showing that Anglican theology is both complex and contested and it is nowhere near as simple as some might claim. As I said at the end of the introduction, this complexity makes it infuriating and exciting. I hope that something of that exciting infuriation has shone through this book.

Notes

1 See Polly Ha and Patrick Collinson (eds), *The Reception of the Continental Reformation in Britain* (Oxford: Oxford University Press for the British Academy, 2010).

2 John Craig, 'Erasmus or Calvin? The Politics of Book Purchase in the Early Modern English Parish' in Ha and Collinson, *The Reception of the Continental Reformation*, pp. 39–62, esp. pp. 45–50. The first volume of Erasmus' Paraphrases was translated by Nicholas Udall and the second volume by Miles Coverdale and others and first published in England during the reign of Edward VI: *The Paraphrase of Erasmus vpon the Newe Testamente* (London, 1548; second volume London, 1549).

3 I have deliberately used the term 'protestant' when referring to the 'evangelical' theology that emerged at the Reformation. While 'evangelical' might be a more accurate term, since protestant has a specific meaning in relation to a number of events in Germany, and was not used a great deal at the time, I use it to differentiate from Evangelicalism, which was the name given to a distinctive Church party that developed in the eighteenth century. See my article, 'Protestant Christianity' in Peter Clarke and Peter Beyer (eds), *The World's Religions: Continuities and Transformations* (London Routledge, 2008), pp. 510–24.

4 Patrick Collinson, 'England', in Robert Scribner, Roy Porter and Mikuláš Teich (eds), *The Reformation in National Context* (Cambridge: Cambridge University Press, 1994), pp. 80–94. For the most wide-ranging survey, see Diarmaid MacCulloch, *Reformation: Europe's House Divided 1490–1700* (London: Penguin, 2004).

5 For this view, see Aubrey Moore, *Lectures and Papers on the History of the Reformation in England and on the Continent* (London: Kegan Paul, Trench, Trübner, 1890).

6 Diarmaid MacCulloch, 'The Myth of the English Reformation' in *Journal of British Studies* 30 (1991), pp. 1–19. See below, Chapter 2.

7 MacCulloch, 'The Myth of the English Reformation', p. 1.

8 The most important theorist of the 'branch theory' was William Palmer, *A Treatise on the Church of Christ* (London: Rivington, 1838).

9 On this, see, for example, E. J. Hobsbawm and T. Ranger (eds), *The Invention of Tradition* (Cambridge: Cambridge University Press, 1983), and E. J. Hobsbawm, *Nations and Nationalism Since 1780* (Cambridge: Cambridge University Press, 1992).

10 For a comparative discussion, see R. W. Franklin, *Nineteenth Century Churches: The History of a New Catholicism in Württemberg, England, and France* (New York: Garland, 1987).

11 John Pearson, *The Exposition of the Creed* (1659), E. Burton (ed.), (Oxford: Oxford University Press, 1843).

12 See M. G. Brock and M. C. Curthoys (eds), *The History of the University of Oxford: Nineteenth-Century Oxford, Part 1* (Oxford: Clarendon Press, 1997), esp. pp. 10, 348.

13 Newman reported that he had begun to read the book in June 1825 (in Gerard Tracey (ed.), *Letters and Diaries of John Henry Newman* (Oxford: Oxford University Press, 2000), vol. 1, p. 238). On Gladstone and Butler, see David Bebbington, *The Mind of Gladstone: Religion, Homer, and Politics* (Oxford: Oxford University Press, 2004), esp. 118.

14 W. E. Gladstone (ed.), *The Works of Joseph Butler, D.C.L. Sometime Lord Bishop of Durham* (Oxford: Clarendon Press, 1897), 2 vols, vol. 1: *The Analogy of Religion, Natural and Revealed, to the Constitution and Course of Nature.*

15 Richard Bancroft, cited in John Craig, 'The politics of Book Purchase', p. 50.

16 Stephen Sykes, *The Integrity of Anglicanism* (London: Mowbray, 1978).

17 See Diarmaid MacCulloch, 'Richard Hooker's Reputation', *English Historical Review* 117 (2002), pp. 773–812.

18 Cited in Standish Meacham, *Lord Bishop: The Life of Samuel Wilberforce: 1805–1873* (Cambridge: Harvard University Press, 1970), p. 221.

19 See, for instance, John Macquarrie, *Principles of Christian Theology* (London: SCM Press, 1966).

Chapter 2

1 J. C. D. Clark, *English Society: 1688–1832: Ideology, Social Structure, and Political Practice During the Ancien Régime* (Cambridge: Cambridge University Press, second edition, 2000), esp. pp. 527–47.

2 J. H. Newman, John Keble and J. B. Mozley (eds), *Remains of the Late Reverend Richard Hurrell Froude, M.A. Fellow of Oriel College, Oxford* (London: Rivington, 1838–1839), 2 parts in 4 volumes; here, part 2, vol. 1, pp. 206–7.

3 P. B. Nockles, 'An Academic Counter-Revolution: Newman and Tractarian Oxford's Idea of a University' in *History of Universities* 10 (1991), pp. 137–97; here, p. 181.

4 Simon Skinner, *Tractarians and the 'Condition of England': The Social and Political Thought of the Oxford Movement* (Oxford: Clarendon, 2004).

5 See Peter Nockles, *The Oxford Movement in Context: Anglican High Churchmanship, 1760–1857* (Cambridge: Cambridge University Press, 1994), ch. 2.

6 Diarmaid MacCulloch, 'The Myth of the English Reformation' in *Journal of British Studies* 30 (1991), pp. 1–19, p. 4.

Notes

7 H. Hensley Henson, *In Defence of the English Church* (London: Hodder & Stoughton, 1923), p. 138.

8 On Froude, see Piers Brendon, *Hurrell Froude and the Oxford Movement* (London: Elek, 1974).

9 *Remains*, vol. 1, p. 433.

10 *Remains*, vol. 1, p. 336.

11 *Remains*, vol. 1, p. 389.

12 Andrew Atherstone, 'The Martyrs' Memorial at Oxford', *Journal of Ecclesiastical History* 54 (2003), pp. 278–301.

13 Keble to Pusey, 18 January 1839 in H. P. Liddon, *The Life of Edward Bouverie Pusey* (London: Longmans, 1894), 4 volumes, vol. 2, p. 71. See also Michael A. McGreevy, 'John Keble on the Anglican Church and the Church Catholic', *Heythrop Journal* 5 (1964), pp. 27–35.

14 Cited in John Henry Newman, *Certain Difficulties Felt by Anglicans in Catholic Teaching* (London: Longmans, 1901), vol. 1, pp. 109–10.

15 Cited in R. B. Martin, *The Dust of Combat: a Life of Charles Kingsley* (London: Faber and Faber, 1959), p. 47.

16 See, for example, the statement by Modern Church at: http://www.inclusivechurch2.net/Anglican-Covenant-and-Communion-755dd12 (accessed 9 March 2011).

17 Eamon Duffy, *The Stripping of the Altars: Traditional Religion in England, 1400–1580* (New Javen: Yale University press, 1992), and A. G. Dickens, *The English Reformation* (London: Batsford, 1964; revised edition 1989).

18 See David Loades, *Revolution in Religion: The English Reformation, 1530–1570* (Cardiff: University of Wales Press, 1992), pp. 4–5.

19 Christopher Haigh, *English Reformations: Religion, Politics and Society under the Tudors* (Oxford: Oxford University Press, 1993).

20 Christopher Haigh (ed.), *The English Reformation Revised* (Cambridge: Cambridge University Press, 1988), p. 29.

21 For a useful account, see Felicity Heal, *Reformation in Britain and Ireland* (Oxford: Oxford University Press, 2003), ch. 4.

22 A. Fox and J. Guy, *Reassessing the Henrician Age: Humanism, Politics and Reform, 1500–1550* (Oxford: Blackwell, 1986), pp. 157–64.

23 T. F. T. Plucknett and J. L. Barton (eds), *St Germain's Doctor and Student* (Selden Society 94, 1974), p. 327. On St Germain and royal supremacy, see Daniel Eppley, *Defending Royal Supremacy and Discerning God's Will in Tudor England* (Aldershot: Ashgate, 2007), ch. 3.

24 Haigh, *English Reformations*, p. 115.

25 See Daniel Eppley, *Defending Royal Supremacy*, ch. 1.

26 Haigh, *English Reformations*, p. 123.

27 Jasper Ridley, *Thomas Cranmer* (Oxford: Clarendon Press, 1962), p. 12.

28 'A collection of Tenets extracted from Canon Law showing the Extravagant Pretensions of the Church of Rome', in J. E. Cox, *The Works of Thomas Cranmer* (Cambridge: Cambridge University Press for the Parker Society, 1846), 2 volumes, vol. 2, pp. 68–75.

29 Dickens, *The English Reformation*, p. 119.

Notes

30 Diarmaid MacCulloch, 'Henry VIII and the Reform of the Church' in MacCulloch, *The Reign of Henry VIII: Politics, Policy and Piety* (Basingstoke: Macmillan, 1995), p. 178.

31 *Die Wittenberger Artikel con 1536 (Artikel der cristlichen lahr, von welchen die legatten aus Engelland mit dem herrn doctor Martnio gehandelt anno 1536)*, ed. Georg Mentz (Darmstadt: Wissenschaftliche Buchgesellschaft, 1968), pp. 48–9.

32 John Stephenson, 'Wittenberg and Canterbury', *Concordia Theological Quarterly* 48 (1984), pp. 165–84.

33 G. W. Bernard, 'The making of religious policy, 1533–1546: Henry VIII and the search for the middle way', *Historical Journal* 41 (1998), pp. 321–49, esp. p. 336.

34 Haigh, *English Reformations*, p. 129.

35 'The Institution of a Christian Man' in Charles Lloyd (ed.), *Formularies of Faith Put Forth by Authority During the Reign of Henry VIII* (Oxford: Oxford University Press, 1856), pp. 21–211; here, p. 121.

36 Alec Ryrie, 'The Strange Death of Lutheran England', *Journal of Ecclesiastical History* 53 (2002), pp. 64–92, esp. p. 82.

37 Patrick Collinson, 'Thomas Cranmer', in Geoffrey Rowell (ed.), *The English Religious Tradition and the Genius of Anglicanism* (Wantage: Ikon, 1992), pp. 79–104, p. 87.

38 G. W. Bernard, 'The making of religious policy, 1533–1546: Henry VIII and the search for the middle way', *Historical Journal* 41 (1998), pp. 321–49, here, p. 333. See also p. 349. See also G. W. Bernard, 'The Church of England, c. 1529–1642', *History* 75 (1990), pp. 183–206, p. 188. See also, *The King's Reformation: Henry VIII and the Remaking of the English Church* (New Haven: Yale University Press, 2005).

39 J. S. Brewer, James Gairdner and R. H. Brodie (eds), *Letters and Papers, Foreign and Domestic, of the Reign of Henry VIII, 1509–1547* (London: Longmans, 1862–1910), 21 volumes, vol. 15, p. 484.

40 Henry VIII, Speech to parliament, 24 December 1545, in *The Parliamentary History of England from the Earliest Period to the Year 1803* (London: Hansard, 1806), vol. 1 (1066–1625), col. 563.

41 Bernard, 'The making of religious policy', p. 339.

42 'A Necessary Doctrine and Erudition for Any Christian Man (King's Book)' in *Formularies of the Faith*, pp. 213–377; here, p. 215.

43 'King's Book', p. 278.

44 Ryrie, 'The Strange Death of Lutheran England', pp. 85–6.

45 S. R. Cattley (ed.), *The Acts and Monuments of John Foxe (Foxe's Book of Martyrs)* (London: Seeley, 1839), vol. 8 (Bk. 12), p. 580.

46 Ryrie, 'The Strange Death of Lutheran England', p. 88.

47 Haigh, *English Reformations*, p. 166.

48 Haigh, *English Reformations*, p. 167.

49 'A Sermon of the Salvation of Mankind, by only Christ our Saviour, from Sin and Death Everlasting' in *Certain Sermons or Homilies Appointed to Be Read in Churches in the Time of the Late Queen Elizabeth of Famous Memory* (Oxford: Oxford University Press, 1840), pp. 17–28, p. 23.

50 P. N. Brooks, *Thomas Cranmer's Doctrine of the Eucharist: An Essay in Historical Development* (London: Macmillan, 1965).

51 See Diarmaid MacCulloch, *Tudor Church Militant: Edward VI and the Protestant Reformation* (London: Penguin, 2001), pp. 87, 167–71.

52 Hastings Robinson (ed.), *Original letters relative to the English Reformation: written during the reigns of King Henry VIII., King Edward VI., and Queen Mary: chiefly from the archives of Zurich* (Cambridge: University Press for the Parker Society, 1846–1847), 2 volumes, vol. 1, pp. 24–5 (hereafter OL).

53 See B. Hall, 'Cranmer, the Eucharist and the Foreign Divines in the reign of Edward VI', in Paul Ayris and David Selwyn (eds), *Thomas Cranmer, Churchman and Scholar* (Woodbridge: Boydell, 1993), pp. 217–58.

54 Joseph Ketley (ed.), *The Two Liturgies, A.D. 1549, and A.D. 1552: with other documents set forth by authority in the reign of King Edward VI: viz. The Order of Communion, 1548; The Primer, 1553; The Catechism and Articles, 1553; Catechismus Brevis, 1553* (Cambridge: Cambridge University Press for the Parker Society, 1844), p. 88.

55 *The Two Liturgies*, PS, p. 79.

56 Bucer and Paul Fagius to the Ministers at Strasbourg, 26 April 1549, OL, ii, p. 535.

57 Samuel Carr (ed.), *Early Writings of John Hooper, D.D. Lord Bishop of Gloucester and Worcester, Martyr, 1555* (Cambridge: Cambridge for the Parker Society, 1843), p. 156.

58 Hooper to Bullinger, 27 March 1550, OL, i, p. 79. See Timothy Rosendale, *Liturgy and Literature in the Making of Protestant England* (Cambridge: Cambridge University Press, 2007).

59 Cited in MacCulloch, *Tudor Church Militant*, pp. 91–2.

60 Basil Hall, 'Martin Bucer in England', in D. E Wright (ed.), *Martin Bucer: Reforming Church and Community* (Cambridge: Cambridge University Press, 1994), pp. 152–4.

61 Henry Jenkyns (ed.), *The Remains of Thomas Cranmer* (Oxford: Oxford University Press, 1833), 4 volumes, vol. 2, pp. 275–463.

62 J. E. Cox, *Writings and Disputations of Thomas Cranmer, Archbishop of Canterbury, Martyr, 1556, Relative to the Sacrament of the Lord's Supper* (Cambridge: Cambridge University Press for the Parker Society, 1844), pp. 1–367.

63 *Defence*, Bk 4, ch. 3, Cranmer, *Remains*, vol. 2, p. 427.

64 *Defence*, Bk 3, ch. 15, Cranmer, *Remains*, vol. 2, p. 422.

65 Diarmaid MacCulloch, *Thomas Cranmer: A Life* (New Haven: Yale University Press, 1996), p. 615.

66 *Defence*, Bk 1, ch. 12, Cranmer, *Remains*, vol. 2, p. 302.

67 Cranmer, *Writings*, PS, p. 11.

68 *Defence*, Bk 3, ch. 15, Cranmer, *Remains*, vol. 2, p. 417.

69 *Defence*, Preface to the Reader, Cranmer, *Remains*, vol. 2, p. 289.

70 *Defence*, Bk 1, ch. 3, Cranmer, *Remains*, vol. 2, p. 346.

71 Henry Christmas (ed.), *The Works of Nicholas Ridley, D.D.: Sometime Lord Bishop of London, Martyr, 1555* (Cambridge: Cambridge University Press for the Parker Society, 1843), p. 322.

72 Hooper to Bullinger, 5 February 1550, Zurich Letters, iii, 76.

73 'An Oversight and Deliberation upon the Holy Prophet Jonas', in *Hooper's Early Writings*, PS, pp. 431–558, esp. p. 479. On this controversy, see MacCulloch, *Cranmer*, pp. 469–84.

74 Hooper to Bucer, 17 October 1550 in John Strype, *Historical Memorials, Chiefly Ecclesiastical, And Such As Concern Religion, The Reformation Of It, And The Progress Made Therein, Under The Reign And. Influence Of King Edward The Sixth* (Oxford: Clarendon Press, 1822), vol. 2, pt 2, pp. 455–65.

75 Bucer to Hooper, no date, in Strype, *Historical Memorials*, pp. 456–65.

76 See esp. John Ayre, *The works of John Whitgift, D.D., Master of Trinity College, Dean of Lincoln, &c. afterwards successively Bishop of Worcester and Archbishop of Canterbury* (Cambridge: Cambridge University Press for the Parker Society, 1851–1853), 3 volumes, vol. 1, pp. 72, 258.

77 Hooper to Bullinger, 29 June 1550, OL, i, p. 87.

78 Cranmer to Bullinger, 20 March 1552, OL, i, p. 23.

79 See Letter of Anne Hooper to Bullinger, 3 April 1551, OL, i, p. 107.

80 Hooper to Bullinger, 1 August 1551, OL, i, pp. 91–5.

81 Whitgift, PS, i, p. 64.

82 MacCulloch, *Cranmer*, p. 525–8.

83 See below, Chapter 3.

84 Gerald Bray (ed.), *Documents of the English Reformation* (Cambridge: James Clarke, 2004) and *Tudor Church Reform: The Henrician Canons of 1535 and the Reformatio Legum Ecclesiasticarum* (Woodbridge: Boydell, 2000).

Chapter 3

1 See Edward Bickersteth, *The Divine Warning to the Church, of our Enemies, Dangers, and Duties, and as to our Future Prospects* (London: Seeley, 1844). See also Donald Lewis, *The Origins of Christian Zionism: Lord Shaftesbury and Evangelical Support for a Jewish Homeland* (Cambridge: Cambridge University Press, 2009); and Martin Spence, 'Time and eternity in British evangelicalism, c. 1820–c.1860', University of Oxford DPhil, 1980.

2 On Bickersteth's suspicion of the Oxford Movement, see T. R. Birks, *Memoir of Edward Bickersteth* (London: Seeley, 1852), 2 volumes, ii, p. 243.

3 Edward Bickersteth, *Progress Of Popery, Including Observations On Its True Character, The Causes of Its Present Progress, its Final Fall, and the Difficulties and Duties of Protestants in These Days* (London: Seeley, 1836), p. 4.

4 See Peter Toon, *Evangelical Theology, 1833–1856: A Response to Tractarianism* (London: Marshall, Morgan & Scott, 1979), esp. pp. 52–3.

5 'The Thirteenth and Final Report of the Council of the Parker Society' in *General Index Publications of The Parker Society* compiled for Henry Gough (Cambridge: Cambridge University Press for the Parker Society, 1855), no page number [p. 2].

Notes

6 Pears' researches led to the publication of two volumes of Hastings Robinson and Steuart Adolphus Pears (eds), *The Zurich Letters: Comprising the Correspondence of Several English Bishops and Others, with Some of the Helvetian Reformers, during the early part of the reign of Queen Elizabeth, translated from authenticated copies of the autographs preserved in the archives of Zurich* (Cambridge: Cambridge University Press for the Parker Society, 1842–45). Hereafter, ZL.

7 Peter Toon, 'The Parker Society', *Historical Magazine of the Protestant Episcopal Church*, 46 (September 1977), pp. 323–32; Andrew Cinnamond, 'The Reformed Treasures of the Parker Society', in *Churchman* 122 (2008), pp. 221–42; Toon, *Evangelical Theology*, pp. 43–4.

8 'Thirteenth and Final Report of the Council of the Parker Society' [p. 1].

9 'Thirteenth and Final Report of the Council of the Parker Society' [p. 1].

10 Linda Colley, *Britons: Forging the Nation, 1707–1837* (London: Vintage, 1996).

11 Diarmaid MacCulloch, *The Later Reformation in England* (Basingstoke: Macmillan, 1990), p. 25.

12 See, for instance, the recent introduction by William Marshall, *Scripture, Tradition and Reason: A Selective View of Anglican Theology Through the Centuries* (Dublin: Columba Press/APCK, 2010).

13 Patrick Collinson, 'The politics of religion and the religion of politics in Elizabethan England', *Historical Research* 82 (2009), pp. 74–92, p. 92.

14 William P. Haugaard, *Elizabeth and the English Reformation: The Struggle for a Stable Settlement of Religion* (Cambridge: Cambridge University Press, 1970), p. 31,

15 Christina H. Garrett, *The Marian Exiles: A Study in the Origins of Elizabethan Puritanism* (Cambridge: Cambridge University Press, 1938; reprint, 1966).

16 Leo F. Solt, *Church and State in Early Modern England, 1509–1640* (New York: Oxford University Press, 1990), p. 65.

17 Jewel to Bullinger, 22 May 1559, ZL, i, p. 33. See N. M. Sutherland, 'The Marian exiles and the establishment of the Elizabethan regime', *Archiv für Reformationsgeschichte* 78 (1987), pp. 253–86.

18 W. H. Frere, *The English Church in the Reigns of Elizabeth and James I* (London: Macmillan, 1904).

19 J. E. Neale, 'The Elizabethan Acts of Supremacy and Uniformity', *English Historical Review* LXV (1950), pp. 304–32; *Elizabeth I and her Parliaments 1559–1581* (London: Cape, 1953), pp. 33–84.

20 Norman L. Jones, *Faith by Statute: Parliament and the Settlement of Religion, 1559* (London: Royal Historical Society, 1982), pp. 83–118.

21 See Patrick Collinson, 'Windows in a woman's soul: questions about the religion of Elizabeth I', *Elizabethan Essays* (London: Hambledon Press, 1994), pp. 87–118. For his judicious assessment that she was not as protestant as Jewel and others but might have been manipulated, see p. 109. See also 'The politics of religion and the religion of politics in Elizabethan England', *Historical Research* 82 (2009), pp. 74–92; 'The Religion of Elizabethan England and of its Queen', in Michele Cilibreto and Nicholas Mann (eds),

Notes

Giordano Bruno 1583–1585: The English Experience (Florence: L.S. Olschki, 1997), pp. 3–22.

22 Collinson, 'Windows in a woman's soul', p. 112.

23 Sandys to Martyr, 1 April 1560, ZL, i, pp. 73–4.

24 Letter to the Queen, 20 December 1576 in William Nicholson (ed.), *The remains of Edmund Grindal, D.D. successively Bishop of London and Archbishop of York and Canterbury* (Cambridge: Cambridge University Press for the Parker Society,1843), p. 382.

25 Collinson, 'Windows in a woman's soul', p. 118. See Eamon Duffy, *The Stripping of the Altars: Traditional Religion in England, c.1400–c.1580* (New Haven and London: Yale University Press, 1992).

26 Collinson, 'Politics of Religion', pp. 74–5.

27 Jewel to Martyr, 20 March 1559, ZL, i, 10.

28 Henry Gee and William John Hardy (eds), *Documents Illustrative of English Church History* (New York: Macmillan, 1896), pp. 416–7. On the role of parliament, see Haugaard, *Elizabeth and the English Reformation*, pp. 81–91.

29 This was the view of John Jewel (Haugaard, *Elizabeth and the English Reformation*, p. 105).

30 1569 Defence cited in Haugaard, *Elizabeth and the English Reformation*, p. 270.

31 A. G. Dickens, *The English Reformation* (London: Batsford, 1964), p. 303.

32 On the complex and much debated passage through parliament, see Haugaard, *Elizabeth and the English Reformation*, pp. 92–103. See Jewel's letter to Peter Martyr, ZL, i, 17–18.

33 Eamon Duffy, *Fires of faith: Catholic England under Mary Tudor* (New Haven: Yale University Press, 2009), p. 23.

34 Matthew Parker, *De Antiquitate Britanniae Ecclesiae* (1572).

35 See Glanmor Williams, *Reformation Views of Church History* (Cambridge: James Clarke, 1970).

36 James Ussher, *Discourse on the Religion Anciently Professed by the Irish and British* (Dublin: J. Jones, 1815), esp. pp. 114–28.

37 On this, see M. Aston, *England's Iconoclasts: Laws Against Images* (Oxford: Clarendon Press, 1988), 298–303.

38 Collinson, 'Windows in a Woman's Soul', p. 110.

39 Percy Dearmer, *The Parson's Handbook; containing practical directions both for parsons and others as to the management of the Parish Church and its Services according to the English Use as set forth in the Book of Common Prayer. With an introductory essay on Conformity to the Church of England* (London: Grant Richards, 1899).

40 On Dearmer see Nan Dearmer, *The Life of Percy Dearmer*, with an introduction by the Very Revd. W. R. Matthews (London: Jonathan Cape, 1940); Donald Gray, *Percy Dearmer: A Parson's Pilgrimage* (Norwich: Canterbury Press, 2000). On Dearmer and the liturgical movement, see Donald Gray, *Earth and Altar: the Evolution of the Parish Communion in the Church of England to 1945* (Norwich: Canterbury Press for the Alcuin Club, 1986), Part Two; see also Christopher Irvine (ed.), *They Shaped Our Liturgy* (London: SPCK for the Alcuin Club, 1998).

218

41 Parson's *Handbook*, p. 207.

42 Jewel to Martyr, no date, ZL i, 23; see Patrick Collinson, *The Elizabethan Puritan Movement* (London: Jonathan Cape, 1967), p. 64.

43 William Cecil to Nicholas Throckmorton, 8 May 1561, cited in W. M. Southgate, *John Jewel and the Problem of Doctrinal Authority* (Cambridge, MA: Harvard University Press, 1962), pp. 56–7.

44 Lancelot Andrewes, *Opuscula Posthuma* (Oxford: Parker, LACT, 1852), p. 91.

45 John Booty, *John Jewel as Apologist of the Church of England* (London: SPCK, 1963), pp. 51–5; See also Gary W. Jenkins, *John Jewel and the English National Church: The Dilemmas of an Erastian Reformer* (Aldershot: Ashgate, 2006).

46 Jenkins, *John Jewel*, p. 59.

47 Martyr to Jewel, 24 August 1562, ZL, i, 339. Haugaard, *Elizabeth and the English Reformation*, p. 243.

48 Haugaard, *Elizabeth and the English Reformation*, p. 244.

49 Southgate, John Jewel, ch. 3. On Paul's Cross, see W. J. Torrance Kirby, 'The Public Sermon: Paul's Cross and the culture of persuasion in England, 1534–1570', *Renaissance and Reformation* 30 (2006), pp. 4–29.

50 Southgate, *John Jewel*, pp. 80–7.

51 R. W. Jelf (ed.), *The Works of Bishop John Jewel* (Cambridge: Cambridge University Press for the Parker Society, 1845–50), 4 volumes, i, p. 20.

52 Jewel, PS, i, p. 365.

53 Jewel, PS, i, p. 25.

54 Jewel, PS, i, p. 25.

55 Jewel to Martyr, 6 April 1559, ZL, i, p. 16; Jenkins, *John Jewel*, p. 22. On the use of the Fathers in Anglican theology, see the detailed study by Jean-Louis Quantain, *The Church of England and Christian Antiquity: The Construction of a Confessional Identity in the 17th Century* (Oxford: Oxford University Press, 2009), esp. ch. 1.

56 Southgate, *John Jewel*, pp. 49–50.

57 Jewel, PS, i, pp. 26–82.

58 Jewel, PS, iii, p. 57.

59 Jewel, PS, i, p. 20.

60 Jewel, PS, iii, p. 62.

61 Jewel, PS, iii, p. 58.

62 On this, see, for instance, Heiko Oberman, '*Quo Vadis, Petre?* Tradition from Irenaeus to Humani Generis' in Heiko Oberman, *The Dawn of the Reformation* (Edinburgh: T&T Clark, 1992).

63 'A Treatise on the Holy Scriptures' (1570), Jewel, PS, iv, p. 1173.

64 Jewel, PS, iii, p. 68.

65 Jewel, PS, iii, p. 56.

66 Jewel, PS, iii, p. 85.

67 Jewel, PS, iii, p. 100.

68 Jewel, PS, iii, p. 106.

69 Jewel, PS, iii, p. 88.

70 Jewel, PS, iii, p. 104.

71 Jewel, PS, iii, p. 60

72 Jewel, PS, iii, p. 79.
73 *Defence of the Apology*, Jewel, PS, iii, p. 229; cf. PS, iv, p. 901.
74 Jewel, PS, iii, p. 91.
75 Jewel, PS, iii, p. 93.
76 Jewel, PS, iii, p. 54.
77 Jewel, PS, iii, p. 106. See also the correspondence with Cole in PS, i, pp. 62, 68, 205, 231.
78 Jewel, PS, iii, p. 106.
79 Jewel, PS, iii, pp. 69–70.
80 See also Calvin's distinction in *Institutes*, Book IV, ch. x.16; x.27.
81 Jewel, PS, iii, p. 65.
82 Jewel, PS, iii, p. 98. This refers to both halves of the Ten Commandments implying that the Christian magistrate was responsible for all law. See Melanchthon, CR, xxi, 553–4 (1535).
83 Jewel, PS, iii, p. 98.
84 W. J. Torrance Kirby, 'The Articles of Religion of the Church of England (1563/1571) commonly called the "Thirty-Nine Articles"', in Eberhard Busch and Mihály Bucsay (eds), *Reformierte Bekenntnisschriften*, vol. 2/1 (Neukirchen: Neukirchener Verlag, 2008). This contains a critical edition of the text in both Latin and English. See also Gerald Bray (ed.), *Documents of the English Reformation* (Cambridge: Lutterworth, 1994) and *Tudor Church Reform: The Henrician Canons of 1535 and the Reformatio legum Ecclesiasticarum* (Woodbridge: Boydell, 2000).
85 The influence of the Augsburg Confession can be easily discerned in Articles I, II, IV, IX, XIV, XVI, XXIII, XXIV, and XXV (of the Thirty-Nine).
86 Martin Brecht und Hermann Ehmer (eds), *Confessio Virtembergica. Das württembergische Bekenntnis von 1552* (Holzgerlingen: Hänssler, 1999), pp. 139–90.
87 Haugaard, *Elizabeth and the English Reformation*, pp. 253–4.
88 The Lutheran influence on the early Elizabethan Settlement has been discussed in detail by Hirofumi Horie in 'The Lutheran Influence on the Elizabethan Settlement, 1558–1563', *Historical Journal* 34 (1991), pp. 519–37. See esp. pp. 530–32.
89 Text in Edward Cardwell (ed.), *Synodalia: A Collection of Articles of Religion, Canons, and Proceedings of Convocations in the Province of Canterbury from the Year 1547 to the Year 1717* (Oxford: Oxford University Press, 1842), 2 volumes, vol. 1, pp. 28–9.
90 John Griffiths (ed.), *The Two Books of Homilies appointed to be read in Churches* (Oxford: Oxford University Press, 1859), pp. 439–52.
91 *Homilies*, pp. 118–33.
92 *Homilies*, pp. 273–8, here, p. 278. On the Elizabethan homilies, see Haugaard, *Elizabeth and the English Reformation*, pp. 273–6.
93 *Homilies*, p. 445.
94 Cranmer to Calvin, 20 March 1552, OL, i, pp. 24–5.
95 See, for instance, Edgar C. S Gibson, *The Thirty-Nine Articles of the Church of England* (London: Methuen, 1912); E. J. Bicknell, *A Theological Introduction to*

the *Thirty-Nine Articles of the Church of England* (London: Longmans, 1946); Oliver O'Donovan, *On the Thirty-Nine Articles. A Conversation with Tudor Christianity* (Exeter: Paternoster, 1986).

96 Haugaard, *Elizabeth and the English Reformation*, p. 255.

Chapter 4

1 Mark Chatfield, *Churches the Victorians Forgot* (Ashbourne: Moorland, 1979);. see also G. W. O. Addleshaw and Frederick Etchells, *The Architectural Setting of Anglican Worship: An Inquiry into the Arrangements for Public Worship in the Church of England from the Reformation to the Present Day* (London: Faber, 1948); J. F. White, *The Cambridge Movement: The Ecclesiologists and the Gothic Revival* (Cambridge: Cambridge University Press, 1962); Geoffrey Rowell, *The Vision Glorious: Themes and Personalities of the Catholic Revival in Anglicanism* (Oxford: Clarendon, 1991), p. 104.

2 See Peter F. Anson, *Fashions in Church Furnishings, 1840–1940* (London: Faith Press, 1960).

3 The Ecclesiological Society, *Instrumenta Ecclesiastica* (London: John Van Voorst, vol. 1, 1847; vol. 2, 1856).

4 *Church Enlargement and Church Arrangement* (Cambridge: Cambridge Camden Society, 1843), p. 12; cited in White, *The Cambridge Movement*, p. 187.

5 Introduction in J. M. Neale and Benjamin Webb (eds), *The Symbolism of Churches and Church Ornaments: A Translation of the First Book of the Rationale Divinorum Officiorum, Written by William Durandus* (Leeds: T. W. Green, 1843), p. xxvi.

6 *The Symbolism of Churches*, p. cxxx.

7 *The Symbolism of Churches*, p. 32.

8 *The Symbolism of Churches*, p. xxvi.

9 *The Symbolism of Churches*, p. xxi–xxii.

10 A. W. N. Pugin, *The Present State of Ecclesiastical Architecture in England* (London: Charles Dolman, 1843), pp. 142–3.

11 Cited in Rowell, *The Vision Glorious*, p. 129.

12 'The Knightsbridge Churches Case' in *The Ecclesiologist* New Series 82 (1857), pp. 116–8; here, p. 118.

13 On this, see esp. Patrick Collinson, *The Elizabethan Puritan Movement* (London: Jonathan Cape, 1967), pp. 59–100; J. H. Primus, *The Vestments Controversy: an Historical Study of the Earliest Tensions Within the Church of England in the Reigns of Edward VI and Elizabeth* (Kampen: J.H. Kok, 1960); William P. Haugaard, *Elizabeth and the English Reformation: The Struggle for a Stable Settlement of Religion* (Cambridge: Cambridge University Press, 1970), pp. 211–32.

14 Walter Phillips, 'Henry Bullinger and the Elizabethan Vestiarian Controversy: An Analysis of Influence', *Journal of Religious History* 11 (1991), pp. 363–84;

Notes

David Keep, 'Bullinger's Intervention in the Vestiarian Controversy of 1566', *The Evangelical Quarterly* 47 (1975), pp. 223–30.

15 Richard Beaumont to Parker, 27 February 1564 in John Bruce and Thomas Perowne (eds), *Correspondence of Matthew Parker, D.D. Archbishop of Canterbury Comprising Letters Written by and to Him, from A.D. 1535, to His Death, A.D. 1575* (Cambridge: Cambridge University Press for the Parker Society, 1853), p. 226.

16 William Cecil to Parker, 25 January 1565, PS, Parker, pp. 223–7.

17 William Cecil to Parker, 25 January 1565, PS, Parker, pp. 223–4.

18 William Cecil to Parker, 25 January 1565, PS, Parker, p. 227.

19 Humphrey to Bullinger, 16 August 1563 in Hastings Robinson and Steuart Adolphus Pears (eds), *The Zurich Letters: Comprising the correspondence of several English bishops and others, with some of the Helvetian reformers, during the early part of the reign of Queen Elizabeth* (Cambridge: Cambridge University Press for the Parker Society, 2 volumes, 1842–5, hereafter ZL), i, p. 34. See also 9 February 1566, p. 152.

20 Sampson to Bullinger, 16 February 1566, ZL, i, pp. 153–4.

21 Bullinger to Humphrey and Sampson, 1 May 1566, ZL, i, pp. 346–7.

22 Bullinger to Humphrey and Sampson, 1 May 1566, ZL, i, P. 348.

23 Bullinger to Humphrey and Sampson, 1 May 1566, ZL, i, P. 349.

24 Bullinger to Grindal, 3 May 1566, ZL, i, p. 356.

25 Grindal to Bullinger, 27 August 1566, ZL, i, pp. 168–9.

26 *A Parte of a Register*, p. 32 cited in Patrick Collinson, *The Elizabethan Puritan Movement*, p. 74.

27 Grindal and others to Bullinger and Gualter, 6 February 1567, ZL, i, p. 175.

28 William Nicholson (ed.), *The remains of Edmund Grindal, D.D. successively Bishop of London and Archbishop of York and Canterbury* (Cambridge: Cambridge University Press for the Parker Society, 1843), p. 207.

29 Humphrey and Sampson to Bullinger, July 1566, ZL, i, p. 158.

30 Humphrey and Sampson to Bullinger, July 1566, ZL, i, pp. 160–1.

31 Humphrey and Sampson to Bullinger, July 1566, ZL, i, pp. 164–5.

32 Bullinger to Grindal, 6 September 1566, ZL, i, p. 358.

33 Bullinger to Grindal, 6 September 1566, ZL, i, p. 359.

34 Bullinger to Grindal, 6 September 1566, ZL, i, p. 361.

35 Haugaard, *Elizabeth and the English Reformation*, p. 216. This may also explain her refusal to assent to the canons of 1571.

36 On Grindal's role in the controversy, see Patrick Collinson, *Archbishop Grindal, 1519–1583: The Struggle for a Reformed Church* (Berkeley, CA: University of California Press, 1979), esp. ch. 9.

37 Parker to Cecil, 3 March 1565, Parker, PS, pp. 233–4.

38 Parker to Cecil, 5 June 1566, Parker, PS, pp. 284.

39 Parker to Cecil, about Easter 1565, Parker, PS, p. 240.

40 Parker to Cecil, 30 April 1565, Parker, PS, pp. 240–1.

41 Parker, PS, p. 272.

Notes

42 Henry Gee and W. J. Hardy (eds), *Documents Illustrative of English Church History* (London: Macmillan, 1896), pp. 171–4.

43 Haugaard, Elizabeth and the English Reformation, p. 223.

44 Parker, PS, p. 270.

45 Collinson, *The Elizabethan Puritan Movement*, p. 73.

46 Jewel to Bullinger, 24 February 1567, ZL, i, p. 185.

47 Grindal, PS, pp. 203–4.

48 Pius V, *Regnans in Excelsis*, 27 April 1570, at: http://www.papalencyclicals.net/Pius05/p5regnans.htm (accessed 16 March 2011).

49 Heal, *The Reformation in Britain and Ireland*, p. 334.

50 J. W. Allen, *A History of Political Thought in the Sixteenth Century* (London: Methuen, 1928), pp. 172–3.

51 Cited in Collinson, *The Elizabethan Puritan Movement*, p. 107.

52 'Journal of the House of Commons: April 1571', *The Journals of all the Parliaments during the reign of Queen Elizabeth* (1682), pp. 155–180, at: http://www.british-history.ac.uk/report.aspx?compid=43684 (accessed 16 March 2011).

53 *The Parliamentary History of England from the Earliest Period to the Year 1803* (London: Hansard, 1806), vol. 1, 1066–625, cols. 733–4. The Bill is reprinted in W. H. Frere and C. E. Douglas, *Puritan Manifestoes: A Study of the Origin of the Puritan Revolt* (London: SPCK, 1907), pp. 149–151.

54 *The Parliamentary History,* col. 762.

55 'Journal of the House of Commons: May 1572', *The Journals of all the Parliaments during the reign of Queen Elizabeth* (1682), pp. 205–21, at: http://www.british-history.ac.uk/report.aspx?compid=43688 (accessed 16 March 2011).

56 On this, see Collinson, *The Elizabethan Puritan Movement*, pp. 101–21.

57 Sermon of 25 February 1570 in Leonard J. Trinterud, *Elizabethan Puritanism* (New York: Oxford, 1971), p. 159.

58 Peter Lake, *Moderate Puritans and the Elizabethan Church* (Cambridge: Cambridge University Press, 1982), p. 20; Peter Lake, *Anglicans and Puritans? Presbyterianism and English Conformist Thought from Whitgift to Hooker* (London: Allen Unwin, 1988), esp. ch. 1.

59 Letter to Burghley, November 1573, cited in Lake, *Moderate Puritans*, pp. 21–2.

60 *An Admonition to Parliament* in W. H. Frere and C. E. Douglas, *Puritan Manifestoes: A Study of the Origin of the Puritan Revolt* (London: SPCK, 1907), pp. 1–39; here, p. 8.

61 *Admonition*, p. 10.

62 *Admonition*, p. 11.

63 *Admonition*, p. 12.

64 *Admonition*, pp. 12–3.

65 *Admonition*, p. 15.

66 *Admonition*, p. 16.

67   *Admonition*, p. 19.

68   *Admonition*, pp. 20–39.

69   Albert Peel (ed.), *The Second Part of a Register* (Cambridge: Cambridge University Press, Reprint 2010), vol. 1, pp. 89–90.

70   *Admonition*, p. 21.

71   In *Puritan Manifestoes*, pp. 40– 56, here pp. 50–1.

72   *Admonition*, p. 17.

73   *Admonition*, p. 18.

74   *A Second Admonition to the Parliament in Puritan Manifestoes*, pp. 79–34

75   *Second Admonition*, p. 93.

76   See Lake, *Moderate Puritans*, pp. 77–92.

77   John Strype, *The Life And Acts of Matthew Parker, The First Archbishop Of Canterbury in the Reign of Queen Elizabeth* (Oxford: Oxford University Press, 1821), 4 volumes, ii, p. 350.

78   Cartwright in John Ayre, *The Works of John Whitgift, D.D., Master of Trinity College, Dean of Lincoln, &c. afterwards successively Bishop of Worcester and Archbishop of Canterbury* (Cambridge: Cambridge University Press for the Parker Society, 3 volumes, 1851–3), i, p. 390.

79   Cartwright in Whitgift, PS, i, p. 329.

80   Whitgift, PS, i, p. 179.

81   Whitgift, PS, i, p. 3.

82   Bullinger to Humphrey and Sampson, 1 May 1566, ZL, i, pp. 346–9.

83   Whitgift, PS, i, p. 72.

84   Whitgift, PS, i, p. 5.

85   Whitgift, PS, i, p. 184.

86   Whitgift, PS, i, p. 184.

87   Whitgift, PS, i, p. 185.

88   Article XIX.

89   Whitgift, PS, i, p. 185.

90   Whitgift, PS, i, p. 182.

91   Whitgift, PS, i, pp. 246–7.

92   Whitgift, PS, i, p. 245. See Calvin, *Institutes* Book IV, ch. x.16; x.27.

93   Whitgift, PS, ii, p. 97.

94   Whitgift, PS, i, p. 335.

95   For a useful summary of the concept, which was adopted by a number of other English theologians, see R. P. C. Hanson, *Tradition in the Early Church* (London: SCM Press, 1962), pp. 93–128.

96   Whitgift, PS, ii, pp. 226–7.

97   Whitgift, PS, ii, p. 227.

98   Whitgift, PS, ii, p. 233.

99   Whitgift, PS, ii, p. 271.

100 Whitgift, PS, ii, p. 234.

101 Whitgift, PS, ii, pp. 236–7.

102 Whitgift, PS, ii, p. 97.

103 Whitgift, PS, ii, p. 248.

104 Whitgift, PS, ii, p. 97.

105   Whitgift, PS, iii, p. 189.
106   Whitgift, PS, i, p. 27.
107   Whitgift, PS, ii, p. 239.
108   Whitgift, PS, iii, p. 160.
109   Patrick Collinson, *Godly People: Essays on English Protestantism and Puritanism* (London: Hambledon, 1983), p. 375.
110   See, for example, Collinson, *The Elizabethan Puritan Movement*, pp. 168–90.
111   Grindal, PS, p. 389.
112   See Patrick Collinson, 'The Downfall of Archbishop Grindal and its place in Elizabethan political and Ecclesiastical History', in *Godly People*, pp. 379–98.
113   Solt, *Church and State*, pp. 96–7.
114   Roger B. Manning, 'The Crisis of Episcopal Authority during the Reign of Elizabeth', *Journal of British Studies* 11 (1971), pp. 1–25.
115   See W. D. J. Cargill Thompson, 'Sir Francis Knollys' Campaign Against the Jure Divino Theory of Episcopacy', in C. Robert Cole and Michael E. Moody (eds), *The Dissenting Tradition* (Athens, OH: Ohio University Press, 1975), pp. 39–77.
116   Members of the University of Oxford, *Tracts For The Times, Volume III, 1835–6* (London: Rivington, 1836), no. 74: 'Catena Patrum, No. I. Testimony Of Writers In The Later English Church To The Doctrine Of The Apostolical Succession', p. 4; Lake, *Anglicans and Puritans*, pp. 126–35.
117   Heal, *Reformation in Britain and Ireland*, p. 421.

Chapter 5

1   For surveys of Hooker reception, see Michael Brydon, *The Evolving Reputation of Richard Hooker: An Examination of Responses, 1600–1714* (Oxford: Oxford University Press, 2006); Diarmaid MacCulloch, 'Richard Hooker's Reputation', *English Historical Review*, 117 (2002), pp. 773–812; Conal Condren, 'The Creation of Richard Hooker's Public Authority: Rhetoric, Reputation and Reassessment', *The Journal of Religious History* 21 (1997), pp. 35–59; John Gascoigne, 'The Unity of Church and State Challenged: Responses to Hooker from the Restoration to the Nineteenth-Century Age of Reform', *The Journal of Religious History* 21 (1997), pp. 60–79.
2   John Booty, 'The Quest for the Historical Hooker', *Churchman* 80 (1966).
3   *The Folger Library Edition of the Works of Richard Hooker* (Cambridge: Belknap Press of Harvard University Press, 1977–93), 7 volumes. See also W. Speed Hill (ed.), *Studies in Richard Hooker: Essays Preliminary to an Edition of his Works* (Cleveland, OH: Press of Case Western Reserve University, 1972).
4   Peter Lake, 'Business as Usual? The Immediate Reception of Hooker's Ecclesiastical Polity', *The Journal of Ecclesiastical History* 52 (2001), pp. 456–86;

Notes

Peter Lake, *Anglicans and Puritans? Presbyterianism and English Conformist Thought from Whitgift to Hooker* (London: Allen Unwin, 1988), p. 229.

5 See John E. Booty, 'Hooker and Anglicanism' in W. Speed Hill (ed.), *Studies in Richard Hooker*, pp. 212, 235.

6 See MacCulloch, 'Richard Hooker's Reputation', pp. 783–4.

7 Louis Weil, 'The Gospel in Anglicanism' in Stephen Sykes and John Booty (eds), *The Study of Anglicanism* (London and Philadelphia: SPCK/Fortress Press, 1988), p. 67; W. J. Torrance Kirby, 'Richard Hooker as an Apologist of the Magisterial Reformation in England' in Arthur Stephen McGrade (ed.), *Richard Hooker and the Construction of the Christian Community* (Tempe, AZ: Medieval & Renaissance Texts & Studies, 1997), pp. 219–33. See also, Lee W. Gibbs, 'Richard Hooker: prophet of Anglicanism or English magisterial reformer?', *Anglican Theological Review* 84 (2002), pp. 943–60.

8 J. S. Marshall, *Hooker and the Anglican Tradition: An Historical and Theological Study of Hooker's Ecclesiastical Polity* (London: A & C Black, 1963), pp. v, vii.

9 Philip Secor, *Richard Hooker: Prophet of Anglicanism* (Tunbridge Wells: Burns & Oates, 1999).

10 J. W. Packer, *The Transformation of Anglicanism: 1643–1660 with special reference to William Chillingworth* (Manchester: Manchester University Press, 1969), p. 173n.

11 Henry McAdoo, 'Richard Hooker' in Geoffrey Rowell, *The English Religious Tradition and the Genius of Anglicanism* (Wantage: Ikon, 1992), pp. 105–26, esp. p. 106.

12 William Haugaard, 'Prelude: Hooker after 400 Years', *Anglican Theological Review* 84 (2002), pp. 875–7.

13 John Keble (ed.), *The Works of that learned and judicious Divine, Mr. Richard Hooker* (Oxford: Clarendon Press, seventh edition revised by R. W. Church and F. Paget, 1888), 3 volumes, vol. 1, i, ii, civ. See MacCulloch, 'Richard Hooker's Reputation', pp. 808–10. References are to this edition throughout in the form: book, chapter, section.

14 F. J. Shirley, *Richard Hooker and Contemporary Political Ideas* (London: SPCK, 1949), pp. 35–6.

15 Newman later wrote in his *Apologia*: 'Anglicanism claimed to hold that the Church of England was nothing else than a continuation in this country of that one Church of which in old times Athanasius and Augustine were members' (*Apologia pro vita sua* (London: Longmans, 1864), p. 231). See Lake, *Anglicans and Puritans*, p. 145.

16 See below, ch. 6.

17 MacCulloch, 'Richard Hooker's Reputation', p. 773.

18 Nigel Voak, *Richard Hooker and Reformed Theology: A Study of Reason, Will, and Grace* (Oxford: Oxford University Press, 2003), p. 2.

19 Nigel Atkinson, *Richard Hooker and the Authority of Scripture, Tradition and Reason* (Carlisle: Paternoster Press 1997).

20 W. J. Torrance Kirby, *Richard Hooker, Reformer and Platonist* (Aldershot: Ashgate, 2005). W. J. Torrance Kirby, *Richard Hooker's Doctrine of the*

Notes

Royal Supremacy (Leiden: E J Brill 1990). More nuanced treatments are W. J. Torrance Kirby, 'Richard Hooker's theory of natural law in the context of Reformation theology', *Sixteenth Century Journal* 30 (1999), pp. 681–703, and W. J. Torrance Kirby in McGrade (ed.), *Richard Hooker and the Construction of the Christian Community*, pp. 219–36.

21 Egil Grislis, 'The Hermeneutical Problem of Richard Hooker', in W. Speed Hill (ed.), *Studies in Richard Hooker*, pp. 159–206; Egil Grislis, 'The Role of Consensus in Richard Hooker's Method of Theological Inquiry', in Robert E. Cushman and Egil Grislis (eds.), *The Heritage of Christian Thought: Essays in Honor of Robert Lowry Calhoun* (New York: Harper & Row, 1965), pp. 64–88; Egil Grislis, 'The Scriptural Hermeneutics of Richard Hooker', in W. J. Torrance Kirby (ed.), *Introduction to Richard Hooker* (Leiden: Brill, 2007).

22 Egil Grislis, 'Jesus Christ – The Centre of Theology in Richard Hooker's *Of the Lawes of Ecclesiastical Polity,* Book V', *Journal of Anglican Studies* 5 (2007), pp. 227–52, esp. p. 234.

23 Lake, *Anglicans and Puritans?*, p. 5.

24 Lake, *Anglicans and Puritans?*, p. 245; White and Tyacke, 'Debate', p. 203.

25 Lake, *Anglicans and Puritans?*, p. 196.

26 Lake, *Anglicans and Puritans?*, p. 160.

27 See Peter White, *Predestination, Policy and Polemic: Conflict and Consensus in the English Church from the Reformation to the Civil War* (Cambridge: Cambridge University Press, 1992), p. 125; Olivier Loyer, *L'Anglicanisme de Richard Hooker* (Lille: Réproduction des Theses, 1979).

28 Gunnar Hillerdal, *Reason and Revelation in Richard Hooker* (Lund: Lund Universitets Arsskrift, 1962), p. 20.

29 Peter Munz, *The Place of Hooker in the History of Thought* (Westport, Conn: Greenwood Press 1971).

30 Kirby, Richard *Hooker's Doctrine of the Royal Supremacy*, pp. 33–7, 126–7.

31 See Egil Grislis, *The Hermeneutical Problem*, p. 163, and Kirby, *Richard Hooker's Doctrine of the Royal Supremacy*, p. 39.

32 Nigel Voak, *Richard Hooker*, p. 4.

33 Nigel Voak, *Richard Hooker*, p. 10.

34 Nigel Voak, 'Richard Hooker and the Principle of Sola Scriptura', *Journal of Theological Studies* 59 (2008), pp. 96–139, esp. p. 138.

35 MacCulloch, 'Richard Hooker's Reputation', p. 778.

36 IV. xiii.9.

37 Walton's biography in published in Keble, *Works*, vol. 1, 1–117; here, p. 77.

38 Walter Travers, *A Full and Plain Declaration of Ecclesiastical Discipline we owe of the word of God, and of the declining of the church of England from the Same*, 1574, p. 9. No further information is given. It was published in Heidelberg by Michael Schirat (Early English Texts Online).

39 *A Full and Plain Declaration*, pp. 26–7.

40 Thomas Fuller, *The Church History of Britain from the Birth of Jesus Christ Until the Year MDCXLVIII* (London: Thomas Tegg, 1842), 3 volumes, vol. 3, p. 129.

41 See Richard Bauckham, 'Hooker, Travers and the Church of Rome in the 1580s', *Journal of Ecclesiastical History*, 29 (1978), pp. 37–50.

42 P. A. Nuttall (ed.), *Dr Fuller's Worthies of England* (London: Thomas Tegg, 1840), 3 volumes, i, p. 423.

43 MacCulloch, 'Richard Hooker's Reputation', p. 776.

44 I.xvi.1.

45 I.xvi.2.

46 I.ii.2.

47 I.iii.2.

48 I.v.1.

49 I.vi.1.

50 I.iii.1.

51 I.vi.5.

52 I.vii.2.

53 I.viii.1.

54 I.viii.8.

55 I.x.1.

56 I.x.4.

57 I.x.6.

58 I.x.7.

59 I.x.8.

60 I.x.8.

61 I.x.10.

62 I.x.10.

63 I.x.11.

64 I.x.10.

65 I.x.12.

66 I.xi.6.

67 I.xi.6.

68 I.xii.2.

69 I.xiv.1.

70 I.xiv.1.

71 I.xiv.2:

72 I.xiv.4 (citing 1 John 5.13). The Bishop's Bible renders the verse: 'These thynges haue I written vnto you that beleue on ye name of the sonne of God, that ye may knowe howe that ye haue eternall lyfe, and that ye may beleue on the name of the sonne of God'.

73 Keble, *Works*, vol. 3, pp. 548–69, esp. p. 559.

74 'Mr Hooker's Answer to the Supplication Mr Travers made to Council', 24, in Keble, *Works*, vol. 3, pp. 570–96; here, pp. 594–5.

75 I.xvi.5.

76 III.vii.1.

77 II.i.4.

78 II.iv.4.

79 II.vii.4.

Notes

80 NigelVoak, 'Richard Hooker and the Principle of Sola Scriptura', p. 138.
81 III.i.11.
82 III.i.14.
83 III.iii.4.
84 III.vii.3.
85 III.vii.4.
86 III.xi.18.
87 VIII.ii.16.
88 IV.ix.1.
89 These books were republished in a series of texts aimed at political studies students: A. S. McGrade (ed.), *Richard Hooker: Of Laws of Ecclesiastical Polity, Preface, Book I, Book VIII* (Cambridge Texts in the History of Political Thought, Cambridge: Cambridge University Press, 1989).
90 McAdoo, 'Richard Hooker', p. 118.
91 V.vii.2.
92 III.xi.6.
93 V.vii.2.
94 V.vii.1–3.
95 MacCulloch, 'Richard Hooker's Reputation', p. 779.
96 V.lxvii.6.
97 V.lxvii.2.
98 V.lvi.11.
99 V.liv.5. On Hooker's sacramental theology, see Bryan D. Spinks, *Two Faces of Elizabethan Anglican Theology: Sacraments and Salvation in the Thought of William Perkins and Richard Hooker* (Lanham, MD and London: Scarecrow Press, 1999). Edmund Newey, 'The Form of Reason: Participation in the Work of Richard Hooker, Benjamin Whichcote, Ralph Cudworth and Jeremy Taylor', *Modern Theology* 18 (2002), pp. 1–26.
100 V.lxvii.12.
101 V.lxxvii.1.
102 V.lxxvi.1.
103 V.lxxvii.2.
104 V.lxxviii.12.
105 VII.xiv.11.
106 7.i.4. On Hooker and bishops, see Richard A. Norris, 'Episcopacy' in Stephen Sykes and John Booty (eds), *The Study of Anglicanism* (London: SPCK, 1988), pp. 296–309.
107 VII.v.1.
108 VII.v.8.
109 VII.v.2.
110 On Hooker and Royal Supremacy, see Daniel Eppley, *Defending Royal Supremacy and Discerning God's Will in Tudor England* (Aldershot: Ashgate, 2007), ch. 5.
111 VIII.i.2.
112 VIII.vi.1, 8.

113 VIII.i.7–ii.1.

114 VIII.vi.8.

115 VIII.ii.1.

116 VIII.vi.14.

117 VIII.i.2.

118 Lake, *Anglicans and Puritans?*, p. 230.

119 Lake, *Anglicans and Puritans?*, p. 227.

Chapter 6

1 T. S. Eliot, 'Lancelot Andrewes', *Times Literary Supplement* (23 September 1926), pp. 621–2. It was reprinted in one of Eliot's most important works of criticism: *For Lancelot Andrewes: Essays on Style and Order* (London: Faber & Gwyer, 1928).

2 The famous opening line of Eliot's 'Journey of the Magi' ('A cold coming we had of it') is drawn from Andrewes, *Sermon 15: Of the Nativitie*.

3 R. W. Church, 'Bishop Andrewes' in *Pascal and Other Sermons* (London: Macmillan, 1896), pp. 52–96; here, pp. 90–1.

4 Church, 'Bishop Andrewes', p. 94.

5 Walter Frere, 'Lancelot Andrewes as a Representative of Anglican Principles: A Lecture Delivered at Holy Trinity, Chelsea, February 28, 1897', *Church Historical Society*, 44 (London: SPCK, 1898).

6 Frere, 'Lancelot Andrewes', pp. 11–2; see also Arthur Middleton, *Fathers and Anglicans: the Limits of Orthodoxy* (Leominster: Gracewing, 2001), esp. pp. 114–38.

7 P. E. More and F. L. Cross, *Anglicanism* (1935) (new edition, Cambridge: James Clarke, 2008). See Nicholas Tyacke, *Anti-Calvinists: The Rise of English Arminianism, c. 1590–1640* (Oxford: Clarendon Press, paperback edition, 1990), p. viii.

8 See, for example, Peter Lake, 'Lancelot Andrewes, John Buckeridge, and Avant-garde Conformity at the Court of James I', in Linda Levy Peck (ed.), *The Mental World of the Jacobean Court* (Cambridge: Cambridge University Press, 1991).

9 Nicholas Tyacke, 'Lancelot Andrewes and the Myth of Anglicanism', in Peter Lake and Michael Questier (eds), *Conformity and Orthodoxy in the English Church c. 1560–1660* (Woodbridge: Boydell, 2000), pp. 5–33.

10 On this, see Peter McCullough, 'Making Dead Men Speak: Laudianism, Print, and the Works of Lancelot Andrewes, 1626–1642', *The Historical Journal* 41 (1998), pp. 401–24.

11 Henry Parry Liddon, *Life of Edward Bouverie Pusey* (London: Longmans, 1894), 4 volumes, vol. 1, ch. 18. See R. W. Pfaff, 'The Library of the Fathers: The Tractarians as Patristic Translators', *Studies in Philology* 70 (1973), pp. 329–44.

12 On this, see Peter Nockles, *The Oxford Movement in Context* (Cambridge: Cambridge University Press, 1994), pp. 104–45.

Notes

13 Cited in Liddon, *Life of Pusey*, vol. 1, p. 422.

14 This prospectus was included at the end of each volume, followed by a list of subscribers. The pagination remained separate from the volumes themselves (Prospectus to the *Library of the Fathers*, p. 2).

15 See the preface to Edward Bouverie Pusey (ed.), *Confessions of St Augustine* (Oxford: Parker, 1838), esp. p. viii. See also Liddon, *Life of Pusey*, vol. 1, p. 423.

16 Cited in Liddon, *Life of Pusey*, vol. 1, p. 435.

17 Nockles, *The Oxford Movement in Context*, p. 145.

18 Nockles, *The Oxford Movement in Context*, p. 128.

19 Gerard Tracey (ed.), *Letters and Diaries of John Henry Newman* (Oxford: Oxford University Press, 1999), vol. 8, Appendix 2, pp. 521–3; Nicholas Tyacke 'Lancelot Andrewes and the Myth of Anglicanism', p. 6.

20 Gerard Tracey (ed.), *Letters and Diaries of John Henry Newman* (Oxford: Oxford University Press, 1995), vol. 7, pp. 191–2.

21 *Letters and Diaries*, vol. 7, pp. 195–6 (reply to a letter of Newman, 1 January 1840).

22 'Anglicanism' was modified to 'Anglo-Catholicism' in later editions of the work from 1838. See John Henry Newman, *The Via Media of the Anglican Church Illustrated in Lectures, Letters and Tracts Written Between 1830 and 1841* (London: Longmans, 1901), vol. 1, p. 17.

23 John Henry Newman, *Lectures on the Prophetical Office of The Church, Viewed Relatively To Romanism And Popular Protestantism* (London: Rivington, 1837), p. 21.

24 Pusey to Newman, 8 January 1841, *Letters and Diaries*, vol. 8, pp. 13–4.

25 See also Newman to S. F. Wood, 7 January 1842, *Letters and Diaries*, vol. 8, p. 416.

26 *Letters and Diaries*, vol. 8, p. 14.

27 Newman to Pusey, 12 January 1841, *Letters and Diaries*, vol. 8, pp. 14–5.

28 See Charles W. A. Prior, *Defining the Jacobean Church: The Politics of Religious Controversy* (Cambridge: Cambridge University Press, 2005).

29 This has been vigorously resisted by Peter White in: *Predestination, Policy and Polemic: Conflict and Consensus in the English Church from the Reformation to the Civil War* (Cambridge: Cambridge University Press, 1992). See also G. W. Bernard, 'The Church of England, c.1529–c.1642', *History* 75 (1990), pp. 183–206.

30 The main protagonist in challenging the old orthodoxy is Tyacke, *Anti-Calvinists* and 'Puritanism, Arminianism and Counter-Revolution' in Tyacke, *Aspects of English Protestantism, c. 1530–1700* (Manchester: Manchester University Press, 2001), esp. pp. 132–59. His entertaining essay, 'Anglican Attitudes' (pp. 176–202) surveys the field. See also Peter Lake, 'Calvinism and the English Church, 1570–1635', *Past and Present* 114 (1987), pp. 32–76. Other useful works are Peter Lake, *Moderate Puritans* (Cambridge: Cambridge University Press, 1982); Anthony Milton, *Catholic and Reformed: The Roman and Protestant Churches in English Protestant Thought, 1600–1640*

Notes

(Cambridge: Cambridge University Press, 1995); Kenneth Fincham, 'Episcopal Government, 1603–1640', in Kenneth Fincham (ed.), *The Early Stuart Church, 1603–1640* (Basingstoke: Macmillan, 1993), pp. 71–8; Kenneth Fincham, *Prelate as Pastor: The Episcopate of James I* (Oxford: Clarendon Press, 1990).

31 Conrad Russell, *The Causes of the English Civil War* (Oxford: Clarendon Press, 1990), p. 84.

32 Felicity Heal, *Reformation in Britain and Ireland* (Oxford: Clarendon Press, 2005), p. 424.

33 C. H. McIlwain (ed.), *The Political Works of James I* (Cambridge, MA: Harvard University Press, 1918), p. 291.

34 Peter McCullough, *Sermons at Court: Politics and Religion in Elizabethan and Jacobean Preaching* (Cambridge: Cambridge University Press, 1998); Lori Anne Ferrell, *Government by Polemic: James I, the King's Preachers, and the Rhetoric of Conformity, 1603–1625* (Stanford: Stanford University Press, 1998).

35 Kenneth Fincham and Peter Lake, 'The Ecclesiastical Policy of King James I', *Journal of British Studies* 24 (1985), pp. 169–207, esp. p. 206.

36 Frederick Shriver, 'Hampton Court Re-visited: James I and the Puritans' in *Journal of Ecclesiastical History* 33 (1982), pp. 48–71; J. R. Tanner, *Constitutional Documents of the Reign of James I, 1603–1625* (Cambridge: Cambridge University Press, 1930), pp. 58–60; Fincham and Lake, 'The Ecclesiastical Policy of King James I', pp. 171–5.

37 Patrick Collinson, 'The Jacobean Religious Settlement: The Hampton Court Conference' in Howard Tomlinson (ed.), *Before the English Civil War* (New York: Macmillan, 1983), pp. 27–51, esp. pp. 45–7.

38 McIlwain (ed.), *The Political Works of James I*, pp. 6–8, 23–4.

39 McIlwain (ed.), *The Political Works of James I*, p. 54.

40 Edward Cardwell, *History of Conferences and other Proceedings Connected with the revision of The Book Of Common Prayer; from the year 1558 to the year 1660* (Oxford: Oxford University Press, 1850), p. 150; see also Fincham and Lake, 'The Ecclesiastical Policy of King James I', p. 172.

41 Shriver, 'Hampton Court Re-visited', p. 70.

42 Cardwell, *History of Conferences*, p. 209.

43 Cardwell, *History of Conferences*, pp. 183–4.

44 McIlwain (ed.), *The Political Works of James I*, p. 24.

45 Shriver, 'Hampton Court Re-visited', p. 70.

46 See, for example, Kenneth Fincham (ed.), *Visitation Articles and Injunctions of the Early Stuart Church* (Woodbridge: Boydell, 1994), COERS, vol. 1. See Leo F. Solt, *Church and State in Early Modern England, 1509–1640* (New York: Oxford University Press, 1990), pp. 153–8.

47 'The Canons of 1603 (1604)' in Gerald Bray, *The Anglican Canons 1529–1947* (Woodbridge: Boydell, 1998), pp. 258–445.

48 Tanner, *Constitutional Documents*, p. 73.

49 Fincham and Lake, 'The Ecclesiastical Policy of King James I', p. 179.

50 See John Spurr, *The Post-Reformation* (Harlow: Pearson, 2006), p. 49.

Notes

51 See Paul A. Welsby, *George Abbot: The Unwanted Archbishop* (London: SPCK, 1962); Kenneth Fincham, 'Prelacy and Politics: Archbishop Abbot's Defence of Protestant Orthodoxy', *Historical Research*, 61 (1988), pp. 36–64; and S. M. Holland, 'George Abbot: The Wanted Archbishop' in *Church History* 56 (1987), pp. 172–87.

52 Fincham and Lake, 'The Ecclesiastical Policy of King James I', p. 191.

53 *The Conclusive Part of the Parliamentary or Constitutional History of England; From the earliest times, to the Dissolution of the Convention Parliament that restored King Charles II. Together with an Appendix of Several Matters relative to the foregoing History, which were either omitted in the Course of it, or have been sent in to the Compilers since the Publication of the former Parts of this Work* (London, 1660), vol. 23, p. 30. See also, Prior, *Defining the Jacobean Church*, p. 17.

54 Andrew Pettegree, 'The Reception of Calvinism in Britain' in Wilhelm Neuser, and Brian Armstrong (eds), *Calvinus Sincerioris Religionis Vindex* (Kirkville, MO: Sixteenth Century Journal Publishers, 1997), pp. 267–89; Tyacke, *Anti-Calvinists*; Peter Lake, 'Calvinism and the English Church, 1570–1635', *Past and Present* 114 (1987), pp. 32–76. Peter Lake, *Moderate Puritans* (Cambridge: Cambridge University Press, 1982).

55 Andrew Pettegree, Alastair Duke, and Gillian Lewis (eds), *Calvinism in Europe, 1540–1620* (Cambridge: Cambridge University Press, 1994); Patrick Collinson, 'England and International Calvinism 1558–1640', in Menna Prestwich (ed.), *International Calvinism 1541–1715* (Oxford: Clarendon Press, 1985), pp. 197–223; Milton, *Catholic and Reformed*, ch. 8.

56 Nicholas Tyacke, *Anti-Calvinists. The Rise of English Arminianism c. 1590–1640* (Oxford: Clarendon Press, 1987).

57 Tyacke, *Anti-Calvinists*, ch. 2.

58 Tyacke, 'The Rise of Arminianism reconsidered', *Aspects of English Protestantism*, pp. 160–175.

59 For a definition of Arminianism, see Tyacke, *Aspects of English Protestantism*, pp. 156–9.

60 Peter White, *Predestination, Policy and Polemic*, pp. 175–202.

61 Anthony Milton (ed.), *The British Delegation and the Synod of Dort (1618–1619)* (Woodbridge: Boydell, 2005), COERS, vol. 13.

62 W. B. Patterson, 'The Synod of Dort and the Early Stuart Church' in Donald S Armentrout (ed.), *This Sacred History: Anglican Reflections for John Booty* (Cambridge, MA: Cowley Publications, 1990), p. 206.

63 Milton, *The British Delegation*, pp. lii–liii.

64 An interesting ideological definition of 'Arminianism' was given in the *Dictionary of English Church History*. It was 'a general term used to cover the whole High Church and Latitudinarian reaction against the intellectual tyranny of Calvinism'.

65 Peter Lake, 'The Laudian style: order, Uniformity and the Pursuit of the Beauty of Holiness in the 1630s', in Fincham (ed.), *Early Stuart Church*, pp. 161–85.

66 Lake, 'The Laudian style', p. 162.

Notes

67 Julian Davies, *The Caroline Captivity of the Church: Charles I and the Remoulding of Anglicanism* (Oxford: Clarendon Press, 1992), p. 3; Kevin Sharpe, *The Personal Rule of Charles I* (New Haven; London: Yale University Press, 1992), pp. 275–6, 284–6.

68 Laud, Works, I, p. 131.

69 Tyacke, *Anti-Calvinists*.

70 Peter White, 'The *via media* in the Early Stuart Church' in Fincham (ed.), *The Early Stuart Church*, pp. 211–30.

71 Hugh Trevor-Roper, *Catholics, Anglicans and Puritans* (Chicago: University of Chicago Press, 1988), p. 114.

72 Tyacke, 'Anglican Attitudes', in *Aspects of English Protestantism*, p. 187.

73 Tyacke, *Anti-Calvinists*, pp. 103–5; 125–8.

74 Conrad Russell, *Parliaments and English Politics, 1621–1629* (Oxford: Clarendon Press, 1982), p. 404.

75 J. P. Kenyon, *The Stuart Constitution, 1603–1688: Documents and Commentary* (Cambridge: Cambridge University Press, 1986), 2nd edn, p. 139.

76 Russell, *Parliaments*, p. 404.

77 'A Relation of the Conference between William Laud and Mr. Fisher the Jesuit' in James Bliss (ed.), *The Works of William Laud* (Oxford: Parker, 1849), 7 volumes, vol. 2, p. 366.

78 'Conference', p. 218.

79 'Conference', p. 247.

80 'Conference', p. 266.

81 'Conference', p. 235.

82 'Conference', pp. 167–8.

83 'Conference', p. 170.

84 'Conference', p. 170.

85 'Conference', p. 168.

86 'Conference', p. 170.

87 'Conference', p. 171.

88 'Conference', p. 189.

89 'Conference', p. 190.

90 'Conference', p. 225.

91 'Conference', pp. 5–6.

92 Davies, *The Caroline Captivity*, p. 86.

93 Laud, *Works*, VI, p. 44.

94 Laud, *Works*, I, p. 83.

95 Edward Cardwell, *Documentary Annals of the Reformed Church of England* (Oxford: Oxford University Press, 1839), vol. 2, p. 159.

96 John Selden (S. H. Reynolds, ed.), *Table Talk* (Oxford: Oxford University Press, 1892), p. 71.

97 Tyacke, 'Archbishop Laud' in *Aspects of English Protestantism*, pp. 203–21; here, p. 203.

98 See Kenneth Fincham, 'The Restoration of Altars in the 1630s', in *The Historical Journal* 44 (2001), pp. 919–40.

99 Thomas Fuller, *The Church History of Britain from the Birth of Jesus Christ until the year 1648* (London: Tegg, 1837), vol. 3, pp. 385–8.

100 See also the works by Thomas Bilson, *The Perpetual Government of Christ's Church* (1593) (Oxford: Oxford University Press, 1842); and later Joseph Hall, *Episcopacy by Divine Right* (1640) (Oxford: Oxford University Press, 1863).

101 J. P. Sommerville, 'The Royal Supremacy and Episcopacy "Jure Divino", 1603–1640', *Journal of Ecclesiastical History* 34 (1983), pp. 548–58. See, for instance, Laud's somewhat functional view of episcopacy: 'Luther, since he would change the name, yet did very wisely that he would leave the thing, and make choice of such a name as was not altogether unknown in the ancient church' (Laud, *Works*, III, p. 386).

102 Laud, *Works*, III, 406–7; see also IV, 311.

103 Laud, *A Speech delivered in the Starre-Chamber, on Wednesday, the XIVth of Iune* (London, 1637), p. 7 in *Works*, VI, 43.

104 See Robert Clifton, 'Fear of Popery' in Conrad Russell (ed.), *The Origins of the English Civil War* (Basingstoke: Macmillan, 1973), pp. 144–67.

105 Bray, *Canons*, pp. 532–52; Canon 16.3, Bray, *Canons*, p. 547.

106 Bray, *Canons*, pp. 553–78. See Davies, *Caroline Captivity*, pp. 251–87.

107 Canon 6.2 in Bray, *Canons*, p. 568. See also Laud, *Works*, V, p. 623.

108 Davies, *Caroline Captivity*, p. 285.

109 On the complexities of the Commonwealth period, see Judith Maltby, 'Suffering and surviving: the Civil Wars, the Commonwealth and the formation of "Anglicanism"', in Stephen Platten (ed.), *Anglicanism and the Western Christian Tradition* (Norwich: Canterbury Press, 2003), pp. 122–43.

110 William Orme, *The Life and Times of Richard Baxter with a critical examination of his writings* (London: J. Duncan, 1830), 2 volumes, vol. 1, p. 68.

111 Milton, 'On the New Forcers of Conscience under the Long Parliament'.

112 See Norman Sykes, *Old New and Priest Presbyter* (Cambridge: Cambridge University Press, 1956).

113 Edward Reynolds, 'Joy in the Lord, 1655', in John Rogers Pitman (ed.), *The whole works of the Right Rev. Edward Reynolds, Lord Bishop of Norwich* (London: Holdsworth, 1826), 6 volumes, vol. 4, p. 377.

114 Oliver Cromwell, *Speeches* (London: Dutton, 1908), pp. 160–1.

115 Maltby, 'Suffering and surviving', p. 143.

Chapter 7

1 Colin McLekvie, 'Jeremy Taylor's recommendations for a library of Anglican theology (1660)', *Irish Booklore* IV (1980), pp. 96–103.

2 'Jeremy Taylor's recommendations', p. 101.

3 'Jeremy Taylor's recommendations', p. 102.

4 Full text in Gerald Bray, *Documents of the English Reformation, 1526–1701* (Cambridge : James Clarke, 2004), pp. 544–5; here, p. 545.

Notes

5 I. M. Green, *The Re-establishment of the Church of England, 1660–3* (Oxford: Oxford University Press, 1977), p. 127. See also Robert S. Bosher, *The Making of the Restoration Settlement: the Influence of the Laudians, 1649–1662* (London: Dacre, 1951); Ronald Hutton, *The Restoration: a Political and Religious History of England and Wales, 1658–67* (Oxford: Clarendon Press, 1985); Paul Seaward, *The Cavalier Parliament and the Reconstruction of the Old Regime, 1661–7* (Cambridge: Cambridge University Press, 1989); John Spurr, *The Restoration Church of England, 1648–89* (New Haven: Yale University Press, 1991).

6 Keeble, *The Restoration*, p. 110; J. P. Cunningham, 'The Eirenicon and the "primitive episcopacy" of James Ussher: an Irish Panacea for Britannia's Ailment' in *Reformation and Renaissance Review* 8 (2006), pp. 128–46. On Ussher, see Alan Ford, *James Ussher: theology, history, and politics in early-modern Ireland and England* (Oxford: Oxford University Press, 2007). On episcopacy, see ch. 10. See also John Lloyd, *Treatise of Episcopacy* (London, 1661).

7 Richard Baxter reminisced after the Declaration that he and Ussher could have reconciled their differences within half an hour. See F. J. Powicke, *A Life of the Reverend Richard Baxter, 1615–1691* (London: Jonathan Cape, 1924), pp. 126–7.

8 John Gauden, κακουργοι, *sive medicastri: Slight Healers of Publique Hurts* (London, 1660), title page.

9 *Slight Healers*, pp. 78–9 (Gauden's emphases).

10 Barry Till, 'The Worcester House Declaration and the Restoration of the Church of England', *Historical Research* 70 (1997), pp. 203–30.

11 N. H. Keeble, *The Restoration: England in the 1660s* (Oxford: Blackwell, 2002), p. 138.

12 'House of Lords Journal Volume 11, 9 November 1660', *Journal of the House of Lords: volume 11: 1660–1666 (1767–1830)*, pp. 178–82, at: http://www.british-history.ac.uk/report.aspx?compid=14056 (accessed: 28 July 2011).

13 Till, 'The Worcester House Declaration', p. 213.

14 'House of Commons Journal Volume 8: 28 November 1660', *Journal of the House of Commons: volume 8: 1660–1667* (1802), p. 194, at: http://www.british-history.ac.uk/report.aspx?compid=26312 (Accessed: 28 July 2011).

15 Keeble, *The Restoration*, p. 115.

16 Richard Baxter, 'The Reformed Liturgy, with the exceptions of the Presbyterian brethren against the present liturgy' (1661) in *The Practical Works of Richard Baxter* (London: James Duncan, 1830), 23 volumes, vol. 15, pp. 451–527.

17 William Orme, *The Life and Times of Richard Baxter with a critical examination of his writings* (London: James Duncan, 1830), 2 volumes, vol. 1, p. 188.

18 N. H. Keeble (ed.), *The Autobiography of Richard Baxter* (London: Dent, 1974), p. 167.

19 Spurr, *The Restoration Church*, p. 42.

20 14 Car. II c. 4. The full text is in Bray, *Documents*, pp. 449–59.

21 Spurr, *The Restoration Church*, p. 42.

22 R. C. Latham and W. Matthews (eds), *The Diary of Samuel Pepys* (London: HarperCollins, 1995), 8 volumes, vol. 3 (1662), pp. 117, 169.

23 One Collect for his feast day on 30 January spoke of Charles as a 'blessed Saint and Martyr'.

24 John Spurr, 'The Church of England, comprehension and the Toleration Act of 1688', *English Historical Review* 104 (1989), pp. 927–46, esp. p. 944; John Spurr, 'From Puritanism to Dissent, 1660–1700' in Christopher Durston and Jacqueline Eales (eds), *The Culture of English Puritanism, 1560–1700* (Basingstoke: Macmillan, 1996), pp. 234–65.

25 *Letter from the Member of Parliament*, cited in Spurr, 'The Church of England', p. 943.

26 Norman Sykes, *The English Religious Tradition* (London: SCM, 1951), p.52.

27 R. Thomas, 'Comprehension and indulgence' in Geoffrey F. Nuttall and Owen Chadwick (eds), *From Uniformity to Unity, 1662–1962* (London: SPCK, 1962), pp. 189–253; here, pp. 192–3.

28 Judith Maltby, *Prayer Book and People in Elizabethan and Early Stuart England* (Cambridge: Cambridge University Press, 1998), p. 235.

29 Spurr, The Restoration Church, p. 103.

30 Hooker, EP VIII.i.2.

31 Sykes, *The English Religious Tradition*, p. 44.

32 The most comprehensive survey is by Peter White, *Predestination, Policy and Polemic*. Such a work is derided as an anachronistic 'Anglican' reading of the past by Nicholas Tyacke. See esp. 'Anglican Attitudes', pp. 180–5.

33 Letter from Richard Montague to John Cosin, 28 June 1624 in George Ornsby (ed.), *Correspondence of John Cosin* (Durham, London and Edinburgh: Surtees Society, vol. 52, 1869), part one, p. 21. See also p. 97.

34 On heroism in the seventeenth century, see Reid Barbour, 'The Caroline Church Heroic: The Reconstruction of Epic Religion in Three Seventeenth-Century Communities', *Renaissance Quarterly* 50 (1997), pp. 771–818, p. 786.

35 Thomas Harrab, *Tessaradelphus, or The foure brothers* (London, 1616), preface to the reader. The book is not paginated. I owe these references to Professor Alec Ryrie.

36 Harrab, *Tessaradelphus*, ch. 7.

37 Harrab, *Tessaradelphus*, preface to the reader.

38 Harrab, *Tessaradelphus*, ch. 7.

39 Harrab, *Tessaradelphus*, ch. 7.

40 The letter is simply signed 'S. P.' but was very likely to have been written by him. *A Brief Account of The New Sect of Latitude-man: Together With Some Reflections Upon The New Philosophy. By S.P. of Cambridge* (London, 1662). References to the 1669 edition where 'Latitude-men' is changed to 'Latitudinarians'. See W. M. Spellman, *The Latitudinarians and the Church of England, 1660–1700* (Athens, GA: University of Georgia Press, 1993).

41 G. R. Cragg, *Cambridge Platonists* (Oxford: Oxford University Press, 1968), p. 83; see also H. R. McAdoo, *The Spirit of Anglicanism: A Survey of Anglican*

Notes

Theological Method in the Seventieth Century (London: A & C Black, 1965), pp. 189–197.

42   *A Brief Account*, p. 7.

43   *A Brief Account*, p. 14.

44   *A Brief Account*, p. 22.

45   *A Brief Account*, p. 24.

46   *A Brief Account*, p. 24.

47   See C. A. Patrides, *Cambridge Platonists* (London: Edward Arnold, 1969). McAdoo, *The Spirit of Anglicanism*, chs 3 and 4.

48   F. T. Campagnac (ed.), *The Cambridge Platonists Being Selections From The Writings Of Benjamin Whichcote, John Smith And Nathanael Culverwel* (Oxford: Clarendon Press, 1901), p. 67.

49   Ralph Cudworth, 'The First Sermon' in *The True Notion of the Lord's Supper* (London, 1670), p. 53.

50   W. R. Inge, *The Platonic Tradition in English Religious Thought* (London: Longman, 1926).

51   McAdoo, *The Spirit of Anglicanism*, ch. 5.

52   John Marshall, 'The ecclesiology of the Latitude-men 1660–1689: Stillingfleet, Tillotson and "Hobbism"', *Journal of Ecclesiastical History* 36 (1985), pp. 407–27; here, p. 408.

53   Edward Fowler, *The Principles and Practices of certain moderate divines of the Church of England (greatly mis-understood), truly represented and defended* (London, 1670).

54   Fowler, *The Principles and Practices*, pp. 18–9.

55   Fowler, *The Principles and Practices*, pp. 308–9.

56   Edward Stillingfleet, *Irenicum: A weapon-salve for the churches wounds, or The divine right of particular forms of church-government: discuss'd and examin'd according to the principles of the law of nature* (London, 1662), preface to the reader.

57   Marshall, 'The ecclesiology of the Latitude-men'.

58   William Stephens, *An Account of the Growth of Deism in England* (London, 1696), p. 8. See Tim Harris, *Politics under the later Stuarts: party conflict in a divided society, 1660–1715* (London: Longman, 1993), p. 153.

59   William Gibson, *The Church of England, 1688–1832: Unity and Accord* (London: Routledge, 2001), ch. 2.

60   Gibson, *The Church of England*, p. 61.

61   Francis Atterbury, *A letter to a convocation-man, concerning the rights, powers, and priviledges of that body* (London, 1697), pp. 6–7.

62   William Wilberforce, *A Practical View of the Prevailing Religious Systems in Higher and Middle Classes in this Country contrasted with Real Christianity* (London, 1797).

63   See esp. Nockles, *The Oxford Movement in Context*.

64   John Henry Newman, *The Via Media of the Anglican Church illustrated in Lectures, Letters and Tracts written between 1830 and 1841* (London: Longman, 1901), 2 volumes, vol. 1, p. 21.

65   *Via Media*, p. 25.

66   *Via Media*, p. 18.
67   *Via Media*, p. 18.

Chapter 8

1   John Walsh, Colin Haydon and Stephen Taylor (eds), *The Church of England, c.1689-c.1833: from Toleration to Tractarianism* (Cambridge: Cambridge University Press, 1993).

2   McAdoo, *The Spirit of Anglicanism*, (London: A & C Black, 1965) ch. 1.

3   See, most recently, Bruce Kaye, *An Introduction to World Anglicanism* (Cambridge: Cambridge University Press, 2008). See also William L. Sachs, *The Transformation of Anglicanism* (Cambridge: Cambridge University Press, 1993).

4   See my *Anglicanism: A Very Short Introduction* (Oxford: Oxford University Press, 2006), ch. 1; Ian T. Douglas and Kwok Pui-Lan (eds), *Beyond Colonial Anglicanism* (New York: Church Publishing Inc., 2001); Kevin Ward, *A History of Global Anglicanism* (Cambridge: Cambridge University Press, 2006), ch. 15. See also Andrew Wingate, Kevin Ward, Carrie Pemberton and Wilson Sitshebo (eds), *Anglicanism: A Global Communion* (New York: Church Publishing Inc., 1998); W. M. Jacob, *The Making of the Anglican Church Worldwide* (London: SPCK, 1997); Rowan Strong, *Anglicanism and the British Empire, c. 1700–1850* (Oxford: Oxford University Press, 2007).

5   The four 'Instruments of Unity' are the Archbishop of Canterbury (established in 597), the Lambeth Conference (1867), the Anglican Consultative Council (1968) and the Primates' Meeting (1978).

6   The 'Primates' consist of the senior archbishops, presiding bishops and primuses of the different churches, who frequently developed very different understandings of primacy.

7   See http://www.anglicancommunion.org/ministry/theological/teac/anglican way/index.cfm (accessed 1 March 2011).

8   Geoffrey Rowell, Kenneth Stevenson and Rowan Williams (eds), *Love's Redeeming Work: the Anglican Quest for Holiness* (Oxford: Oxford University Press, 2001).

9   The bibliography can be found at http://www.anglicancommunion.org/ ministry/theological/teac/anglicanway/keytexts.cfm (accessed 1 March 2011).

10   See http://www.lutheranworld.org/lwf/index.php/who-we-are/faith (accessed 1 March 2011).

11   See, for example, Inter-Anglican Theological and Doctrinal Commission, *The Virginia Report: The Report of the Inter-Anglican Theological and Doctrinal Commission*, included in James M. Rosenthal and Nicola Currie (eds), *Being Anglican in the Third Millennium* (Harrisburg, PA: Morehouse, 1997), pp. 211–81, sect. 3.3.

Notes

12 *Virginia Report*, ch. 5.

13 Stephen Sykes, *The Integrity of Anglicanism* (Oxford: Mowbray, 1978), pp. 8–25.

14 Sykes, *The Integrity of Anglicanism*, p. 19.

15 Sykes, *The Integrity of Anglicanism*, p. 19.

16 Stephen Sykes and John Booty (eds), *The Study of Anglicanism* (London: SPCK, 1988), p. 177.

17 H. Hensley Henson, *In Defence of the English Church* (London: Hodder & Stoughton, 1923), p. 43.

18 *Doctrine in the Church of England: the report of the Commission on Christian Doctrine appointed by the Archbishops of Canterbury and York in 1922* (London: SPCK, 1938).

19 *Doctrine in the Church of England*, p. 25.

20 'The Renewal of the Church in Unity' in *The Lambeth Conference 1968* (London: SPCK, 1968), p. 140.

21 Sykes, *The Integrity of Anglicanism*, p. 19.

22 Sykes, *The Integrity of Anglicanism*, p. 34.

23 Stephen Sykes, *Unashamed Anglicanism* (London: DLT, 1995).

24 F. D. Maurice, *The Kingdom of Christ or Hints on the Principles, Ordinances and Constitution of the Catholic Church in letters to a Member of the Society of Friends* (reprint of 2nd edn, London: James Clarke, 1959), 2 volumes, vol. 2, p. 314.

25 Maurice, *The Kingdom of Christ*, vol. 2, p. 329.

26 Maurice, *The Kingdom of Christ*, vol. 2, p. 316.

27 A. Michael Ramsey, *The Gospel and the Catholic Church* (London: Longmans, Green and Co., 1936), p. 41.

28 Ramsey, *The Gospel and the Catholic Church*, p. 66.

29 Ramsey, *The Gospel and the Catholic Church*, p. 135.

30 Rowan Williams, 'Theology and the Churches' in Robin Gill and Lorna Kendall (eds), *Michael Ramsey as Theologian* (London: DLT, 1995), pp. 9–28, p. 22.

31 'What Is Catholic Orthodoxy?' in R. D. Williams and Kenneth Leech (eds), *Essays Catholic and Radical* (London: Bowardean Press, 1983), pp. 11–25, p. 25.

32 'What is Catholic Orthodoxy?', p. 18.

33 'Does it make sense to speak of a pre-Nicene Orthodoxy?' in Rowan Williams (ed.), *The Making of Orthodoxy* (Cambridge: Cambridge University Press, 1989), pp. 1–23; here, pp. 17–8.

34 On Colenso see the standard biographies by George Cox, *The Life of John William Colenso, D.D., Bishop of Natal* (London: Ridgway, 1888); Peter Hinchliff, *John William Colenso. Bishop of Natal* (London: Nelson, 1964); and Jeff Guy, *The Heretic: A Study of the Life of John William Colenso, 1814–1883* (Pietermaritzburg: University of Natal Press, 1983). A collection of essays was published to mark the 150th anniversary of his consecration: Jonathan A. Draper (ed.), *The Eye of the Storm* (Pietermaritzburg: Cluster Publications, 2004).

Notes

35 J.W. Colenso, *Two Weeks in Natal. A Journal of a first tour of Visitation among the colonists and Zulu Kafirs of Natal* (London: Macmillan, 1855).

36 J.W. Colenso, *The Epistle of St. Paul to the Romans. Newly translated and explained from a Missionary Point of View* (London: Macmillan, 1863). New edition edited by Jonathan A. Draper: *Commentary on Romans* (Pietermaritzburg: Cluster Publications, 2003).

37 J.W. Colenso, *Romans*, p. 107.

38 J.W. Colenso, *A Letter to the Archbishop of Canterbury. Upon the Proper Treatment of Polygamist Converts from Heathenism* (London: Macmillan, 1862).

39 On this see John Rogerson, *Old Testament Criticism in the Nineteenth Century: England and Germany* (London: SPCK, 1984), esp. pp. 180–220.

40 In *Essays and Reviews* (1860). References are to the tenth edition (London: Longmans, 1862), pp. 399–527. On the controversies surrounding *Essays and Reviews*, see Ieuan Ellis, *Seven against Christ: A Study of Essays and Reviews* (Leiden: Brill, 1980), and Josef L. Altholz, *Anatomy of a Controversy: The Debate over Essays and Reviews* (Aldershot: Scolar Press, 1994). See also Basil Willey, *More Nineteenth Century Studies: A Group of Honest Doubters* (Cambridge: Cambridge University Press, 1956), ch. 4; and A. O. J. Cockshut, *Anglican Attitudes* (London: Collins, 1959), ch. 4. I have discussed liberalism and the philosophy of education, particularly in relation to Frederick Temple's essay, 'The Education of the World' (pp. 1–58) in 'The Authority of Reason? The Importance of Being Liberal' in Mark D. Chapman (ed.), *The Hope of Things to Come* (London: Mowbray, 2010), pp. 45–68.

41 'The Interpretation of Scripture', pp. 407–8.

42 'The Interpretation of Scripture', p. 487.

43 E. Abbott and L. Campbell, *The Life and Letters of Benjamin Jowett* (London: James Murray, 1897), 2 volumes, vol. 1, p. 275.

44 John Octavius Johnston, *Life and Letters of Henry Parry Liddon* (London: Longmans, 1904), pp. 63–4.

45 Johnston, *Life and Letters of Henry Parry Liddon*, p. 64.

46 *The Times*, 14 September 1867, p. 8.

47 See Alan Stephenson, *The First Lambeth Conference, 1867* (London: SPCK, 1967), ch. 11.

48 See also Mark D. Chapman, 'Where is it all going? A plea for humility?' in Kenneth Stevenson (ed.), *A Fallible Church* (London: DLT, 2008), pp. 122–41.

49 See Robert Prichard, *A History of the Episcopal Church* (Harrisburg, PA: Morehouse, 1999), pp. 188–90. On the origins of the national church idea, see Paul T. Phillips, 'The Concept of a National Church in Late Nineteenth-century England and America', *Journal of Religious History* 14 (1986), pp. 26–37, esp. pp. 31–2.

50 On Maurice, see Jeremy Morris, *F. D. Maurice and the Crisis of Christian Authority* (Oxford: Oxford University Press, 2005).

51 F. D. Maurice, *Theological Essays* (1853) (London: James Clarke, 1957), p. 403.

Notes

52 Frederick Maurice, *Life of Frederick Denison Maurice* (London: Macmillan, 1885), 2 volumes, vol. 1, pp. 306–7.

53 F. D. Maurice, *The Kingdom of Christ or Hints on the Principles, Ordinances and Constitution of the Catholic Church. In Letters to a Member of the Society of Friends* (1st edn, 1837–8) (new edition based on second edition of 1842, Cambridge: James Clarke, 1958), 2 volumes, vol. 1, p. 279.

54 F. D. Maurice, *Lincoln's Inn Sermons* (London: Longmans, 1891), 6 volumes, vol. 1, p. 251.

55 William Reed Huntington, *The Church-Idea: An Essay Towards Unity* (New York: E. P. Dutton, 1870; 4th edn, Charles Scribner's Sons, 1899), p. 169.

56 William Reed Huntington, *A National Church* (New York: Charles Scribner's Sons, 1899), pp. 52–3.

57 *The Church-Idea*, p. 1.

58 *The Church-Idea*, p. 2.

59 *The Church-Idea*, p. 124.

60 *The Church-Idea*, pp. 124–5.

61 On the origins of the North American Churches and the American Revolution, see, Peter Doll, *Revolution, Religion and National Identity* (Madison: Farleigh Dickinson, 2000).

62 *The Church-Idea*, pp. 125–6.

63 *The Church-Idea*, p. 169.

64 Huntington, *A National Church*, pp. 52–3.

65 *A National Church*, p. 14.

66 *A National Church*, p. 13.

67 *A National Church*, p. 16.

68 *A National Church*, pp. 31–3.

69 *A National Church*, p. 36.

70 *A National Church*, p. 51.

71 *A National Church*, p. 52.

72 *A National Church*, p. 66.

73 *A National Church*, pp. 71–2.

74 Resolution of the General Convention 1886 at: http://anglicansonline.org/basics/Chicago_Lambeth.html (accessed 18 July 2011).

75 Ibid.

76 Resolution 11 of the Lambeth Conference of 1888. Cf. Roger Coleman, *Resolutions of the Twelve Lambeth Conferences* (Toronto: Anglican Book Centre, 1992), p. 13; Alan M. G. Stephenson, *Anglicanism and The Lambeth Conferences* (London: SPCK, 1978). Cf. Jonathan Draper (ed.), *Communion and Episcopacy. Essays to Mark the Centenary of the Chicago-Lambeth Quadrilateral* (Oxford: RCC, 1988).

77 Gillian R. Evans, 'Permanence in the Revealed Truth and Continuous Exploration of its Meaning', in J. Robert Wright (ed.), *Quadrilateral at One Hundred* (London: Mowbray, 1998), pp. 111–25, esp. pp. 114–5.

78 'Growing Unity' in Edward White Benson, *Living Theology* (London:

Sampson Low, Marston, 1893), pp. 131–45; here, p. 139.

79 'Growing Unity', p. 133.

80 Visitation Charge of 1885 in A. C. Benson, *The Life of Edward White Benson, Sometime Archbishop of Canterbury* (London: Macmillan, 1899), 2 volumes, vol. 2, pp. 465–6.

81 See William Croswell Doane, 'The Historic Episcopate' in *The Church Review* 59 (1890), pp. 158–64; William Stevens Perry, 'Church Reunion Discussed on the Basis of the Lambeth Propositions of 1888', *The Church Review* 59 (1890), pp. 165–73.

82 Perry, 'Church Reunion Discussed', p. 173.

83 Mark D. Chapman, 'The politics of episcopacy' in *Bishops, Saints and Politics: Anglican Studies* (London: T & T Clark, 2007), pp. 9–32.

84 Lambeth Conference 1920, 'Appeal to All Christian People' in Coleman, *Resolutions*, pp. 45–8. See also Wright, 'Heritage and Vision' in *Quadrilateral at One Hundred*, pp. 8–45; here, p. 26.

85 *The Lambeth Conference Report 1930* (London: SPCK, 1930), p. 115. Cf. Resolution 9 of the 1920 Conference: 'An Appeal to All Christian People', esp. §7: 'we would urge that [the episcopate] is now and will prove to be in the future the best instrument for maintaining the unity and continuity of the Church'.

86 *The Meissen Agreement Texts* (London: Council for Christian Unity, 1992), § 16. See also Henry Chadwick, 'The Quadrilateral in England', in Wright, *Quadrilateral at One Hundred*, pp. 140–55, esp. p. 149.

87 Norman Sykes (ed.), *Church and State: Report of the Archbishop's Commission on the Relations Between Church and State* (London: Church Assembly, 1936), p. 301.

88 *The Lambeth Conference Report 1920* (London: SPCK, 1920), p. 14.

89 Paul Avis, 'Anglican Ecclesiology' in Gerard Mannion and Lewis Mudge (eds), *The Routledge Companion to the Christian Church* (London: Routledge, 2008), pp. 210–2; see also *The Identity of Anglicanism* (London: T&T Clark, 2007), esp. ch. 4.

90 Avis, *Identity*, pp. 19–21.

Chapter 9

1 Henry Luke Orombi, 'What is Anglicanism?' in *First Things* (August/September 2007) at http://firstthings.com/article.php3?id_article=6002 (accessed 1 August 2011).

2 Ian T. Douglas and Kwok Pui-Lan (eds), *Beyond Colonial Anglicanism* (New York: Church Publishing Inc., 2001).

3 Miranda K. Hassett, *Anglican Communion in Crisis: How Episcopal Dissidents and Their African Allies are Reshaping Anglicanism* (Princeton: Princeton University Press, 2007).

4 Ephraim Radner and Philip Turner, *The Fate of Communion: The Agony of Anglicanism and the Future of a Global Church* (Grand Rapids: Eerdmans, 2006),

Notes

pp. 20–1. There are many bitter asides. See, for example, p. 125, n. 21, which sees the use of gender-neutral language with reference to the Trinity as 'the most serious issue in respect to ecclesial integrity and tolerable diversity that faces the Anglican Communion'.

5   See Kevin Ward, *A History of Global Anglicanism*, ch. 15.

6   The most useful set of texts from the American Church (formerly ECUSA and now The Episcopal Church) was published as an appendix to *To Set Our Hope on Christ: A Response to the Invitation of Windsor Report §135* (New York: The Episcopal Church Center, 2005), pp. 63–130.

7   Lambeth 1978, Resolution 10.3. This was reaffirmed at 1988 (Resolution 34). Details for this section are taken from ACNS at http://www.anglicancommunion.org/acns/ (accessed 2 August 2011).

8   Ward, *A History of Global Anglicanism*, pp. 308–18.

9   Ward, *A History of Global Anglicanism*, p. 310.

10 Ward, *A History of Global Anglicanism*, p. 315.

11 Lambeth 1998, Resolution 1.10 at http://www.lambethconference.org/resolutions/1998/1998-1-10.cfm, (accessed 20 October 2011)

12 This appears to have been done only twice before, once on a sexual matter, with Resolution 19 from 1930 noting that 'illicit and irregular unions are wrong and contrary to the revealed will of God', and once on the illegitimacy of racism and tribalism (1978, Resolution 3).

13 See my *Bishops, Saints, and Politics* (London: T & T Clark, 2007), ch. 3.

14 Radner and Turner, *The Fate of Anglicanism*, p. 15.

15 Inter-Anglican Theological and Doctrinal Commission, *The Virginia Report: the Report of the Inter-Anglican Theological and Doctrinal Commission* (included in James M. Rosenthal and Nicola Currie (eds), *Being Anglican in the Third Millennium* (Harrisburg PA: Morehouse, 1997), pp. 211–81.

16 Primates' Statement, 16 October 2003 at: http://www.anglicancommunion.org/acns/news.cfm/2003/10/16/ACNS3633 (Accessed 1 August 2011).

17 The Lambeth Commission on Communion, *The Windsor Report* (London: Anglican Communion Office, 2004).

18 *The Windsor Report* Appendix 2, Art. 4.

19 *The Windsor Report*, Appendix 2, Art. 6.

20 Available at http://www.globalsouthanglican.org/index.php/comments/the_road_to_lambeth_presented_at_capa/ (accessed 2 August 2011).

21 A slightly modified version was issued in April 2007: Anglican Communion Office, *An Anglican Covenant: A Draft for Discussion* (April 2007), available at http://www.anglicancommunion.org/commission/d_covenant/docs/Draft%20Covenant%20Text%20070504.pdf (accessed 2 August 2011).

22 Peter Akinola, address at the opening of Gafcon, 22 June 2008 at http://www.evangelicals.org/news.asp?id=886 (accessed 2 August 2011).

23 http://www.gafcon.org/news/gafcon_final_statement/ (accessed 2 August 2011).

24 'The Archbishop's Retreat Addresses Parts III, IV & V', 18 July 2008 at http://www.archbishopofcanterbury.org/articles.php/1739/the-archbishops-retreat-addresses-parts-iii-iv-v (accessed 2 August 2011).

Notes

25 Concluding Presidential Address to the Lambeth Conference, 3 August 2008 at: http://www.archbishopofcanterbury.org/articles.php/1350/concluding-presidential-address-to-the-lambeth-conference (accessed 2 August 2011).

26 The so-called Ridley Hall Draft was produced in April 2009 at: http://www.anglicancommunion.org/commission/covenant/ridley_cambridge/commentary.cfm (accessed 2 August 2011), and the final draft for consideration by the constituent churches of the Anglican Communion was published in 2010 at: http://www.anglicancommunion.org/commission/covenant/final/text.cfm (accessed 1 August 2011). For the history of the different drafts, see http://www.anglicancommunion.org/commission/covenant/index.cfm (accessed 2 August 2011).

27 *Draft Covenant*, Intro, sect. 4 and sect. 3.

28 *Draft Covenant*, sect. 4.3.

29 J. N. Figgis, *Studies in Political Thought from Gerson to Grotius* (Cambridge: Cambridge University Press, 1907), p. 35.

30 See esp. Christopher Hill and Edward Yarnold SJ (eds), *Anglicans and Roman Catholics: The Search for Unity* (London: SPCK/CTS, 1994).

Bibliography

Pre nineteenth-century Primary Sources

Lancelot Andrewes, *Opuscula Posthuma* (Oxford: Parker, 1852).

Francis Atterbury, *A letter to a convocation-man, concerning the rights, powers, and priviledges of that body* (London, 1697).

Richard Baxter, 'The Reformed Liturgy, with the exceptions of the Presbyterian brethren against the present liturgy' (1661) in *The Practical Works of Richard Baxter* (London: James Duncan, 1830), 23 volumes, vol. 15, pp. 451–527.

Gerald Bray, *The Anglican Canons 1529–1947* (Woodbridge: Boydell, 1998).

—. (ed.), *Documents of the English Reformation, 1526–1701* (Cambridge: James Clarke, 2004).

—. (ed.), *Tudor Church Reform: The Henrician Canons of 1535 and the Reformatio legum Ecclesiasticarum* (Woodbridge: Boydell, 2000).

Martin Brecht and Hermann Ehmer (eds), *Confessio Virtembergica. Das württembergische Bekenntnis von 1552* (Holzgerlingen: Hänssler, 1999).

Robert Henry Brodie (eds), *Letters and Papers, Foreign and Domestic, of the Reign of Henry VIII, 1509–1547* (London: Longmans, 1862–1910), 21 vols.

Joseph Butler (ed. W. E. Gladstone), *The works of Joseph Butler, D.C.L. sometime Lord Bishop of Durham* (Oxford: Clarendon Press, 1897), 2 vols.

Edward Cardwell, *Documentary Annals of the Reformed Church of England* (Oxford: Oxford University Press, 1839).

—. *History of Conferences and Other Proceedings Connected with the Revision of the Book of Common Prayer; from the Year 1558 to the Year 1660* (Oxford: Oxford University Press, 1850).

—. (ed.), *Synodalia: A Collection of Articles of Religion, Canons, and Proceedings of Convocations in the Province of Canterbury from the Year 1547 to the Year 1717* (Oxford: Oxford University Press, 1842), 2 vols.

The Conclusive Part of the Parliamentary or Constitutional History of England; From the earliest times, to the Dissolution of the Convention Parliament that restored King Charles II. Together with an Appendix of Several Matters relative to the foregoing History, which were either omitted in the Course of it, or have been sent in to the Compilers since the Publication of the former Parts of this Work (London, 1660).

John Cosin (ed. George Ornsby), *Correspondence of John Cosin* (Durham, London and Edinburgh: Surtees Society, 1869), vol. 52.

Thomas Cranmer (ed. Henry Jenkyns), *The Remains of Thomas Cranmer* (Oxford: Oxford University Press, 1833), 4 vols.

—. (ed. John Edmund Cox.), *The Works of Thomas Cranmer* (Cambridge: Cambridge University Press for the Parker Society, 1846), 2 vols.

Bibliography

—. (ed. John Edmund Cox.), *Writings and Disputations of Thomas Cranmer, Archbishop of Canterbury, Martyr, 1556, Relative to the Sacrament of the Lord's Supper* (Cambridge: Cambridge University Press for the Parker Society, 1844).

Oliver Cromwell, *Speeches* (London: Dutton, 1908).

Desiderius Erasmus, *The Paraphrase of Erasmus vpon the Newe Testamente* (London, 1548, vol. 2: London, 1549).

Edward Fowler, *The Principles and Practices of Certain Moderate Divines of the Church of England (Greatly Mis-understood), Truly Represented and Defended* (London, 1670).

John Foxe (ed. S. R. Cattley), *The Acts and Monuments of John Foxe (Foxe's Book of Martyrs)* (London: Seeley, 1839).

Walter Howard Frere and Charles Edward Douglas (eds), *Puritan Manifestoes: A Study of the Origin of the Puritan Revolt* (London: SPCK, 1907), pp. 1–39.

Thomas Fuller, *The Church History of Britain from the Birth of Jesus Christ Until the Year MDCXLVIII* (London: Thomas Tegg, 1842), 3 vols.

—. (ed. P. Austin Nuttall), *Dr Fuller's Worthies of England* (London: Thomas Tegg, 1840), 3 vols.

John Gauden, kakourgoi, *sive medicastri: Slight Healers of Publique Hurts* (London, 1660).

Edmund Grindal (ed. William Nicholson.), *The Remains of Edmund Grindal, D.D. Successively Bishop of London and Archbishop of York and Canterbury* (Cambridge: Cambridge University Press for the Parker Society, 1843).

Joseph Hall, *Episcopacy by Divine Right* (1640) (Oxford: Oxford University Press, 1863).

Thomas Curson Hansard, *The Parliamentary History of England from the Earliest Period to the Year 1803* (London: Hansard, 1806), vol. 1 (1066–1625).

Thomas Harrab, *Tessaradelphus, or The foure brothers* (London, 1616).

[Books of Homilies], *Certain Sermons or Homilies Appointed to be Read in Churches in the Time of the Late Queen Elizabeth of Famous Memory* (Oxford: Oxford University Press, 1840).

[Books of Homilies] (ed. John Griffiths), *The Two Books of Homilies Appointed to be Read in Churches* (Oxford: Oxford University Press, 1859).

John Hooper (ed. Samuel Carr), *Early Writings of John Hooper, D.D. Lord Bishop of Gloucester and Worcester, Martyr, 1555* (Cambridge: Cambridge for the Parker Society, 1843).

Richard Hooker, *The Folger Library Edition of the Works of Richard Hooker* (Cambridge: Belknap Press of Harvard University Press, 1977–1993), 7 vols.

—. (ed. A. S. McGrade), *Richard Hooker: Of Laws of Ecclesiastical Polity, Preface, Book I, Book VIII* (Cambridge Texts in the History of Political Thought, Cambridge: Cambridge University Press, 1989).

—. (ed. John Keble), *The Works of that Learned and Judicious Divine, Mr. Richard Hooker* (Oxford: Clarendon Press, seventh edition revised by R. W. Church and F. Paget, 1888), 3 vols.

John Jewel (ed. Richard William Jelf), *The Works of Bishop John Jewel* (Cambridge: Cambridge University Press for the Parker Society, 1845–1850), 4 vols.

Bibliography

Joseph Ketley (ed.), *The Two Liturgies, A.D. 1549, and A.D. 1552: With Other Documents Set Forth by Authority in the Reign of King Edward VI: viz. The Order of Communion, 1548; The Primer, 1553; The Catechism and Articles, 1553; Catechismus Brevis, 1553* (Cambridge: Cambridge University Press for the Parker Society, 1844).

William Laud (ed. James Bliss), *The Works of William Laud* (Oxford: Parker, 1849), 7 vols.

Charles Lloyd (ed.), *Formularies of Faith Put Forth by Authority During the Reign of Henry VIII* (Oxford: Oxford University Press, 1856).

John Lloyd, *Treatise of Episcopacy* (London, 1661).

Georg Mentz (ed.), *Die Wittenberger Artikel con 1536 (Artikel der cristlichen lahr, von welchen die legatten aus Engelland mit dem herrn doctor Martnio gehandelt anno 1536)*, (Darmstadt: Wissenschaftliche Buchgesellschaft, 1968).

Paul E. More and Frank L. Cross (eds), *Anglicanism* (1935) (new edition, Cambridge: James Clarke, 2008).

Matthew Parker, *De Antiquitate Britanniae Ecclesiae* (London, 1572).

—. (eds. John Bruce and Thomas Perowne), *Correspondence of Matthew Parker, D.D. Archbishop of Canterbury Comprising Letters Written by and to Him, from A.D. 1535, to His Death, A.D. 1575* (Cambridge: Cambridge University Press for the Parker Society, 1853).

—. (ed. John Strype), *The Life And Acts of Matthew Parker, The First Archbishop Of Canterbury in the Reign of Queen Elizabeth* (Oxford: Oxford University Press, 1821), 4 vols.

[Simon Patrick], *A Brief Account of the New Sect of Latitude-Man: Together with Some Reflections Upon the New Philosophy. By S.P. of Cambridge* (London, 1662).

John Pearson (ed. Edward Burton), *The Exposition of the Creed* (1659) (Oxford: Oxford University Press, 1843).

Albert Peel (ed.), *The Second Part of a Register* (Cambridge: Cambridge University Press, Reprint 2010).

Edward Reynolds (ed. John Rogers Pitman), *The Whole Works of the Right Rev. Edward Reynolds, Lord Bishop of Norwich* (London: Holdsworth, 1826), 6 vols.

Nicholas Ridley (ed. Henry Christmas), *The Works of Nicholas Ridley, D.D.: Sometime Lord Bishop of London, Martyr, 1555* (Cambridge: Cambridge University Press for the Parker Society, 1843).

Hastings Robinson (ed.), *Original Letters Relative to the English Reformation: Written During the Reigns of King Henry VIII., King Edward VI., and Queen Mary: Chiefly from the Archives of Zurich* (Cambridge: University Press for the Parker Society, 1846–1847), 2 vols (OL).

Hastings Robinson and Steuart Adolphus Pears (eds), *The Zurich Letters: Comprising the Correspondence of Several English Bishops and Others, with Some of the Helvetian Reformers, During the Early Part of the Reign of Queen Elizabeth, Translated from Authenticated Copies of the Autographs Preserved in the Archives of Zurich* (Cambridge: Cambridge University Press for the Parker Society, 1842–1845) (ZL).

Bibliography

Christopher St German (ed. T. F. T. Plucknett and J. L. Barton), *St German's Doctor and Student* (London: Selden Society, 1974), vol. 94.

William Stephens, *An Account of the Growth of Deism in England* (London, 1696).

Edward Stillingfleet, *Irenicum: A Weapon-Salve for the Churches Wounds, or the Divine Right of Particular Forms of Church-Government: Discuss'd and Examin'd According to the Principles of the Law of Nature* (London, 1662).

Walter Travers, *A Full and Plain Declaration of Ecclesiastical Discipline We Owe of the Word of God, and of the Declining of the Church of England from the Same* (Heidelberg, 1574).

James Ussher, *Discourse on the Religion Anciently Professed by the Irish and British* (Dublin: J. Jones, 1815).

John Whitgift (ed. John Ayre), *The works of John Whitgift, D.D., Master of Trinity College, Dean of Lincoln, &c. Afterwards Successively Bishop of Worcester and Archbishop of Canterbury* (Cambridge: Cambridge University Press for the Parker Society, 1851–1853), 3 vols.

William Wilberforce, *A Practical View of the Prevailing Religious Systems in Higher and Middle Classes in this Country Contrasted with Real Christianity* (London, 1797).

Secondary Sources

Evelyn Abbott and Lewis Campbell, *The Life and Letters of Benjamin Jowett* (London: James Murray, 1897), 2 vols.

G. W. O. Addleshaw and Frederick Etchells, *The Architectural Setting of Anglican Worship: An Inquiry Into the Arrangements for Public Worship in the Church of England from the Reformation to the Present Day* (London: Faber 1948).

Josef L. Altholz, *Anatomy of a Controversy: The Debate Over Essays and Reviews* (Aldershot: Scolar Press, 1994).

Peter F. Anson, *Fashions in Church Furnishings, 1840–1940* (London: Faith Press, 1960).

Margaret Aston, *England's Iconoclasts: Laws Against Images* (Oxford: Clarendon Press, 1988).

Andrew Atherstone, 'The Martyrs' Memorial at Oxford', *Journal of Ecclesiastical History* 54 (2003), pp. 278–301.

Nigel Atkinson, *Richard Hooker and the Authority of Scripture, Tradition and Reason* (Carlisle: Paternoster Press, 1997).

Paul Avis, 'Anglican Ecclesiology', in Gerard Mannion and Lewis Mudge (eds), *The Routledge Companion to the Christian Church* (London: Routledge, 2008), pp. 210–22.

—. *The Identity of Anglicanism* (London: T & T Clark, 2007).

Reid Barbour, 'The Caroline Church Heroic: The Reconstruction of Epic Religion in Three Seventeenth-Century Communities', *Renaissance Quarterly* 50 (1997), pp. 771–818.

Richard Bauckham, 'Hooker, Travers and the Church of Rome in the 1580s', *Journal of Ecclesiastical History* 29 (1978), pp. 37–50.

Bibliography

David Bebbington, *The Mind of Gladstone: Religion, Homer, and Politics* (Oxford: Oxford University Press, 2004).

Edward White Benson, 'Growing Unity', in Edward White Benson, *Living Theology* (London: Sampson Low, Marston, 1893), pp. 131–45.

Arthur Christopher Benson, *The Life of Edward White Benson, Sometime Archbishop of Canterbury* (London: Macmillan, 1899), 2 vols.

George W. Bernard, 'The Church of England, c.1529–c.1642', *History* 75 (1990), pp. 183–206.

—. *The King's Reformation: Henry VIII and the Remaking of the English Church* (New Haven, CT: Yale University Press, 2005).

—. 'The Making of Religious Policy, 1533–1546: Henry VIII and the Search for the Middle Way', *Historical Journal* 41 (1998), pp. 321–49.

Edward Bickersteth, *The Divine Warning to the Church, of Our Enemies, Dangers, and Duties, and as to Our Future Prospects* (London: Seeley, 1844).

—. *Progress of Popery, Including Observations On Its True Character, the Causes of Its Present Progress, Its Final Fall, and the Difficulties and Duties of Protestants in These Days* (London: Seeley, 1836).

Edward John Bicknell, *A Theological Introduction to the Thirty-Nine Articles of the Church of England* (London, 1946).

Thomas Bilson, *The Perpetual Government of Christ's Church* (1593) (Oxford: Oxford University Press, 1842).

Thomas Rowson Birks, *Memoir of Edward Bickersteth* (London: Seeley, 1852), 2 vols.

Robert S. Bosher, *The Making of the Restoration Settlement: The Influence of the Laudians, 1649–1662* (London: Dacre, 1951).

Gerald Bray, *The Anglican Canons 1529–1947* (Woodbridge: Boydell, 1998).

—. (ed.), *Documents of the English Reformation, 1526–1701* (Cambridge: James Clarke, 2004).

—. (ed.), *Tudor Church Reform: The Henrician Canons of 1535 and the Reformatio legum Ecclesiasticarum* (Woodbridge: Boydell, 2000).

Piers Brendon, *Hurrell Froude and the Oxford Movement* (London: Elek, 1974).

Michael George Brock and Mark Charles Curthoys (eds), *The History of the University of Oxford: Nineteenth-Century Oxford, Part 1* (Oxford: Clarendon Press, 1997).

Peter Newman Brooks, *Thomas Cranmer's Doctrine of the Eucharist: An Essay in Historical Development* (London: Macmillan, 1965).

Michael Brydon, *The Evolving Reputation of Richard Hooker: An Examination of Responses, 1600–1714* (Oxford: Oxford University Press, 2006).

Cambridge Camden Society, *Church Enlargement and Church Arrangement* (Cambridge: Cambridge Camden Society, 1843).

Ernest Trafford Campagnac (ed.), *The Cambridge Platonists Being Selections from the Writings of Benjamin Whichcote, John Smith and Nathanael Culverwel* (Oxford: Clarendon Press, 1901).

Henry Chadwick, 'The Quadrilateral in England', in J. Robert Wright, *Quadrilateral at One Hundred*, pp. 140–55.

Mark D. Chapman, *Anglicanism: A Very Short Introduction* (Oxford: Oxford University Press, 2006).

Bibliography

—. 'The Authority of Reason? The Importance of Being Liberal', in Mark D. Chapman (ed.), *The Hope of Things to Come* (Mowbray, 2010), pp. 45–68.

—. 'The Politics of Episcopacy', in *Bishops, Saints and Politics: Anglican Studies* (London: T & T Clark, 2007), pp. 9–32.

—. 'Protestant Christianity', in Peter Clarke and Peter Beyer (eds), *The World's Religions: Continuities and Transformations* (London Routledge, 2008), pp. 510–24.

—. 'Where Is It all Going? A Plea for Humility?', in Kenneth Stevenson (ed.), *A Fallible Church* (London: DLT, 2008), pp. 122–41.

Mark Chatfield, *Churches the Victorians Forgot* (Ashbourne: Moorland 1979).

Richard William Church, 'Bishop Andrewes', in *Pascal and Other Sermons* (London: Macmillan, 1896).

Andrew Cinnamond, 'The Reformed Treasures of the Parker Society', *Churchman* 122 (2008), pp. 221–42.

Jonathan C. D. Clark, *English Society: 1688–1832: Ideology, Social Structure, and Political Practice During the Ancien Régime* (Cambridge: Cambridge University Press, 2000), 2nd edn.

Robert Clifton, 'Fear of Popery', in Conrad Russell (ed.), *The Origins of the English Civil War* (Basingstoke: Macmillan, 1973), pp. 144–67.

A. O. J. Cockshut, *Anglican Attitudes* (London: Collins, 1959).

Roger Coleman, *Resolutions of the Twelve Lambeth Conferences* (Toronto: Anglican Book Centre, 1992).

John Williams Colenso, *The Epistle of St. Paul to the Romans. Newly Translated and Explained from a Missionary Point of View* (London: Macmillan, 1863). New edition edited by Jonathan A. Draper: *Commentary on Romans* (Pietermaritzburg: Cluster Publications, 2003).

—. *A Letter to the Archbishop of Canterbury. Upon the Proper Treatment of Polygamist Converts from Heathenism* (London: Macmillan, 1862).

—. *Two Weeks in Natal. A Journal of a first tour of Visitation among the colonists and Zulu Kafirs of Natal* (London: Macmillan, 1855).

Linda Colley, *Britons: Forging the Nation, 1707–1837* (London: Vintage 1996).

Patrick Collinson, *Archbishop Grindal, 1519–1583: The Struggle for a Reformed Church* (Berkeley, CA: University of California Press, 1979).

—. *The Elizabethan Puritan Movement* (London: Jonathan Cape, 1967).

—. 'England', in Robert Scribner, Roy Porter and Mikuláš Teich (eds), *The Reformation in National Context* (Cambridge: Cambridge University Press, 1994), pp. 80–94.

—. 'England and International Calvinism 1558–1640', in Menna Prestwich (ed.), *International Calvinism 1541–1715* (Oxford: Clarendon Press, 1985), pp. 197–223.

—. *Godly People: Essays on English Protestantism and Puritanism* (London: Hambledon, 1983).

—. 'The Jacobean Religious Settlement: The Hampton Court Conference', in Howard Tomlinson (ed.), *Before the English Civil War* (New York: Macmillan 1983), pp. 27–51.

Bibliography

—. 'The Politics of Religion and the Religion of Politics in Elizabethan England', *Historical Research* 82 (2009), pp. 74–92.

—. 'The Religion of Elizabethan England and of its Queen', in Michele Cilibreto and Nicholas Mann (eds), *Giordano Bruno 1583–1585: The English Experience* (Florence: L.S. Olschki, 1997), pp. 3–22.

—. 'Thomas Cranmer', in Geoffrey Rowell (ed.), *The English religious tradition and the genius of Anglicanism* (Wantage: Ikon, 1992), pp. 79–104.

—. 'Windows in a Woman's Soul: Questions About the Religion of Elizabeth I', *Elizabethan Essays* (London: Hambledon Press, 1994), pp. 87–118.

Conal Condren, 'The Creation of Richard Hooker's Public Authority: Rhetoric, Reputation and Reassessment', *The Journal of Religious History* 21 (1997), pp. 35–59.

George Cox, *The Life of John William Colenso, D.D., Bishop of Natal* (London: Ridgway, 1888).

Gerald R. Cragg, *Cambridge Platonists* (Oxford: Oxford University Press, 1968).

John Craig, 'Erasmus or Calvin? The Politics of Book Purchase in the Early Modern English Parish', in Polly Ha and Patrick Collinson, *The Reception of the Continental Reformation,* pp. 39–62.

Jack Patrick Cunningham, 'The Eirenicon and the "primitive episcopacy" of James Ussher: An Irish Panacea for Britannia's Ailment', *Reformation and Renaissance Review* 8 (2006), pp. 128–46.

Julian Davies, *The Caroline Captivity of the Church: Charles I and the Remoulding of Anglicanism* (Oxford: Clarendon Press, 1992).

Nan Dearmer, *The Life of Percy Dearmer,* with an introduction by the Very Revd. W. R. Matthews (London: Jonathan Cape, 1940).

Percy Dearmer, *The Parson's Handbook; Containing Practical Directions Both for Parsons and Others as to the Management of the Parish Church and Its Services According to the English Use as Set forth in the Book of Common Prayer. With an Introductory Essay on Conformity to the Church of England* (London: Grant Richards, 1899).

Arthur G. Dickens, *The English Reformation* (London: Batsford, 1964; revised edition 1989).

William Croswell Doane, 'The Historic Episcopate', *The Church Review* 59 (1890), pp. 158–64.

Doctrine in the Church of England: The Report of the Commission on Christian Doctrine Appointed by the Archbishops of Canterbury and York in 1922 (London: SPCK, 1938).

Peter Doll, *Revolution, Religion and National Identity* (Madison: Farleigh Dickinson, 2000).

Ian T. Douglas and Kwok Pui-Lan (eds), *Beyond Colonial Anglicanism* (New York: Church Publishing Inc., 2001).

Jonathan Draper (ed.), *Communion and Episcopacy. Essays to Mark the Centenary of the Chicago-Lambeth Quadrilateral* (Oxford: RCC, 1988).

Jonathan A. Draper (ed.), *The Eye of the Storm* (Pietermaritzburg: Cluster Publications, 2004).

Eamon Duffy, *Fires of Faith: Catholic England Under Mary Tudor* (New Haven, CT: Yale University Press, 2009).

Bibliography

—. *The Stripping of the Altars: Traditional Religion in England, c.1400–c.1580* (New Haven and London: Yale University Press, 1992).

The Ecclesiological Society, *Instrumenta Ecclesiastica* (London: John Van Voorst, vol. 1, 1847, vol. 2, 1856).

Thomas Stearns Eliot, *For Lancelot Andrewes: Essays on Style and Order* (London: Faber & Gwyer, 1928).

—. 'Lancelot Andrewes', *Times Literary Supplement* (23 September 1926), pp. 621–2.

Ieuan Ellis, *Seven against Christ: A Study of Essays and Reviews* (Leiden: Brill, 1980).

Daniel Eppley, *Defending Royal Supremacy and Discerning God's Will in Tudor England* (Aldershot: Ashgate, 2007).

Essays and Reviews (1860). References are to the tenth edition (London: Longmans, 1862), pp. 399–527.

Gillian R. Evans, 'Permanence in the Revealed Truth and Continuous Exploration of its Meaning', in J. Robert Wright (ed.), *Quadrilateral at One Hundred* (London: Mowbray, 1998), pp. 111–25.

Lori Anne Ferrell, *Government by Polemic: James I, the King's Preachers, and the Rhetoric of Conformity, 1603–1625* (Stanford, CA: Stanford University Press, 1998).

John Nevile Figgis, *Studies in Political Thought from Gerson to Grotius* (Cambridge: Cambridge University Press, 1907).

Kenneth Fincham, 'Prelacy and Politics: Archbishop Abbot's Defence of Protestant Orthodoxy', *Historical Research*, 61 (1988), pp. 36–64.

—. (ed.), *The Early Stuart Church, 1603–1640* (Basingstoke: Macmillan, 1993).

—. 'Episcopal Government, 1603–1640', in Kenneth Fincham (ed.), *The Early Stuart Church, 1603–1640* (Basingstoke: Macmillan, 1993), pp. 71–8.

—. *Prelate as Pastor: The Episcopate of James I* (Oxford: Clarendon Press, 1990).

—. 'The Restoration of Altars in the 1630s', *The Historical Journal* 44 (2001), pp. 919–40.

—. (ed.), *Visitation Articles and Injunctions of the Early Stuart Church* (Woodbridge: Boydell, 1994).

Kenneth Fincham and Peter Lake, 'The Ecclesiastical Policy of King James I', *Journal of British Studies* 24 (1985), pp. 169–207.

Alan Ford, *James Ussher: Theology, History, and Politics in Early-Modern Ireland and England* (Oxford: Oxford University Press, 2007).

Alistair Fox and John Guy, *Reassessing the Henrician Age: Humanism, Politics and Reform, 1500–1550* (Oxford: Blackwell, 1986).

R. William Franklin, *Nineteenth Century Churches: The History of a New Catholicism in Württemberg, England, and France* (New York: Garland, 1987).

Walter Howard Frere, *The English Church in the Reigns of Elizabeth and James I* (London: Macmillan, 1904).

—. 'Lancelot Andrewes as a Representative of Anglican Principles: A Lecture Delivered at Holy Trinity, Chelsea, February 28, 1897', *Church Historical Society*, 44 (London: SPCK, 1898).

Christina H. Garrett, *The Marian Exiles: A Study in the Origins of Elizabethan Puritanism* (Cambridge: Cambridge University Press, 1938; reprint, 1966).

Bibliography

John Gascoigne, 'The Unity of Church and State Challenged: Responses to Hooker from the Restoration to the Nineteenth-Century Age of Reform', *The Journal of Religious History* 21 (1997), pp. 60–79.

Henry Gee and William John Hardy (eds), *Documents Illustrative of English Church History* (New York: Macmillan, 1896).

Lee W. Gibbs, 'Richard Hooker: Prophet of Anglicanism or English Magisterial Reformer?', *Anglican Theological Review* 84 (2002), pp. 943–60.

William Gibson, *The Church of England, 1688–1832: Unity and Accord* (London: Routledge, 2001).

Edgar C. S Gibson, *The Thirty-Nine Articles of the Church of England* (London: Methuen, 1912).

Donald Gray, *Earth and Altar: The Evolution of the Parish Communion in the Church of England to 1945* (Norwich: Canterbury Press for the Alcuin Club, 1986).

—. *Percy Dearmer: A Parson's Pilgrimage* (Norwich: Canterbury Press, 2000).

I. M. Green, *The Re-establishment of the Church of England, 1660–1663* (Oxford: Oxford University Press, 1977).

Egil Grislis, 'The Hermeneutical Problem of Richard Hooker', in W. Speed Hill (ed.), *Studies in Richard Hooker: Essays Preliminary to an Edition of His Works* (Cleveland, OH: Press of Case Western Reserve University, 1972), pp. 159–206.

—. 'Jesus Christ – The Centre of Theology in Richard Hooker's *Of the Lawes of Ecclesiastical Polity*, Book V', *Journal of Anglican Studies* 5 (2007), pp. 227–52.

—. 'The Role of Consensus in Richard Hooker's Method of Theological Inquiry', in Robert E. Cushman and Egil Grislis (eds), *The Heritage of Christian Thought: Essays in Honor of Robert Lowry Calhoun* (New York: Harper & Row, 1965), pp. 64–88.

—. 'The Scriptural Hermeneutics of Richard Hooker', in W. J. Torrance Kirby (ed.), *Introduction to Richard Hooker* (Leiden: Brill, 2007).

Jeff Guy, *The Heretic: A Study of the Life of John William Colenso, 1814–1883* (Pietermaritzburg: University of Natal Press, 1983).

Polly Ha and Patrick Collinson (eds), *The Reception of the Continental Reformation in Britain* (Oxford: Oxford University Press for the British Academy, 2010).

Christopher Haigh (ed.), *The English Reformation Revised* (Cambridge: Cambridge University Press, 1988).

—. *English Reformations: Religion, Politics and Society Under the Tudors* (Oxford: Oxford University Press, 1993).

Basil Hall, 'Cranmer, the Eucharist and the Foreign Divines in the Reign of Edward VI', in Paul Ayris and David Selwyn (eds), *Thomas Cranmer, Churchman and Scholar* (Woodbridge: Boydell, 1993), pp. 217–58.

Richard P. C. Hanson, *Tradition in the Early Church* (London: SCM Press, 1962).

Tim Harris, *Politics Under the Later Stuarts: Party Conflict in a Divided Society, 1660–1715* (London: Longman, 1993).

Miranda K. Hassett, *Anglican Communion in Crisis: How Episcopal Dissidents and Their African Allies are Reshaping Anglicanism* (Princeton, NJ: Princeton University Press, 2007).

William P. Haugaard, *Elizabeth and the English Reformation: The Struggle for a Stable Settlement of Religion* (Cambridge: Cambridge University Press, 1970).

Bibliography

William Haugaard, 'Prelude: Hooker after 400 Years', *Anglican Theological Review* 84 (2002), pp. 875–7.

Felicity Heal, *Reformation in Britain and Ireland* (Oxford: Oxford University Press, 2003).

H. Hensley Henson, *In Defence of the English Church* (London: Hodder & Stoughton, 1923).

Christopher Hill and S. J. Edward Yarnold (eds), *Anglicans and Roman Catholics: The Search for Unity* (London: SPCK/CTS, 1994).

Gunnar Hillerdal, *Reason and Revelation in Richard Hooker* (Lund: Lund Universitets Arsskrift, 1962).

Peter Hinchliff, *John William Colenso. Bishop of Natal* (London: Nelson, 1964).

Eric Hobsbawm, *Nations and Nationalism Since 1780* (Cambridge: Cambridge University Press, 1992).

Eric Hobsbawm and T. Ranger (eds), *The Invention of Tradition* (Cambridge: Cambridge University Press, 1983).

S. M. Holland, 'George Abbot: The Wanted Archbishop', *Church History* 56 (1987), pp. 172–87.

Hirofumi Horie, 'The Lutheran Influence on the Elizabethan Settlement, 1558–1563', *Historical Journal* 34 (1991), pp. 519–37.

William Reed Huntington, *The Church-Idea: An Essay Towards Unity* (New York: E. P. Dutton, 1870, 4th edn., Charles Scribner's Sons, 1899).

—. *A National Church* (New York: Charles Scribner's Sons, 1899).

Ronald Hutton, *The Restoration: A Political and Religious History of England and Wales, 1658–1667* (Oxford: Clarendon Press, 1985).

William Ralph Inge, *The Platonic Tradition in English Religious Thought* (London: Longmans, 1926).

Inter-Anglican Theological and Doctrinal Commission, *The Virginia Report: The Report of the Inter-Anglican Theological and Doctrinal Commission*, included in James M. Rosenthal and Nicola Currie (eds), *Being Anglican in the Third Millennium* (Harrisburg, PA: Morehouse, 1997), pp. 211–81.

Christopher Irvine (ed.), *They Shaped Our Liturgy* (London: SPCK for the Alcuin Club), 1998.

William Jacob, *The Making of the Anglican Church Worldwide* (London: SPCK, 1997).

John Octavius Johnston, *Life and Letters of Henry Parry Liddon* (London: Longmans, 1904).

Norman L. Jones, *Faith by Statute: Parliament and the Settlement of Religion, 1559* (London: Royal Historical Society, 1982).

Bruce Kaye, *An Introduction to World Anglicanism* (Cambridge: Cambridge University Press, 2008).

N. H. Keeble (ed.), *The Autobiography of Richard Baxter* (London: Dent, 1974).

—. *The Restoration: England in the 1660s* (Oxford: Blackwell, 2002).

David Keep, 'Bullinger's Intervention in the Vestiarian Controversy of 1566', *The Evangelical Quarterly* 47 (1975), pp. 223–30.

John Philipps Kenyon, *The Stuart Constitution, 1603–1688: Documents and Commentary* (Cambridge: Cambridge University Press, 1986), 2nd edn.

Bibliography

W. J. Torrance Kirby, 'The Articles of Religion of the Church of England (1563/1571) Commonly Called the "Thirty-Nine Articles"', in Eberhard Busch and Mihály Bucsay (eds), *Reformierte Bekenntnisschriften* (Neukirchen: Neukirchener Verlag, 2008), vol. 2/1.

—. 'The Public Sermon: Paul's Cross and the Culture of Persuasion in England, 1534–1570', *Renaissance and Reformation* 30 (2006), pp. 4–29.

—. 'Richard Hooker as an Apologist of the Magisterial Reformation in England', in A. S. McGrade (ed.), *Richard Hooker and the Construction of the Christian Community* (Tempe, AZ: Medieval & Renaissance Texts & Studies, 1997), pp. 219–33.

—. *Richard Hooker's Doctrine of the Royal Supremacy* (Leiden: E J Brill 1990).

—. *Richard Hooker, Reformer and Platonist* (Aldershot: Ashgate, 2005).

—. 'Richard Hooker's Theory of Natural Law in the Context of Reformation Theology', *Sixteenth Century Journal* 30 (1999), pp. 681–703.

'The Knightsbridge Churches Case', *The Ecclesiologist*. New Series 82 (1857), pp. 116–18.

Peter Lake, *Anglicans and Puritans? Presbyterianism and English Conformist Thought from Whitgift to Hooker* (London: Allen Unwin, 1988).

—. 'Business as Usual? The Immediate Reception of Hooker's Ecclesiastical Polity', *The Journal of Ecclesiastical History* 52 (2001), pp 456–86.

—. 'Calvinism and the English Church, 1570–1635', *Past and Present* 114 (1987), pp. 32–76.

—. 'Lancelot Andrewes, John Buckeridge, and Avant-garde Conformity at the Court of James I', in Linda Levy Peck (ed.), *The Mental World of the Jacobean Court* (Cambridge: Cambridge University Press, 1991).

—. 'The Laudian Style: Order, Uniformity and the Pursuit of the Beauty of Holiness in the 1630s', in Fincham (ed.), *Early Stuart Church*, pp. 161–85.

—. *Moderate Puritans and the Elizabethan Church* (Cambridge: Cambridge University Press, 1982).

Lambeth Commission on Communion, *The Windsor Report* (London: Anglican Communion Office, 2004).

The Lambeth Conference Report 1920 (London: SPCK, 1920).

The Lambeth Conference Report 1930 (London: SPCK, 1930).

The Lambeth Conference 1968 (London: SPCK, 1968).

Robert C. Latham and William Matthews (eds), *The Diary of Samuel Pepys* (London: HarperCollins, 1995), 8 vols.

Donald Lewis, *The Origins of Christian Zionism: Lord Shaftesbury and Evangelical Support for a Jewish Homeland* (Cambridge: Cambridge University Press, 2009).

Henry Parry Liddon, *Life of Edward Bouverie Pusey* (London: Longmans, 1894), 4 vols.

David Loades, *Revolution in Religion: The English Reformation, 1530–1570* (Cardiff: University of Wales Press, 1992).

Olivier Loyer, *L'Anglicanisme de Richard Hooker* (Lille: Réproduction des Theses, 1979).

Henry R. McAdoo, *The Spirit of Anglicanism: A Survey of Anglican Theological Method in the Seventieth Century* (London: A & C Black, 1965).

Bibliography

—. 'Richard Hooker', in Geoffrey Rowell, *The English Religious Tradition and the Genius of Anglicanism* (Wantage: Ikon, 1992), pp. 105–26.

Diarmaid MacCulloch, *Reformation: Europe's House Divided 1490–1700* (London: Penguin, 2004).

—. *The Later Reformation in England* (Basingstoke: Macmillan, 1990).

—. 'The Myth of the English Reformation', *Journal of British Studies* 30 (1991), pp. 1–19.

—. *The Reign of Henry VIII: Politics, Policy and Piety* (Basingstoke: Macmillan, 1995).

—. 'Richard Hooker's Reputation', *English Historical Review*, 117 (2002), pp. 773–812.

—. *Thomas Cranmer: A Life* (New Haven, CT: Yale University Press, 1996).

—. *Tudor Church Militant: Edward VI and the Protestant Reformation* (London: Penguin, 2001).

John Macquarrie, *Principles of Christian Theology* (London: SCM Press, 1966).

Judith Maltby, *Prayer Book and People in Elizabethan and Early Stuart England* (Cambridge: Cambridge University Press, 1998).

Judith Maltby, 'Suffering and Surviving: The Civil Wars, the Commonwealth and the Formation of "Anglicanism"', in Stephen Platten (ed.), *Anglicanism and the Western Christian Tradition* (Norwich: Canterbury Press, 2003), pp. 122–43.

Peter McCullough, 'Making Dead Men Speak: Laudianism, Print, and the Works of Lancelot Andrewes, 1626–1642', *The Historical Journal* 41 (1998), pp. 401–424.

—. *Sermons at Court: Politics and Religion in Elizabethan and Jacobean Preaching* (Cambridge: Cambridge University Press, 1998).

Arthur Stephen McGrade (ed.), *Richard Hooker and the Construction of the Christian Community* (Tempe, AZ: Medieval & Renaissance Texts & Studies, 1997).

—. (ed.), *Richard Hooker: Of Laws of Ecclesiastical Polity, Preface, Book I, Book VIII* (Cambridge Texts in the History of Political Thought, Cambridge: Cambridge University Press, 1989).

Michael A. McGreevy, 'John Keble on the Anglican Church and the Church Catholic', *Heythrop Journal* 5 (1964), pp. 27–35.

Colin McLekvie, 'Jeremy Taylor's Recommendations for a Library of Anglican Theology (1660)', *Irish Booklore* IV (1980), pp. 96–103.

Charles Howard McIlwain (ed.), *The Political Works of James I* (Cambridge, MA, Harvard University Press, 1918).

Roger B. Manning, 'The Crisis of Episcopal Authority During the Reign of Elizabeth', *Journal of British Studies* 11 (1971), pp. 1–25.

John Marshall, 'The Ecclesiology of the Latitude-Men 1660–1689: Stillingfleet, Tillotson and "Hobbism"', *Journal of Ecclesiastical History* 36 (1985), pp. 407–27.

John Sedberry Marshall, *Hooker and the Anglican Tradition: An Historical and Theological Study of Hooker's Ecclesiastical Polity* (London: A & C Black, 1963).

William Marshall, *Scripture, Tradition and Reason: A Selective View of Anglican Theology Through the Centuries* (Dublin: Columba Press/APCK, 2010).

Bibliography

Robert Bernard Martin, *The Dust of Combat: A Life of Charles Kingsley* (London: Faber and Faber, 1959).

Frederick D. Maurice, *The Kingdom of Christ or Hints on the Principles, Ordinances and Constitution of the Catholic Church. In Letters to a Member of the Society of Friends* (1st edn., 1837–1838) (new edition based on second edition of 1842, Cambridge: James Clarke, 1958), 2 vols.

——. *Life of Frederick Denison Maurice* (London: Macmillan, 1885), 2 vols.

——. *Lincoln's Inn Sermons* (London: Longmans 1891), 6 vols.

——. *Theological Essays* (1853) (London: James Clarke, 1957).

Standish Meacham, *Lord Bishop: The Life of Samuel Wilberforce: 1805–1873* (Cambridge: Harvard University Press, 1970).

Members of the University of Oxford, *Tracts for the Times, Volume III, 1835–1836* (London: Rivington, 1836), no. 74: 'Catena Patrum, No. I. Testimony of Writers in the Later English Church to the Doctrine of the Apostolical Succession'.

Arthur Middleton, *Fathers and Anglicans: The Limits of Orthodoxy* (Leominster: Gracewing, 2001).

Anthony Milton (ed.), *The British Delegation and the Synod of Dort (1618–1619)* (Woodbridge: Boydell, 2005), COERS, vol. 13.

——. *Catholic and Reformed: The Roman and Protestant Churches in English Protestant Thought, 1600–1640* (Cambridge: Cambridge University Press, 1995).

Aubrey Moore, *Lectures and Papers on the History of the Reformation in England and on the Continent* (London: Kegan Paul, Trench, Trübner, 1890).

Jeremy Morris, *F. D. Maurice and the Crisis of Christian Authority* (Oxford: Oxford University Press, 2005).

Peter Munz, *The Place of Hooker in the History of Thought* (Westport, CT: Greenwood Press, 1971).

John E. Neale, 'The Elizabethan Acts of Supremacy and Uniformity', *English Historical Review* LXV (1950), pp. 304–32.

——. *Elizabeth I and her Parliaments 1559–1581* (London: Cape, 1953).

John Mason Neale and Benjamin Webb (eds), *The Symbolism of Churches and Church Ornaments: A Translation of the First Book of the Rationale Divinorum Officiorum, Written by William Durandus* (Leeds: T. W. Green, 1843).

Edmund Newey, 'The Form of Reason: Participation in the Work of Richard Hooker, Benjamin Whichcote, Ralph Cudworth and Jeremy Taylor', *Modern Theology* 18 (2002), pp. 1–26.

John Henry Newman, *Certain Difficulties Felt by Anglicans in Catholic Teaching* (London: Longmans, 1901).

——. *Lectures on the Prophetical Office of the Church, Viewed Relatively To Romanism and Popular Protestantism* (London: Rivington, 1837).

——. (ed. Gerard Tracey), *Letters and Diaries of John Henry Newman*, vol. 1 (Oxford: Oxford University Press, 2000).

——. (ed. Gerard Tracey), *Letters and Diaries of John Henry Newman*, vol. 7 (Oxford: Oxford University Press, 1995).

Bibliography

—. (ed. Gerard Tracey), *Letters and Diaries of John Henry Newman*, vol. 8 (Oxford: Oxford University Press, 1999).

—. *The Via Media of the Anglican Church illustrated in Lectures, Letters and Tracts Written Between 1830 and 1841* (London: Longmans, 1901).

J. H. Newman, John Keble and J. B. Mozley (eds), *Remains of the Late Reverend Richard Hurrell Froude, M.A. Fellow of Oriel College, Oxford* (London: Rivington, 1838–1839), 2 parts in 4 volumes.

Peter B. Nockles, 'An Academic Counter-Revolution: Newman and Tractarian Oxford's Idea of a University', *History of Universities* 10 (1991), pp. 137–97.

—. *The Oxford Movement in Context: Anglican High Churchmanship, 1760–1857* (Cambridge: Cambridge University Press, 1994).

Richard A. Norris, 'Episcopacy', in Stephen Sykes and John Booty (eds), *The Study of Anglicanism* (London: SPCK, 1988), pp. 296–309.

Oliver O'Donovan, *On the Thirty-Nine Articles. A Conversation with Tudor Christianity* (Exeter: Paternoster, 1986).

Heiko Oberman, *The Dawn of the Reformation* (Edinburgh: T & T Clark, 1992).

William Orme, *The Life and Times of Richard Baxterwith a Critical Examination of his Writings* (London: J. Duncan, 1830), 2 vols.

John W. Packer, *The Transformation of Anglicanism: 1643–1660 with Special Reference to William Chillingworth* (Manchester, IN: Manchester University Press, 1969).

William Palmer, *A Treatise on the Church of Christ* (London: Rivington, 1838).

Parker Society, 'The Thirteenth and Final Report of the Council of the Parker Society', in *General Index Publications of The Parker Society* compiled for Henry Gough (Cambridge: Cambridge University Press for the Parker Society, 1855).

C. A. Patrides, *Cambridge Platonists* (London: Edward Arnold, 1969).

W. B. Patterson, 'The Synod of Dort and the Early Stuart Church', in Donald S Armentrout (ed.), *This Sacred History: Anglican Reflections for John Booty* (Cambridge, MA: Cowley Publications, 1990).

William Stevens Perry, 'Church Reunion Discussed on the Basis of the Lambeth Propositions of 1888', *The Church Review* 59 (1890), pp. 165–73.

Andrew Pettegree, Alastair Duke, and Gillian Lewis (eds), *Calvinism in Europe, 1540–1620* (Cambridge: Cambridge University Press, 1994).

—. 'The Reception of Calvinism in Britain', in Wilhelm Neuser, and Brian Armstrong (eds), *Calvinus Sincerioris Religionis Vindex* (Kirkville, MO: Sixteenth Century Journal Publishers, 1997), pp. 267–89.

Richard W. Pfaff, 'The Library of the Fathers: The Tractarians as Patristic Translators', *Studies in Philology* 70 (1973), pp. 329–44.

Paul T. Phillips, 'The Concept of a National Church in Late Nineteenth-century England and America', *Journal of Religious History* 14 (1986), pp. 26–37.

Walter Phillips, 'Henry Bullinger and the Elizabethan Vestiarian Controversy: An Analysis of Influence', *Journal of Religious History* 11 (1991), pp. 363–84.

Frederick J. Powicke, *A Life of the Reverend Richard Baxter, 1615–1691* (London: Jonathan Cape, 1924).

Bibliography

Robert Prichard, *A History of the Episcopal Church* (Harrisburg, PA: Morehouse, 1999), pp. 188–90.

John Henry Primus, *The Vestments Controversy: An Historical Study of the Earliest Tensions Within the Church of England in the Reigns of Edward VI and Elizabeth* (Kampen: J.H. Kok, 1960).

Charles W. A. Prior, *Defining the Jacobean Church: The Politics of Religious Controversy* (Cambridge: Cambridge University Press, 2005).

Augustus Welby Northmore Pugin, *The Present State of Ecclesiastical Architecture in England* (London: Charles Dolman, 1843).

Edward Bouverie Pusey (ed.), *Confessions of St Augustine* (Oxford: Parker, 1838).

Jean-Louis Quantain, *The Church of England and Christian Antiquity: The Construction of a Confessional Identity in the 17th Century* (Oxford: Oxford University Press, 2009).

Ephraim Radner and Philip Turner, *The Fate of Communion: The Agony of Anglicanism and the Future of a Global Church* (Grand Rapids: Eerdmans, 2006).

A. Michael Ramsey, *The Gospel and the Catholic Church* (London: Longmans, Green and Co., 1936).

Jasper Ridley, *Thomas Cranmer* (Oxford: Clarendon Press, 1962).

John Rogerson, *Old Testament Criticism in the Nineteenth Century: England and Germany* (London: SPCK, 1984).

Timothy Rosendale, *Liturgy and Literature in the Making of Protestant England* (Cambridge: Cambridge University Press, 2007).

Geoffrey Rowell (ed.), *The English Religious Tradition and the Genius of Anglicanism* (Wantage: Ikon, 1992).

—. *The Vision Glorious: Themes and Personalities of the Catholic Revival in Anglicanism* (Oxford: Clarendon, 1991).

Geoffrey Rowell, Kenneth Stevenson and Rowan Williams (eds), *Love's Redeeming Work: The Anglican Quest for Holiness* (Oxford: Oxford University Press, 2001).

Conrad Russell, *The Causes of the English Civil War* (Oxford: Clarendon, 1990).

—. *Parliaments and English Politics, 1621–1629* (Oxford: Clarendon Press, 1982).

Alec Ryrie, 'The Strange Death of Lutheran England', *Journal of Ecclesiastical History* 53 (2002), pp. 64–92.

William L. Sachs, *The Transformation of Anglicanism* (Cambridge: Cambridge University Press, 1993).

Paul Seaward, *The Cavalier Parliament and the Reconstruction of the Old Regime, 1661–1667* (Cambridge: Cambridge University Press, 1989).

Philip Secor, *Richard Hooker: Prophet of Anglicanism* (Tunbridge Wells: Burns & Oates, 1999).

Kevin Sharpe, *The Personal Rule of Charles I* (New Haven; London: Yale University Press, 1992).

F. J. Shirley, *Richard Hooker and Contemporary Political Ideas* (London: SPCK, 1949).

Frederick Shriver, 'Hampton Court Re-visited: James I and the Puritans', *Journal of Ecclesiastical History* 33 (1982), pp. 48–71.

Bibliography

Simon Skinner, *Tractarians and the 'Condition of England': The Social and Political Thought of the Oxford Movement* (Oxford: Clarendon 2004).

Leo F. Solt, *Church and State in Early Modern England, 1509–1640* (New York: Oxford University Press, 1990).

Johann P. Sommerville, 'The Royal Supremacy and Episcopacy "Jure Divino", 1603–1640', *Journal of Ecclesiastical History* 34 (1983), pp. 548–58.

William M. Southgate, *John Jewel and the Problem of Doctrinal Authority* (Cambridge, MA: Harvard University Press, 1962).

W. Speed Hill (ed.), *Studies in Richard Hooker: Essays Preliminary to an Edition of his Works* (Cleveland, OH: Press of Case Western Reserve University, 1972).

William M. Spellman, *The Latitudinarians and the Church of England, 1660–1700* (Athens, GA: University of Georgia Press, 1993).

Martin Spence, *Time and Eternity in British Evangelicalism, c. 1820-c.1860'*, University of Oxford DPhil, 2008..

Bryan D. Spinks, *Two Faces of Elizabethan Anglican Theology: Sacraments and Salvation in the Thought of William Perkins and Richard Hooker* (Lanham, MD and London: Scarecrow Press, 1999).

John Spurr, 'The Church of England, Comprehension and the Toleration Act of 1688', *English Historical Review* 104 (1989), pp. 927–46, esp. p. 944.

—. 'From Puritanism to Dissent, 1660–1700', in Christopher Durston and Jacqueline Eales (eds), *The Culture of English Puritanism, 1560–1700* (Basingstoke: Macmillan, 1996), pp. 234–265.

—. *The Post-Reformation* (Harlow: Pearson, 2006).

—. *The Restoration Church of England, 1648–1689* (New Haven, CT: Yale University Press, 1991).

Alan M. G. Stephenson, *Anglicanism and the Lambeth Conferences* (London: SPCK, 1978).

—. *The First Lambeth Conference, 1867* (London: SPCK, 1967).

John Stephenson, 'Wittenberg and Canterbury', *Concordia Theological Quarterly* 48 (1984), pp. 165–84.

Rowan Strong, *Anglicanism and the British Empire, c. 1700–1850* (Oxford: Oxford University Press, 2007).

John Strype, *Historical Memorials, Chiefly Ecclesiastical, and Such as Concern Religion, the Reformation of It, and the Progress Made Therein, Under the Reign and. Influence of King Edward the Sixth* (Oxford: Clarendon Press, 1822).

N. M. Sutherland, 'The Marian Exiles and the Establishment of the Elizabethan Regime', *Archiv fur Reformationsgeschichte* 78 (1987), pp. 253–86.

Norman Sykes (ed.), *Church and State: Report of the Archbishop's Commission on the Relations Between Church and State* (London: Church Assembly, 1936).

—. *The English Religious Tradition* (London: SCM, 1951).

—. *Old New and Priest Presbyter* (Cambridge: Cambridge University Press, 1956).

Stephen Sykes, *The Integrity of Anglicanism* (London: Mowbray, 1978).

—. *Unashamed Anglicanism* (London: DLT, 1995).

Stephen Sykes and John Booty (eds), *The Study of Anglicanism* (London and Philadelphia: SPCK/Fortress Press, 1988).

Bibliography

J. R. Tanner, *Constitutional Documents of the Reign of James I, 1603–1625* (Cambridge: Cambridge University Press, 1930).

Roger Thomas, 'Comprehension and Indulgence', in Geoffrey F. Nuttall and Owen Chadwick (eds), *From Uniformity to Unity, 1662–1962* (London: SPCK, 1962), pp. 189–253.

W. D. J. Cargill Thompson, 'Sir Francis Knollys' Campaign Against the Jure Divino Theory of Episcopacy', in C. Robert Cole and Michael E. Moody (eds), *The Dissenting Tradition* (Athens, OH: Ohio University Press, 1975), pp. 39–77.

Barry Till, 'The Worcester House Declaration and the Restoration of the Church of England', *Historical Research* 70 (1997), pp. 203–30.

To Set Our Hope on Christ: A Response to the Invitation of Windsor Report §135 (New York: The Episcopal Church Center, 2005).

Peter Toon, *Evangelical theology, 1833–1856: A Response to Tractarianism* (London: Marshall, Morgan & Scott, 1979).

—. 'The Parker Society', *Historical Magazine of the Protestant Episcopal Church*, 46 (September 1977), pp. 323–32.

Hugh Trevor-Roper, *Catholics, Anglicans and Puritans* (Chicago, IL: University of Chicago Press, 1988).

Leonard J. Trinterud, *Elizabethan Puritanism* (New York: Oxford, 1971).

Nicholas Tyacke, *Anti-Calvinists: The Rise of English Arminianism, c. 1590–1640* (Oxford: Clarendon, 1987; paperback edition, 1990).

—. *Aspects of English Protestantism, c. 1530–1700* (Manchester, IN: Manchester University Press, 2001).

—. 'Lancelot Andrewes and the Myth of Anglicanism', in Peter Lake and Michael Questier (eds), *Conformity and Orthodoxy in the English Church c. 1560–1660* (Woodbridge: Boydell, 2000), pp. 5–33.

Nigel Voak, 'Richard Hooker and the Principle of Sola Scriptura', *Journal of Theological Studies* 59 (2008), pp. 96–139.

—. *Richard Hooker and Reformed Theology: A Study of Reason, Will, and Grace* (Oxford: Oxford University Press, 2003).

John Walsh, Colin Haydon, and Stephen Taylor (eds), *The Church of England, c. 1689–c. 1833: From Toleration to Tractarianism* (Cambridge: Cambridge University Press, 1993).

Kevin Ward, *A History of Global Anglicanism* (Cambridge: Cambridge University Press, 2006).

Paul A. Welsby, *George Abbot: The Unwanted Archbishop* (London: SPCK, 1962).

James F. White, *The Cambridge Movement: The Ecclesiologists and the Gothic Revival* (Cambridge: Cambridge University Press, 1962).

Peter White, *Predestination, Policy and Polemic: Conflict and Consensus in the English Church from the Reformation to the Civil War* (Cambridge: Cambridge University Press, 1992).

—. 'The *Via Media* in the Early Stuart Church', in Fincham (ed.), *The Early Stuart Church*, pp. 211–30.

Basil Willey, *More Nineteenth Century Studies: A Group of Honest Doubters* (Cambridge: Cambridge University Press, 1956).

Bibliography

Glanmor Williams, *Reformation Views of Church History* (Cambridge: James Clarke, 1970).

Rowan Williams, 'Does It Make Sense to Speak of a Pre-Nicene Orthodoxy?', in Rowan Williams (ed.), *The Making of Orthodoxy* (Cambridge: Cambridge University Press, 1989), pp. 1–23.

—. 'Theology and the Churches', in Robin Gill and Lorna Kendall (eds), *Michael Ramsey as Theologian* (London: DLT, 1995), pp. 9–28.

—. 'What is Catholic Orthodoxy?', in R. D. Williams and Kenneth Leech (eds), *Essays Catholic and Radical* (London: Bowardean Press, 1983), pp. 11–25.

Andrew Wingate, Kevin Ward, Carrie Pemberton and Wilson Sitshebo (eds), *Anglicanism: A Global Communion* (New York: Church Publishing Inc., 1998).

David F. Wright (ed.), *Martin Bucer: Reforming Church and Community* (Cambridge: Cambridge University Press, 1994).

J. Robert Wright (ed.), *Quadrilateral at One Hundred* (London: Mowbray, 1998).

Index

Index

Index

Index

Index

29418465R00156

Made in the USA
San Bernardino, CA
21 January 2016